Michael Hutchence

Vincent Lovegrove began as co-singer with Bon Scott and moved on to manage the up-and-coming rock legends, Cold Chisel. In 1980, Lovegrove moved to Sydney to write a rock column for *The Sun* and to manage The Divinyls, a job which took him to work and live in New York. He has co-produced two documentaries, *Suzi's Story* and *A Kid Called Troy*, both of which were sold internationally and won more than 30 awards between them. In 1994, Lovegrove moved to London and became a full-time writer. He was one of the last journalists to interview Hutchence at length before he died.

Michael Hutchence

Vincent Lovegrove

ALLEN & UNWIN

Every effort has been made to contact the copyright holders of material used in this book. However, where an omission has occurred, the author and publisher will gladly include acknowledgement in any future editions.

Copyright © Vincent Lovegrove 1999

All rights reserved. No part of this book may be reproduced or transmitted in any form or by any means, electronic or mechanical, including photocopying, recording or by any information storage and retrieval system, without prior permission in writing from the publisher.

First published in 1999 by
Allen & Unwin
9 Atchison Street, St Leonards NSW 1590 Australia
Phone: (61 2) 8425 0100
Fax: (61 2) 9906 2218
E-mail: frontdesk@allen-unwin.com.au
Web: http://www.allen-unwin.com.au

National Library of Australia
Cataloguing-in-Publication entry:

Lovegrove, Vincent.
    Michael Hutchence.

    Includes index.
    ISBN 1 86448 894 8.

    1. Hutchence, Michael. 2. Rock musicians—Australia—Biography. 3. Singers—Australia—Biography. I. Title.

781.66092

Set in 10.5/14 pt Adobe Caslon by Bookhouse Digital, Sydney
Printed and bound by Griffin Press, Adelaide

10 9 8 7 6 5 4 3 2 1

Contents

Preface ix

1 Eight husbands, the lovers, the brothers, the stepdaughter, the seed 1
2 The Hong Kong connection 12
3 Escape to Hollywood, stranded in Sydney 28
4 The Farriss Brothers, Doctor Dolphin, Guinness, the Nullarbor and Manila 45
5 Thrusting clenched fists, wiggling arses: INXS and Australian music 63
6 *Dogs in Space*, Max Q 90
7 Kicking arse 1986–1992, saving arse 1992–1997 119
8 The cavalier sex god, Kylie, Helena, Paula 143
9 Paula, Michael, Tiger, Bob 169
10 Suicide or not—that is the question 195
11 The funeral, the eulogy, the wake 229
12 Money, that's what I want 256
13 The christening, the photos, the money, the mag 273
14 The ashes: torn apart 282
Appendix: The coroner's report 288

Acknowledgements and sources 293
Index 298

*This book is for Heavenly Hiraani Tiger Lily.
May Michael shine over you—he was a beautiful,
good man. His soft, soft heart, wandering spirit,
intense soul and open mind remain a collective
inspiration and beacon to many.*

Preface

A series of coincidences led me to this point. In July of 1997, Tim Farriss sent me an email, inviting me to get in touch with him in London, as INXS were in town and about to promote their most recent album, *Elegantly Wasted*. The band and I had known each other since about 1981. We weren't close friends, but some of us were very good acquaintances. If I had been a close friend, I could not have written this book.

I hooked up with Farriss and the other members of the band, spent a couple of days with them, saw their performance at Wembley Stadium, and after the show chatted for hours with Michael back at his hotel. He was a troubled man that night. In the early hours of the morning, both of us a little worse for wear, his revelations floored me and he gave me his nod of approval to write about the things he told me.

At around the same time, I had appointed Jane Burridge from Sydney as my agent. Jane had a literary agency at the time, The Other Woman. I wanted her to represent me for another book I had begun writing, a book of twelve short fiction stories about women. Strong, tough women. A few months later I interviewed Michael again, via email and facsimile, coordinated by his manager Martha Troup, he in New York and Los Angeles, me in London.

Eight days after that final interview with Michael, my close friend Peter Carrette called me in the early hours of a dark, cold, windy London Saturday morning. Peter was calling from Sydney to tell me Michael had tragically died. A few weeks later I was contacted by Jane Burridge who told me that the publishers Allen & Unwin were interested in a book about Michael, a biography. At the time, there were supposedly a dozen books being written, so we all hesitated for a moment, but then decided to write the book, in an attempt to find out about his life, to find out what led the charismatic and popular singer to his tragic end. Thus far there have been three books released about Hutchence, a fourth, written by his mother, is yet to be released.

Every story from every friend displays another facet of Michael's complex character: happiness, frustration, anger, wisdom; he had a heart as big as the ocean, a wicked sense of humour—he was witty, naughty, sexy and sad.

Everyone who knew him saw a different aspect of his personality, a hundred people with a hundred different Michaels, each of them seeming to be real. But the common threads that everyone shared about Michael Hutchence were warmth, charisma, a reckless charm, a unique ability to grant friendship without boundaries. And sex and drugs and rock'n'roll.

During the time spent on this project I have learned once more that when troubled matters of the heart take over our lives, emotions rule. Matters of the heart can be a positive force; they can be a negative force. But nothing is more passionately negative than the hotbed of emotions that pervades all parties as a marriage or intimate relationship disintegrates. When there are children involved, the situation is magnified, and in some cases spirals out of control—personal war erupts. Cruel, vicious words are spoken on both sides. When death is thrown into the equation, chaos rules.

Each of us has the capacity to be at least four people: the person we think we are, the person we'd like others to see, the person others think we are, and the person we really are. Appearances can be deceiving, and life is shades of grey, not black and white. Truth is not always clear-cut and singular. All of us have stories to be told, and with most, quite a few perspectives are available, yet each would be a true version.

This book then, is just one version of events in Michael's life, and the pathway along which his destiny led him. To the inescapable black hole in the corner of his mind. I understand the overpowering feeling and confused thought patterns of the desire to commit suicide, the desire to escape reality. I can relate to emotional baggage, family conflict, to the death of a son and the death of a partner, to drugs, to the amorous addiction of sex and the pain and heartache of divorce, separation and all that goes with it. I have forged friendships during the writing of this book, and I have grown to love Michael Hutchence. He was one of the good guys, but a victim of his own circumstances.

Many people have asked me if this book is authorised. My answer has been to ask the question: exactly who is going to authorise the book? Who has the right to authorise the book? Only Michael, and he is dead. But in attempting to unravel the paradox that was Michael Hutchence, I sought the help of those who thought they knew him best, who knew him the longest, who saw the drama of his life unfold before their very eyes—those who shared the most intimate moments with him. The good, the bad and the ugly. I thank all who have helped me try to find an answer, but Michael is the only one who has the real answers.

Life is about exploration, resolution and conciliation. Life is for living, for making mistakes, for learning from our mistakes, for helping our young avoid our mistakes as they stumble and make new ones of their own. Life is about preparing our spirit and soul for death. Life is about all this and more.

It is easy to judge others' lives, far more difficult trying to understand in non-judgemental fashion. Whilst many have been preoccupied with the question mark of how Michael died, I was more concerned with how he lived. Why he died rather than how. And in time, Michael will be remembered for who he was in life, rather than who he was in death.

Vincent Lovegrove
January, 1999

one

Eight husbands, the lovers, the brothers, the stepdaughter, the seed

> You might know of the Original Sin
> You might know how to play with fire
>
> 'Original Sin'
> *The Swing* 1983
> MICHAEL HUTCHENCE AND
> ANDREW FARRISS

December, 1958, in the Newcastle pub at the bottom of George Street in Sydney, not far from the centre of bustling Circular Quay. Kelland Hutchence had had a phone call earlier that afternoon from his friend Johnny Walker, whom he knew from his Melbourne days. The pair had lived in the same boarding house in St Kilda Road before Hutchence resigned from his job of four years and moved to Sydney, to work for Guthrie & Co., an old English plantation and trading company.

The two bachelors, then in their mid-twenties, had spent many an evening trawling the Melbourne nightclubs, restaurants and bars, drinking whiskey, mostly on the lookout for wild, wild women. Now on a business trip to Sydney, Walker was accompanied by his girlfriend, the current Miss Australia, Leah McCartney.

'What are you up to tonight, Kell?' Walker had queried. 'I'm with Leah and another woman called Patricia Kennedy. Maybe you'd like to join us for a drink and make it a foursome? Patricia's a really nice lady and I'd like you to meet her.'

Kell, being in the market, told him to bring her along.

Walker chose the Newcastle pub because it contained one of the few bars in Sydney at the time where women were allowed to enter. The 34-year-old Kelland Hutchence was immediately and absolutely besotted by 29-year-old Patricia Kennedy as she sauntered into the bar on that hot, steamy night, her carefully coiffured dark hair almost to her shoulders, a capricious look of adventure in her brown-green eyes.

'In walks Patricia looking like a million bloody dollars, a gorgeous-looking woman,' Hutchence remembers, 'and that was virtually that. I just fell in love with her very, very quickly. I mean, she was some lady.'

After a brief romance, Patricia Kennedy and Kelland Hutchence were married on 31 January 1959. Like all newly married couples they were blissful, excited, passionate and locked together; but the seeds of their romance hid fundamental differences that later exploded into full-scale personal war. The Hutchence family would eventually see the battle lines being drawn, with ensuing dramas on a mammoth scale. The best soap-opera writers in Hollywood could not have written a more bizarre story, and even if they had, nobody would have believed them.

During the next thirty-seven years, the Hutchence family would be involved in death, divorce, heroin addiction, custody battles, a kidnap, an attempted murder charge, the bright lights and tainted glamour of the music industry, money battles, deceit, lies, infidelities, a suicide, and traded insults and tirades.

As with many feuding relations, the Hutchence family would paradoxically also witness affection, loyalty, remorse, romance, tenderness, devotion and hope. But the complex issues of love, morality and ethics would be truly put to the test. In time, the glue that loosely kept the estranged family members together would become Michael Hutchence. When he died the adhesive came unstuck.

Michael's parents first met at the end of the fifties, a time of unrest and major change, and of heroes who would burn out too soon—James Dean, Elvis Presley, Marilyn Monroe. It was the beginning of the space age, post-war political tension, new technology, a questioning of social barriers and limits, the threat of nuclear war. The air was thick with the whiff of social and political upheaval on every level of life, and the first signs of the fifties' social shackles being released came with the raucous new, devil-inspired music known as rock'n'roll, a black American term for fucking. This new music form was slowly infiltrating world society, enthusiastically embraced by a listless, downtrodden and bored teenage generation, who rejected the confused morals thrust upon them by hypocritical parents. Before it even began, rock'n'roll was hysterically scorned by a paranoid adult generation. The double standards set in the fifties had proven to be repressive, oppressive and sanctimonious. It was time for a changing of the guard.

Rock'n'roll's infectious, rebellious sound, message and

feel spread like wildfire throughout the United States, and eventually the globe. The world was confused. Mr Jones didn't know what was happening, and neither did anyone else.

Prior to meeting Pat, bachelor Kell Hutchence had travelled throughout South-East Asia representing his employers. He established himself as a credible, competent expatriate in the region, eventually using Hong Kong as his main base during the sixties, seventies and eighties. Contrary to some reports, Hutchence was never a rich man. He was a trader, he moved a lot of product for a lot of people, and a lot of money changed hands. But he was never financially rich.

Kell was raised in the home of a sea captain, and was used to his father being away and his mother running the home and attending to the kids. He expected his wife to do the same but this was not to be. 'Eventually, after we were married and I was travelling in my various jobs, she didn't seem to like it because it meant she had to spend more time on the home front instead of working on her make-up jobs.'

Patricia had been married twice before meeting Kell. Her first marriage was a disaster, having occurred in her late teens. It was from this marriage that her daughter Tina Burgess was born, in November 1947. Patricia was modelling at the time, and after the breakdown of her marriage found herself travelling Australia to pursue her career. She was full of zest and ambition, a single, independent career woman with a child. Her mother Kate looked after young Tina while Pat worked the demanding modelling circuit.

She soon met the established make-up expert Joan Von Addlestein and began learning the art of make-up, a trade that would stay with her for the rest of her life. She was very good at her job.

Pat's second husband, Roger Smith, was an extremely good-looking American television executive who had come to Australia to help with the birth of television Down Under. As it happened, Smith was also a bigamist, and when Pat eventually discovered the lie, he took an overdose of sleeping pills and killed himself.

'At the time, I felt very sorry for her,' Kell states.

Pat became pregnant just a few months after she and Kell were married, and Kell's mother Mabel offered the newlyweds her home, an English-style bungalow with leadlight windows. They packed up and left their Neutral Bay apartment and moved to 24 Howell Avenue, Lane Cove, excited with the move, excited with the coming of their first child, and by the prospect of a full family life ahead.

As soon as they settled in, Pat wanted her daughter Tina to move to Sydney and be part of the family. 'Tina came up from Melbourne and joined us, aged twelve or thirteen. She was such a happy, delightful little girl back then. She'd never known her father because he left her a month after she was born. Her name was Burgess, Tina Burgess. I said to her, You use my name, you're a Hutchence now. Tina and I had a great relationship. I used to call her my little princess, which she loved. She was quite a darling, and she and I got on well together.'

Kell's first major argument with Patricia was over education. 'I wanted the kids to have some kind of academic background, to go to university and all that stuff, and that's what I wanted for Tina, too.'

Later on, when Tina was about fifteen, she left school

and became an assistant make-up artist. Tina was looking for a good bloke to get married and settle down.

That attitude appears to have prevailed throughout Tina's life: by 1998 she had had three husbands. Between them, Patricia and Tina have had eight marriages. Husband number one for Tina was Jim Lewis from San Jose; her second husband was Jeff Bushelman from Burbank, Los Angeles; her third, also from Los Angeles, was scrap-metal merchant Ken Schorr, who left her in February 1998.

Patricia Hutchence became Mrs Mollenberg during her fourth marriage, and her fifth and current husband is millionaire ex-airforce group captain, Ross Glassop.

Although Tina has used the surname of Hutchence at various stages of her life, she was never actually adopted by Kelland. According to him, this has always been a sore point with her. He never adopted her because his marriage started to go shaky after only a couple of years. His lawyer advised him against adoption if the marriage was unsound.

• • •

Michael Kelland John Hutchence was born on 22 January 1960 at the Mater Misericordiae Hospital, North Sydney. His third Christian name, John, was the name of Patricia's brother, who was killed in a shooting accident on a hunting trip.

The labour was a short one. As Patricia recovered from the birth, Michael's father pressed his face against the window in the maternity ward, longing to hold his tiny, beautiful baby.

'You don't have to drive this slowly,' Kelland recalls Pat telling him as he painstakingly drove his wife and Michael home from the hospital. 'I didn't want to have any accidents, any brushes with other cars. This was our little baby. I drove slowly all the way down River Road, up all the back streets until we arrived at Lane Cove.'

Patricia had put up new curtains in the nursery, selected a beautiful bassinet, and there were toys and rattles and soft teddy bears all over the room. It was freshly painted. As a baby, Michael had everything he could ever wish for.

To celebrate the occasion, Kell and Pat held a barbecue in the backyard, underneath the camphor laurel trees. Their guests included Diana Gregory, a top glamour girl at the time. 'I remember Diana going over to look at Mike lolling back in his pram,' Kell says, 'and as she picked him up to help with a nappy change he peed right into her face, giving her a big, gummy smile and a chuckle in the process.'

Tina, thirteen and firmly entrenched in the Hutchence home, was ecstatic when Michael was born. According to Kell she was terrific around the baby. She helped wash him, changed his nappies, and generally supported her parents with regards to Michael. He was her baby brother. Her first baby brother.

Patricia had stopped working for a while after the birth and life was joyous. Lots of friends came to visit and enjoy the congenial hospitality of the Hutchence family. They were both good hosts and had a wide variety of glamorous friends; make-up artists, models, photographers, businessmen. They were part of Sydney's swinging cocktail set.

Meanwhile, Kell was still working for Guthrie & Co., one of the most successful distributors of Australian products, especially flour and sugar, in Singapore, Malaysia and Borneo. The company represented the Anchor Mills company of Sydney, which was one of the premium selling brands in South-East Asia. In 1961 Guthrie bought a louvre-window factory in Brisbane and asked Kell to move there to oversee it. His export savvy was starting to be recognised and he was set the task of developing the export section of the company, in addition to overseeing production. All of Guthrie's sales were overseas, with none whatsoever in Australia.

Kell subsequently bought a modern home in Brisbane, a rectangled, elevated dwelling on three levels with a garage underneath the bedrooms at the front of the house. Because of its shape and style, it was dubbed the Hollywood house by the neighbours. It was mid-1961 and Michael was eighteen months old when the family moved to Wongabel Estate in the brand new suburb of Kenmore, in Brisbane, Queensland.

Towards the end of that year, Michael's younger brother Rhett was conceived, even though the cracks were already starting to show in the Hutchence marriage.

Rhett Bradley Hutchence was born in Brisbane on 21 August 1962, and Patricia once again had no problems during the pregnancy or birth.

'It was a big day when Rhett came back from hospital. We'd fitted out his nursery, just like we had with Michael's when he was born. New bassinet, new sheets and pillows, the works. Rhett was a good baby, too. He was a big sleeper and was no trouble at all,' recalls Kell.

Rhett's birth marked the beginning of a brotherly love and attachment that would be truly put to the test during the next thirty-five years, with both brothers wearing each other's guilt, each other's despair, frustrations and elation. Rhett and Michael would run the gauntlet of compassion and understanding, and as the years rolled by, each tried to delve into their family past and figure out exactly what went wrong and when. Michael found partial refuge in his rock'n'roll lifestyle, expressing his angst in his lyrics, while Rhett found an asylum of sorts in his wandering. The empathy they had for each other was deep, devoted and pushed to the limits. Their relationship, and indeed that of his entire family, would be Michael's inspiration for some of his more introspective and poignant lyrics.

The following eighteen months saw Kell expand his employer's business interests. He started an assembly plant in Pretoria, South Africa, and another in Nigeria, and then another in Jamaica. He was travelling the world, visiting more than fifty countries a year.

Then, around mid-1963, Kelland Hutchence was offered a job with an old friend, Sonny Marshall. Marshall had made a fortune building a successful lighting business, Daydream Lamps. His uniquely styled lamps became quite the rage, and Marshall sold the company for millions just as it started to reach its peak. He now decided he wanted to repeat his success and start up in competition with the company he'd sold. Kell sold the family home in Brisbane and they moved back to Sydney, to Bantry Road, Frenchs Forest. But the original company Marshall had created proved to be too strong, and neither Hutchence nor Marshall could make a dent in the market place. The project failed.

With Michael aged three and a half and Rhett eighteen months, Patricia was bursting to get back into her career as she saw Kelland's working life come to a temporary but screeching halt. Following the failure of the lighting company he set up his own export consulting business and started to represent manufacturers in South-East Asia. It wasn't as successful as he had hoped. Patricia began working again, and it was her money which helped pay the bills at this time.

'Pat helped out with her make-up earnings,' Kell recalls. 'I think that was one of the main problems with our marriage. I felt inadequate even though we had a comfortable home, food, clothing, the lot. I know I provided well.'

If both parents were working late, or if they travelled away from Sydney in their respective jobs, Kelland's sister Croy Magee sometimes came to the rescue and looked after the two young boys. Kell's mother Mabel also looked after them from time to time, and Tina pitched in too, helping out with babysitting on countless occasions. 'I must say, she was a wonderful help with the boys in those days, particularly when Pat and I went out. Some people thought we did it too often, and on reflection they may well have been right,' says Kell.

One evening, following one of Pat and Kell's many arguments, Kell came back to his Frenchs Forest home to find Patricia and his two sons not there. He panicked, made a few phone calls, and discovered that she'd taken the boys down to Melbourne, where she'd left them with her mother, Kate.

Kell jumped on a plane, flew down to Melbourne, picked up the boys and returned to Sydney. He felt that leaving them with Pat's mother was not the right thing to do. When he returned to Sydney he got some help and started looking for a new job.

In October 1964 Kell successfully applied for a job as a general manager and director with the huge Australian trading company, Swift and Company, to be based in Hong Kong. They offered Kell a great deal, with a flat, car, amahs, and an expense account thrown in, and they wanted him to move to Hong Kong immediately and settle into the job first, before his family came to join him a few months later.

Kell didn't think he could pull off the job because there was so much drama going on between him and Pat. At one stage he thought seriously about taking the boys with him to Hong Kong and leaving Pat behind. 'I thought, with the help of amahs, that I could survive in Hong Kong with the boys because I knew the city well. But somebody told me I couldn't get them out of the country without their mother's permission. Then I realised that it would not look good with the company if I rolled up with two children, telling them I had split with my wife. So I told Pat about the job, and she was on the next plane out of Melbourne, headed for Sydney.

Kell ended up leaving for Hong Kong in November 1964, with Patricia leaving with Michael, Rhett and Tina only two months later. Instead of easing into his job and then finding a home for his family, Kell Hutchence soon moved his entire brood into a suite at the Hilton Hotel, at great cost to the company. It was not the best start to his new career. The family stayed in the hotel for around six weeks.

The move to Hong Kong proved to be the beginning of the end of the Hutchence family unit. It would struggle on for more than a decade. The marriage was finally dissolved twelve bitter, turbulent and tearful years later.

two

The Hong Kong connection

> My mother ran
> My father left town
> But we still have
> What's necessary to go on
> Flesh and blood
> Flesh and blood
> My brother's sane
> His heart is so strong
> Sweet sister T
> She loved so long and hard
>
> 'I'm just a man'
> *Elegantly Wasted* 1997
> MICHAEL HUTCHENCE
> AND ANDREW FARRISS

The white, second-hand 1962 Jaguar sedan careered around the bend, thin wire-spoked wheels glistening in the sun, Rhett and Michael rolling from one side of the back seat to the other, Kelland's hands gripped tightly on the wheel.

It was 1965 in Hong Kong, and a Sunday ritual for the three Hutchence males was well under way. Up Tai Tam Road into the steep hills of Hong Kong, rollicking around the twisting bends, cruising down the straight stretch, Kell and his two young sons let their imaginations run wild, playing pretend Grand Prix.

The Hutchence family had now settled into Hong Kong. After leaving the Hilton, they temporarily moved into a flat in Pine Court, Old Peak Road, then to a 'leave house' in the suburb of Stanley. The correspondent for *Time* magazine lived there, but was leaving for six months. It was a common thing for expatriate workers based in Hong Kong to vacate the place for six months, renting out their home. For the Hutchence family it was unsettling to live somewhere for such a short period of time, but they gradually slipped into the bustling, social Hong Kong lifestyle. The fact that their temporary home was a two-story house with a cook and two servants thrown in no doubt sweetened their transient stay. 'What would you like for dinner tonight,' Kelland remembers being asked on a daily basis, 'Russian, Hungarian, French, Australian, or American?'

He kept his eyes and ears open for a suitable, more enduring abode, and was particularly keen on a luxurious apartment block with large rooms, also on Old Peak Road, called Kam Yuen. Eventually, at one of the many parties he and Pat attended, he met an Australian who leased a very large apartment in the block and who was soon to return home permanently. Kell approached the owners and negotiated a deal, signing on for a three-year lease. A stone's throw from where Kell worked in Alexandra House, the flat was just above the city in a very nice part of town. He could walk to work from Old Peak Road.

He soon hired two amahs. Amahs were an intricate part of the Hong Kong lifestyle of the expats, and in many ways gave the young Hutchence lads a rose-coloured view of life. Rhett Hutchence fondly remembers the amahs. 'It was a surreal way to grow up,' he told me. 'They were the old type of amah and they wore their hair in a long plaited pigtail down their back. They had names like Ah Tang—whatever their last name was, they would put an Ah in front of it, like Ah Ha. One, I remember, was called Ha, and we used to call her Ahah . . . ha, ha! We grew up in a place where you didn't have to make your bed. We got to Hong Kong at such a young age, we didn't really know the difference between that and growing up in Australia, where we would have had to do things for ourselves. We had everything done for us in Hong Kong because of the amahs.'

A grassy park was situated at the end of the street, which was lined with lush, leafy trees. The Glenealy Primary School, where Michael was enrolled, was in the road behind the apartment block and it took just a couple of minutes to walk there.

Kell laments that while Pat was supposed to look after Rhett when Michael started school, increasingly the amahs did the job. Now that she had the assistance of two amahs, Pat had returned to her make-up work, moving primarily into commercials, television, and the occasional movie. Tina was already working with her mother on make-up jobs, or doing hairdressing on sets. She was also, according to Michael years later, doing spots as a go-go dancer. There were thousands of American soldiers taking R&R from Vietnam in Hong Kong at that time, demanding night life.

Kell settled into his job with gusto. When Swift acquired the wine and liquor company, Gande Price Ltd, Kell had to meet the owners and managers of all the principal companies, which meant travelling all over Europe for six to eight weeks. His flair for importing and exporting was increasingly coming to the fore, and much of his time was spent expanding the various business interests of Swift, which had also opened a retail store in Hong Kong. Being a comprehensive hands-on man, he naturally took charge of extra duties associated with the store, such as organising brochures, leaflets, advertising, the promotion and display of Christmas bargains.

Hong Kong at the time was bristling, governed by the British. Unrest was spreading throughout the island, causing widespread fear and speculation. 'I can remember when the riots were in full swing, I used to warn Michael and Rhett not to open the letterbox because letter bombs were daily items,' Kell recollects. The riots actually started over a price increase of 10 cents on the ferry fare between Kowloon and Hong Kong, and were initiated and fanned by communists sympathetic to China's cause living in Hong Kong.

People thought it was the end of the Hong Kong boom time, that democracy was in danger, that the revolution in mainland China would spread quickly to the colony. They were leaving in droves; properties were being sold for a song, only to skyrocket in price during the early seventies. Those with enough money who stayed and bought property eventually made a fortune.

Asia, and particularly South-East Asia, was a political hot spot. The Americans were stepping up their activities in Vietnam and eventually, with an increase in the number of soldiers invading Vietnam, a trader with deftness in South-East Asia could bargain himself into plenty of opportunities. Kelland Hutchence was shrewd enough to pull a few deals on behalf of his company.

'I chanced upon a big contract with the American forces,' he remembers, 'when a colonel and a lieutenant accidentally knocked on my door one morning wanting meat supplies for the troops. Being a trader I didn't say no.'

He subsequently made a deal with a New Zealand meat

company, and began importing eight tons of meat on every Air New Zealand flight into Hong Kong. 'I had a freezer near the airport so I could take it off the New Zealand flight, run it to the freezer, then bring in an old DC4 I acquired from Air Vietnam, and load it up.' From midnight until 2 am, with the help of a hundred Chinese crew, Kell would load the lot onto the old DC4. When necessary, he would board the five-and-a-half-hour flight to Saigon, ensuring the safe arrival and unloading of the meat.

'I remember flying in over Da Nang, Phantoms going past us, action on the ground. We'd fly through the valleys over Da Lat and down into Saigon. Sometimes we'd get stacked up in the air for an hour and couldn't get in because there was so much activity on that air strip. But we always got there,' he says. 'The Americans would be at the air strip in Saigon, on the ready with the freezer trucks. The Yanks acting as agents were such shysters, the whole pack of them. I called them camp followers—they'd done the Korean War and made a fortune, and now they were into the Vietnam War. The agents and a few of the American sergeants and officers were arrogant, and some of them I'd rather forget. They were rude, ill-mannered, boring, money-grabbing types.'

That they were, but they were also enterprising capitalists always ready with a deal, always looking for a dealer, and one day Kelland received another call from the US army, this time with regard to 'mobile baskets on wheels'—they were to be part of a new supermarket being opened for the US troops.

'Supermarkets were relatively new, and so, therefore, were push trolleys. They needed fifty of them, so I found some in Australia and flew them into Saigon via Singapore.

Imagine the space they took up. They were expensive in the end, I think each one cost about a thousand dollars, and then I put a profit on them. They must have been the most expensive trolleys ever to leave Australia. They were crazy days, I tell you.'

One of his biggest competitors was an American agent with the unlikely name of Billy Crum, a semi-hunchbacked character who walked with a limp, could talk under wet cement, had made a lot of money from the war in Korea and now Saigon, and who dealt always in high stakes. Kell went to his home one evening to discuss a questionable business deal. They were sitting by the pool with a few girls and Kell felt as if the war was all around. 'C47s were flying above us, and we could hear the gun ships just half a mile away firing wildly into the jungle, not knowing what they were hitting. There were flares lighting up the sky as if it were daytime.' Years later Crum was murdered. He had set up house in the New Territories in Hong Kong and someone poured gasoline over it, inside and out, then ignited it.

Whenever Kell Hutchence returned from his adventures, Rhett and Michael would be eager to hear his stories. Kell is a great raconteur; he has dozens of exciting yarns about his days as a trader, and in later years he continued to reminisce, recounting them to the absolute joy of his sons. So impressed was Michael with his father's exploits that he bought him a journal for Christmas in 1994 and told him to start writing down his experiences. It was his wish that Kelland write a book about his days in South-East Asia.

While Kell and Pat were making a good living in Hong Kong, the strains in their marriage were now very apparent. Patricia was travelling all over the world, her make-up assignments taking her on location work. She went to Guam for a movie, she went to Rome and then Los Angeles. Kelland was beside himself during this time. 'I had good servants but it just wasn't the same. I found trying to deal with work and the kids just too much, and eventually Pat and I fell out to such a degree that it seemed almost impossible to reconcile.'

Patricia was in some ways a woman ahead of her time, a career woman following her own path. Kelland, on the other hand, came from the old school, leaning more towards the idea that a mother's place is in the home.

The increasing arguments between Kell and his wife were just not the right environment for the kids. 'On top of that I was having troubles at work concerning the direction of the company, so I eventually resigned. I received a reasonable package, but nothing like what they get today.'

Exhausted by the arguments and concerned at the effects the acrimony between himself and Pat were having on his family, Kelland decided to ship them all back to Sydney. After almost two years in Hong Kong, he reluctantly booked a boat passage on the *Nanking* for Tina, Patricia, Michael and Rhett. 'I hated sending the boys back but I just had to, I had to get my head together and get myself a job. I could have gone back to Sydney, I suppose, but I loved Hong Kong and I just didn't want it to beat me.'

So, for better or worse, four members of the Hutchence family were shipped off to live in their Frenchs Forest home in Sydney.

• • •

Kelland had a hard time of it emotionally, as did the rest of the family. He began a new job with Mandarin Textiles, one of the more famous Hong Kong textile and clothing manufacturers and exporters, their brand name being Dynasty. In the early 1950s, Kell had had some experience with selling clothing in New South Wales, driving from town to town with his samples in a suitcase in the back of his Hudson car. Mandarin Textiles needed an administration man, the company having boomed during the mid to late sixties. Kell, his reputation well intact, was just the man to oversee everything from an increase in production to exporting and shipping arrangements.

Dynasty was the couture house of Hong Kong, with five salons in the city, a showroom in New York, and a showcase factory near the airport. The company was owned by two Americans, and the factory was unique—an ultra-streamlined building with doors coated in pearl shell, gold-plated doorknobs, huge sumptuous rooms. Under Kelland's guidance, the company expanded even further and he eventually became its general manager.

Kell now began planning the return of his two sons, anticipating becoming a single parent. The idea of getting into a long lease was not so attractive, the future of his family set-up being unknown, so he found a temporary sublet.

Fed up with bickering over the phone and feeling discontent, Kell told Pat to put the boys on the plane to Hong Kong. There was only one big bedroom with a queen-sized bed in the flat, and when they first returned the boys would bunk in with their dad. After a few months Kell looked around for another house, and found one in Dorset Crescent, off Waterloo Road, Kowloon Tong, one of the better areas of Hong Kong. It had a front and back garden, big balconies, a large lounge and dining room, three bedrooms, two bathrooms and amah quarters at the back. There was a back gate that opened onto a park, and, as with their first Hong Kong home, it was a hop, step and jump to Michael's new school, Beacon Hill Primary School, part of the English School Foundation.

The boys' Hong Kong social life picked up speed. Aged nine and seven, they met new friends at school and joined the Boy Scouts movement. One of the more famous meeting places in Hong Kong was the Ladies Recreation Club, and the family often met friends there for Sunday brunch, the boys running off to play. It was here, and later on at the United Services Club, that the Hutchence brothers learned to swim. A former Olympic champion from Belgium took an interest and started coaching them, both boys demonstrating a natural flair. But it was Michael who, according to the coach, was a top talent, destined to go far in the swimming world. He had an excellent stroke and a strong leg kick, inspiring people to comment that he swam like a fish. Swimming was for Michael a natural aptitude, one of his many talents; he was blessed with the ability to excel at almost anything he attempted.

The boys entered regular swimming meets around the island and Michael won countless medals. Rhett wasn't too bad either, but lacked the drive and ambition already emerging in his elder brother. Three days a week Kelland would pick up Mike and Rhett from school and take them to swimming training. The trio also entered a few father-and-son swimming meets.

One Sunday afternoon, Rhett came running through the back gate, across the backyard and into the house yelling, 'Dad, Dad, Mike's broken his arm, come quickly.' Kell tore through the yard and into the park, where he found his eldest son sprawled on the ground with scratches all over his body and his left arm clearly out of shape. Michael had fallen while attempting to hurdle one of the many rosebeds placed systematically throughout the park. It was a Sunday and the nearest hospital open didn't have an emergency ward. Nor could they send an ambulance because there was no driver rostered on that day. Kell was in the house receiving instructions on the telephone from the duty doctor, while Rhett was consoling and nursing Michael who was spreadeagled on the ground in the park.

After making several more phone calls, Kell discovered that the Queen Elizabeth public hospital, most of the patients of which were local Chinese, was open for business. As delicately as they could, Rhett and Kell took Mike from the park and placed him in the car, then drove to the hospital. Michael's broken elbow was set, but not very successfully, and as a consequence he was never able to fully straighten his left arm again. 'That was a great shame because it put to an end what could have been a great swimming career,' Kell sighs.

• • •

Almost six months after the boys had settled in with Kell, he received a phone call from Patricia. 'I want to come back to Hong Kong,' she told him.

Pat had been regularly talking to the boys on the telephone after she and Tina had flown them back from Australia, and Kelland started to get an inkling that something was up when Rhett and Mike began asking when their mother was coming. Despite the siege mentality between the couple, something magnetic was still there and Kell finally invited Patricia to come back and rejoin the family.

'What could I do? I still thought she was terrific, that she was a doll. These things happen.'

Michael had meanwhile settled into Beacon Hill Primary School, which Kell had chosen because he felt it offered the best education outside of a private school. He didn't want his sons to attend one of the private schools because he felt they had a drug problem. He had heard of young boys the age of ten and eleven becoming hooked on drugs. 'One of our closest friends lost his son to drugs and he attended a private school,' Kell recalls.

Michael and Rhett were at this time already very close. Their personalities and characters were taking shape, Michael tending a little to the shy, self-conscious side, but determined and aware. He was already looking lanky, his distinctive loping walk in place. He appeared to know what he wanted, what he enjoyed, while he was quietly getting on with life. Conversely, Rhett was more outgoing, a little more raucous, a bit cheeky, not quite having the direction that Michael was developing. No matter which way you cut it though, Michael was the elder brother and Rhett, as the younger one, was destined to live in his shadow. 'It was probably when we had a "normal" relationship,' Rhett said. 'The shadow was yet to arrive.'

• • •

Six months after she returned to Hong Kong with her daughter, Patricia decided she'd had enough of her rocky marriage and announced she was leaving.

Strong rumours suggested that Patricia was having an affair with American actor John Russell, one of the stars of the television series *The Lawman*. They met on location in Guam and then again in Hong Kong. Kelland thought he wanted a divorce, but subsequently put it on hold. He was still in love with Pat, and he hoped the separation would not last, that the marriage would eventually resume for the sake of the boys.

Working in the entertainment industry, Pat was invited to many parties and it was through an advertising friend of hers that Michael had his first contact with recording, when he was around eleven years old. Michael used to sing in a casual folk outfit. They did not perform often, and certainly not in public—it was a fun, home group. When Pat's advertising friend heard about this, he recruited Michael to sing a song for an ad. Thus it was that on his first record Michael Hutchence sang 'Jingle Bells'. The finished recording was placed on a continuous tape inside the stomach of a plastic, battery-powered Father Christmas. It was a hit. Years later, when Michael had his first taste of American success with INXS, he did an interview for the English magazine, *Mix*, recalling the toy doll and his 'big break'. It was October 1986, and the band was just starting to happen in the UK. He remembered the Hong Kong doll as his first sell-out. 'If anyone out there has a copy, please send me one,' he said.

It was through his mother, according to Michael in the same interview, that he first brushed with stardom, when he realised that stars were given special treatment. In 1971 he met Klaus Kinski, and remembers trying to frolic with his daughter Nastassja, who was ten years old. 'I tried to play doctors but I didn't get very far,' he told the magazine, adding, 'she was extremely intelligent and didn't want to waste her time on boys.'

Michael and his brother met many celebrities in Hong Kong, mainly due to Pat's make-up work and the entertainment crowd she mixed with. 'She was in line for all the top international movies being made in Hong Kong,' Kell reflects.

In the 1986 *Mix* interview, Michael referred to his father as one of the last of the colonials. 'He's waiting for the Chinese to come over the border to attack him. He'll be standing on the roof.' This was not true—Kell had strong, respectful business and friendship ties with the Chinese, but was about as far from being colonial as one could get—and perhaps the interview was a sign of Michael's evasive way of dealing with the media, creating smoke screens for the truth, putting a twist on reality.

Typhoons were a regular occurrence in Hong Kong. There were usually about three hits between April and August, and an air of excitement and adventure would envelop the three Hutchence males, now living alone, when a big one struck the city. Exposed as their house was to the howling winds, Rhett, Mike and Kell would eagerly await the typhoon. As soon as the level-one signal on the typhoon warning system went up, the servants would start placing sticking tape on the windows to stop them shattering, and when the level-three warning was reached, people would start flocking home. If level five was reached, everyone had to get off the streets and take shelter inside the nearest safe building. Should the warning level reach ten, all hell would be let loose and Kell and his sons would huddle together in the bathroom, praying that none of the windows would break, that none of the balcony doors would be ripped off their hinges.

'Suddenly the wind would stop roaring and the eye off the typhoon would pass over, and all would be calm. But after about half an hour, the other half of the blast would hit and we'd wait until it passed over again. I can remember

Rhett and Michael pointing out the window, following a typhoon in Dorset Crescent, at the huge trees ripped out of the ground, the yard and the street littered with debris, strewn with branches,' Kell recalls.

Rhett was showing early signs of being the tearaway kid. One day Ah Chan came racing into the house screaming, 'Quick, master, quickly, much blood, blood everywhere!' Kell raced into the backyard, through the gate and into the park to where Rhett had been playing with one of Kell's spears from New Guinea. He and his friend were throwing the spears at each other when Rhett threw it a little harder than he should have and the spear pierced one of the main veins in his friend's arm. Kell grabbed his arm, placed a ligature around it, and took him to hospital.

On another occasion, Michael came running into the house yelling out that Rhett had his head stuck in the swing. Kell rushed outside, only to find Rhett had wedged his head through the steel back rest of the swing seat. He was in a kneeling position, body on the ground, his head stuck, unable to move.

'I phoned the emergency police and before long they and the fire brigade arrived; the ambulance arrived, lights flashing, siren sounding. The guy in charge of emergency rushed towards the swing, huge steel cutters in his hand. Suddenly, Rhett moved his head slightly and out he came, away from the back of the seat. Everyone had stunned looks of surprise on their faces. It was a hoot, really like a cartoon,' Kell says.

A few months later, there was a knock on the front door. It was the police, wanting to know whether Kell had a young son called Rhett. It transpired that Rhett had been nearly killed by some Chinese boys. He had been at the back of Kowloon Tong, a rough area with even rougher kids, and had started throwing rocks at the Chinese kids. They'd chased after him and nearly got him. Somehow or other, Rhett had escaped. He was starting to be the wild one, while Michael was more pensive, more introverted, a little moody, and at times sickly.

'I was the younger brother,' Rhett recalls. 'What's the role for the younger brother? Fooling around, I guess.'

Kelland was now a single father, working full-time. He finally decided to take a break and go back to Australia for a holiday with his sons. It proved to be hard work, and a little impractical. They lived with Kell's mother Mabel for a while and then stayed in a hotel in Manly Beach. Kell was agitated, unable to fully relax, and felt compelled to return to Hong Kong.

On his arrival, he discovered that Tina had fallen in love with an American man and went with him back to the States. It didn't work out, and Tina started working as a nanny in San Jose for a man called Jim Lewis, who would become her first husband. They had a son, Brent, with whom Michael forged a good friendship in later life.

Tina had only been gone from Hong Kong for a few months when Kell received a phone call from his estranged wife proposing that she return yet again to the family unit.

The two brothers had been missing their mother. Like most children of separated parents, Rhett and Michael longed for a reunion. They were happy with their father, but wanted the family together again. Pat became increasingly upset and teary, saying she wanted to see the boys, so Kelland went for the hat trick and took her back for a third time.

It was 1972 and they decided to take a family holiday

together, travelling to Bali for the first time, en route to Sydney. For both Rhett and Michael it was the start of an intermittent, long-term relationship with the spirituality of the island. The family stayed for five days before travelling on to Sydney for a good, long break. Midway through their holiday, Kell received a phone call from his employer at Dynasty. The British real-estate moguls Slater Walker had made an enormous offer to buy the company. Although he was offered a separate job during his stay in Sydney, Kell wanted to go back to Hong Kong to discuss the British offer.

It turned out that the company wanted to keep Kell on after the sale, and he was made a lucrative offer as managing director. But he declined, taking instead a large pay-out. With Tina gone and Pat back, the family decided to leave Hong Kong permanently and live in Australia.

Michael was twelve years old and about to enter a phase of his life that would change his destiny.

three

Escape to Hollywood, stranded in Sydney

> I was just like a child
> With my eyes wide open
> I'm closing off the lies
> Making my own mind up
> When I can I will
> How many dirty little secrets
> Were kept behind my back
> Men and women
> Giving each other the sham
>
> 'Men and Women'
> *Welcome to Wherever You Are* 1992
> MICHAEL HUTCHENCE

Christmas Day, 1973. Michael, now almost fourteen years old, Kell, Pat and Rhett were settled back in Sydney. The return to Australia had given the boys a feeling of freedom and open spaces, a whole new experience after the geographical confines of Hong Kong, where they'd nevertheless enjoyed a cosmopolitan lifestyle. Despite the trials of the preceding years, the Hutchence family was still together.

On Christmas morning Michael awoke to find a red ribbon dangling from the end of his bed, across the floor, along the passageway, down the stairs, through the kitchen, into the family room by way of the Christmas tree, out to the garage and onto the gift—a Honda XR75. His first motorbike.

'Mike had shown an intense interest in motocross during that year,' Kell remembers. 'He was totally mad about motorbikes so I decided to get him one. I bought it and stored it in the boot of my LTD for about four days. On Christmas Eve, after he'd gone to bed, Pat and I wrapped the bike up in cellophane. You know, it was a great gift and a big surprise for him. Next thing we know, he's tearing around the house on this Honda 75, a peppy little thing it was, too, jumping over logs and things. Oh, it was unbelievable.'

That motorbike was the start of a passion that stayed with Michael for the rest of his life. In later years he'd periodically buy bikes, blasting off into the distance on two-wheeled escapades. Some of his various girlfriends would share his enthusiasm, and stories of his bike bravado abound. The details are always hazy, no matter who tells the story, and it's difficult to detect fact from myth. One commonly told story has him, at the peak of his fame, tearing at 145kmh towards a brick wall, current girlfriend astride the back, and coming to a screeching halt by pulling off a perfect side wheely, just a few feet from the wall. Not showing off, just indulging his adrenaline-pumped need for action and walking the fine line.

Pat and Kell bought Rhett a punching-bag that Christmas.

'It wasn't even a good punching-bag, it was a lousy punching-bag,' Rhett remembers. 'I don't know why they thought I needed a punching-bag. It was a bit of plywood with an extension coming out of it, and a punching-bag hanging from the extension. You had to stand on the bit of plywood placed on the floor to hit the bag, and if you didn't stand on it the whole thing fell over. It was totally impractical. I got a motorbike the next year, and that was the end of my punching days.' Rhett had hounded his father for the intervening twelve months to buy him a motorbike.

'I relented,' says Kell, 'and got him a bike, too, a Yamaha 80. They were all mini-bikes, you couldn't put them on the road or anything like that.' On the weekends, Kell took them to a brick pit in Terrey Hills that Michael had heard about from some of his like-minded mates. It had lots of hills, plenty of clay, and was perfect for motocross. Kell had to get a trailer made to transport both bikes to their various weekend excursions. Then the chains and heavy-duty screws to steady the bikes on the trailer; then it was helmets, boots, the clothes, the whole kit and caboodle.

The family had been settled for almost a year in Belrose, just past Frenchs Forest on the way to Terrey Hills, part of the laced-up web that is Sydney's North Shore suburban slouch. Decidedly middle class, and white. The new Hutchence home had four bedrooms, two bathrooms, a playroom, double garage, air-conditioning, and a large backyard. Pat and Kell sold their home in Frenchs Forest to help finance the purchase. The boys were well ensconced in the local schools, Mike in Davidson High School after a short spell at Killarney Heights while the new school was being built, and Rhett in Belrose Primary School.

During their intensive schooling in Hong Kong, or Hongkers as Michael often called the city, the lads had developed a distinctly non-Australian, British colonial accent, non-clipped, non-nasal, and rounded. Rhett managed to keep his, but Michael's changed as he travelled more extensively. 'Mike seemed to include all accents in his speaking voice. He was a good mimic, and several accents were integrated into his speech,' Kell says. In middle-class Australia, however, the boys' slightly snobbish-sounding accents stood out like a shag on a rock. As open and gregarious as Australians would like to be seen to be, the fact is that in many sections of the community there has always been a subtle, unspoken prejudice towards accents, success, Aborigines, anyone who comes to live in Australia from overseas, anyone who has a non-white skin, the English, the French, the Americans, anyone who is slightly different.

When Michael returned to Sydney from Hong Kong, he was already cosmopolitan, having tasted the exotica of life in Hong Kong and attended with his parents many outrageous parties on the fringe of show business, meeting actors and the like. His was not the normal Australian upbringing, and that, perhaps, was one of the things that helped shape his ambivalent attitude towards Australia. Like many Australian artists who achieve international success, in later years Michael and INXS had a love–hate relationship with their own country.

In an interview with the American magazine *Spin* in February 1988, Michael spoke of his attitude towards Australia after returning from Hong Kong. 'I'm Australian for sure, but I lived in Hong Kong until I was about twelve or thirteen. I had a problem with Australia. In the first place, I hated it. I had all the same prejudices in my head the English have about it, cork screws and cork hats and kangaroos. Once I got there I realised it was different, but I couldn't believe the people where I went to school. I just hated the place.'

He was talking about Davidson High School, the same

school that the Farriss brothers attended. There were fourteen hundred kids at the school, according to Andrew Farriss, and the older kids had a game for newcomers whereby they would saunter around the schoolyard with tennis balls and pummel them. Tennis balls were effective because they didn't leave obvious bruises on the body.

'That went on every day for a while,' Farriss said in the same *Spin* interview. 'Finally, me and the other new kids said to each other, Let's get these fucking people, so we got everything we could find in the way of fruit and food and went in and just threw it on everyone, teachers, everything.'

One of the new kids was Michael Hutchence, the one with the Pommy accent, 'the toffy-nosed little prick from Hong Kong'.

'My friend Paul and I were standing around the courtyard one day and saw Michael being hassled by all these guys,' Andrew Farriss went on. 'He'd only just arrived the day before and I remember watching him, thinking, Boy, this guy doesn't know what this place is like, does he? I just felt sorry for him, I guess. So my friend Paul, who was quite big for his age, he was about six foot two, he just went over and pushed these guys away and said, "Leave him alone." After that incident I didn't really talk to Michael or have anything to do with him for almost a year.

'Older guys have this thing in Australia where they all like to scare the shit out of you and tell you how they're gonna do this or that to you. There's this horrible anticipation of violence that's going to await you at school. It's all exaggerated but it also depends on how quickly you stand up and say "Fuck you" to all these people.'

This was the basic attitude that INXS and its management would successfully apply to the world music industry in later years if told they could not do something the way they wanted to do it.

At fourteen Michael was showing signs of rebellion, albeit in an introverted, cerebral, poetic way, often sneaking off into a corner of a room, or sitting outside, putting pen to paper. In basic words, basic poems, he expressed himself in the same way many kids do. Part of Michael's demeanour was moody, quiet, slightly sullen, and these elements of his character would in his final years develop into radical mood swings, temper tantrums, and frustrated tearful bouts of depression. But at that time, at fourteen, Michael was mostly happy, effervescent, congenial, his wicked sense of humour always shining through. He didn't seem to be detrimentally affected by his slight lisp or his developing acne.

* * *

In 1974 Kelland Hutchence began a new job at Vanbro Pty Ltd, a development company owned and run by Barry Loiterton. Loiterton's son David would later work in the music industry, at one stage for RooArt, the record label and publishing company started and once owned by INXS manager Chris Murphy. Loiterton senior was an entrepreneur who bought failing companies and built them back into viable businesses, among them John Serafino's in Double Bay, an inner city suburb that is often compared to Rodeo Drive in Los Angeles. Serafino had since re-opened his clothing business and today it is one of Double Bay's foremost thriving businesses. Vanbro was based in Bay Street, Double Bay, a stone's throw from where Michael would die twenty-three years later.

Patricia was garnering attention as her reputation as a make-up artist grew. She worked extensively with APA

Studios in Neutral Bay, and was generally in demand. Kell helped with Pat's independence and bought her a car, a small Ford Prefect. 'Under-powered little thing it was,' Kell recalls, 'but at least she had her own wheels'.

The Hutchence family still hosted many parties, and at one of these Kell's old friend Sonny Marshall turned up. Marshall was the man who had made millions from his Daydream Lamps years before. According to Kell, Patricia and Marshall appeared to take a shine to each other.

There had been quite a cultivation of friendship between the two. Kell and Pat were suddenly joining Marshall and his partner Lorraine for dinner and lunch, and they were often going to visit Kell and Pat. Pat and Sonny were always very attentive to each other. One afternoon, Kelland noticed for the first time that there was an obvious attraction between the two. Later that night, Pat and Kell had a huge argument, one that really set off a whole chain of events.

As it turned out, the chain of events proved to be irreversible, and in family terms catastrophic. Next day, Kell telephoned Marshall at his home and had some heated words in his ear, and it wasn't long before Marshall left the country for London.

At exactly the same time as his marriage looked set to finally crack, the company Kell was working for collapsed, going into liquidation. He didn't quite know what to do, but eventually took over one of Vanbro's acquisitions, Solomon's trouser factory in Maitland, a sleepy country town a few hours' drive from Sydney. The factory was well equipped, had a good reputation and retail outlets in the city, so Kell mortgaged his home and re-entered the clothing trade, this time in manufacturing. He didn't have his own range of clothing but he did have a lot of contract work. Under stress from his collapsing marriage, he wasn't able to apply the time and concentration he usually gave to his work, and soon realised that he'd have to start spending time in Maitland to ensure the factory was cost effective. He rented a small, renovated terrace house and two or three evenings a week he would stay in Maitland, always ensuring he phoned the boys, who were back in Sydney with their mother.

After Marshall moved to London, Pat was upset and remote. For three or four weeks during September 1974, Kell reckons he felt uneasy. 'I sensed something was about to happen, but I just did not know what it was.'

One day, in the month of October, something monumental did happen, and it changed the dynamics and individual relationships of the Hutchence family members forever more. Rhett was probably the most radically affected.

'I remember walking home from school with Michael one day, and we walked into the house and I saw half of the stuff in the house packed up in the front room. Mum's stuff was packed,' Rhett recalled. 'I had no idea at all that something like this was going on, and I asked Mum what was happening. She told Michael to go and pack his things, and then told me they were both going to America, that I wasn't going, and that I would be staying in the house with someone from a babysitting company. And that's pretty much all I remember. I was sort of emotional that day, and I've kind of wiped it all out.'

Rhett has probably spent his whole life trying to wipe it all out, the shock, the pain of that afternoon. He was only twelve years old. But in 1996, twenty-two years after the event, during an intense ten-day meditation course, Rhett slowly saw some of the images return. His recollection now is that he did go to the airport that day, along with his mother, his brother, and his mother's sister Maureen. 'I was screaming to my mother to let me go with them. I promised that I would be good. "Please take me with you," I was crying, "I promise I'll be good. I'll change."'

Rhett was left totally bewildered. His father was in the country at his factory, not even aware of what was happening, while his mother rushed through the ticketing process, his brother in tow. Auntie Maureen was dragging suitcases behind them as they moved towards customs. Rhett knew full well that in a moment he'd see his mother and his brother walk towards the plane. He didn't know when he'd be seeing them again, and he didn't know why he was being left behind.

'I think everyone had a responsibility that day to make sure I was okay, and taken care of. I was screaming at the airport. Apparently Michael was trying to drag Mum through customs and onto the plane because he just couldn't handle it and didn't understand what was happening. He just wanted to run away from the situation so that it would be over. He wasn't trying to get away from me. In a way I'll never really know what happened that day. My mother's the only one who really knows. I don't remember the whole story and I don't think I ever will.'

In retrospect, Patricia very much regretted her decision. I am told by Rhett's partner Mandy Nolan that Pat felt Rhett's behaviour was more challenging than Michael's, and that he therefore needed to be with his father. Mandy says that it was a big decision for Pat and she was faced with only being able to take one child and that child happened to be Michael.

'The story just kind of came up in a conversation when Pat and I were having coffee during Rhett's meditation course,' Mandy told me. 'She certainly regretted her decision. She really thought she was doing the best she could in the situation. The end of her marriage had left her stressed and perhaps not able to fully comprehend how much it would end up affecting Rhett.

'Michael was older and easier to manage for a woman on her own, and Rhett certainly seemed to need the guidance of a father. When I spoke with Pat she recalled the most painful memory was Rhett begging to come on the plane with them. He was crying and screaming, Pat told me. She said she was distressed and upset and just wanted to get on the plane. In the midst of the emotional situation she couldn't turn back. The logic of the situation was out of control.

'When Rhett returned from his meditation course I told him about my meeting with his mother. He wept uncontrollably for a long, long time. Hearing of his mother's story and her deep regret touched him very deeply.'

Kell, in Maitland, had been unable to intervene. 'I remember getting a phone call from Rhett. He told me that Mummy and Michael had gone. He was sobbing and crying. I said, "Mummy and Michael have what?" I immediately phoned Maureen, who confirmed that Pat had left for Hollywood and taken Michael with her.

'I just wasn't able to drive, I was beside myself, so I called a friend of mine who came all the way from Marrickville, Sydney, to pick me up in Maitland. A few hours later we arrived back in Belrose and I raced up to the front of the house, and a female stranger opened the front door.

'"Who are you?" I asked her.

"'My name is Mrs Hunter. Who are you?'
'I'm Mr Hutchence.'
'What?'
'I'm Mr Hutchence.'
'No, no, that couldn't be right, your wife told me she was going overseas to meet you in America.'
'Well, I'm not in America, I'm right here, right now.''

Rhett was upstairs in his bedroom, in shock, crying his eyes out. Kell did his best to console him, at the same time trying to work out what he should do. There was no instruction manual for this one.

'Rhett has never gotten over it,' Kell says sadly.

The emotional repercussions of this event had a telling effect on the relationships both boys had with women in later years. It would hammer home to Rhett that he would always be in his brother's shadow in the eyes of his mother. Michael would always feel a certain amount of guilt for the effect his mother's deed had on Rhett, and Rhett would sometimes play on that guilt, perhaps subconsciously. Kell would always wish it had never happened. Pat has not spoken publicly about what drove her to finally leave her marriage.

That day marked the beginning of an unspoken link between Rhett and Michael. No matter what Michael might have felt about different members of his family at later, more divergent times of his transient life, no matter what the distraction, no matter what the drama or emergency, no matter what part of him was being tugged, he loved his family, deeply loved each one of them.

While researching this book, many people told me passionately about how they felt Michael was emotionally and financially held to ransom by some members of his family, driving him sometimes to distraction, sometimes to become reclusive. At various times during his brief life, following his success, he helped out family members in financial, legal, or emotional ways. But this is family say others, this is what family is all about. Others claim that it was mostly one way, that the cost to Michael was emotionally deep, and that he never turned his back on his family, no matter what the cost—financially or emotionally.

• • •

So now it was Rhett and Kell in Sydney, and Michael and Pat in Hollywood.

There is not a great deal of first-hand information about Michael's Hollywood days, a few whispers here, a rumour there. He doesn't appear to have said too much publicly about his twelve-month stay in Tinsel Town and when he did, it was cryptic.

'While Michael and Mum were away I heard from them every now and then,' Rhett recalls. 'I'd get packages, candy and bubble-gum, things like that, you know.'

According to Richard Lowenstein, the Melbourne director of the cult movie *Dogs in Space*—Michael's acting debut—and one of Michael's closest friends for some twelve years, Michael was 'quite proud of some of the experiences his mother took him through, especially in Hollywood'.

'He was hanging around his mother on set. There seems to have been this kind of golden time with his mother in Hollywood. It was an era he would speak about fondly and proudly.'

There has been talk of wild Hollywood parties attended by Michael and his mother; there's the story about Michael having to sell newspapers and take on a part-time cleaner's job to help pay the rent. Rumours have been rife about his introduction to smoking pot while in Hollywood; then there's the one about him breaking into rich Beverly Hills homes to play on their pool tables. Ordinary stories, nothing out of the usual, normal life for a teenager, given that it was Hollywood.

Even from his early Hong Kong days Michael seemed more attracted to fame by way of acting, rather than rock'n'roll. On the surface of it, then, one would imagine that going to the Mecca of the movie world and attending the hottest school in town, North Hollywood High, would just about be nirvana. But his life in Hollywood, which lasted for a little more than a year, was probably quite the opposite. Sure, he had some fun, recalling vague incidents with little detail when given the platform during early INXS interviews, but it appears that it was also an extremely unstable time. Michael jumped from a reasonably stable, middle-class family atmosphere, as troubled as it was, into a nomadic existence. He was now fifteen, he missed his father and his father's balance, his solidarity, his attention, his emotional equilibrium. He missed his brother. Hollywood was an expensive place to live. Pat and Kell were not yet divorced, and this was a further source of uncertainty for both boys.

Back in Sydney, Rhett's babysitter was replaced by a live-in, 24-year-old woman, full of life and willing to be a kind of mate for Rhett. Kell was totally naive about hard drugs at this stage, and he didn't notice at first that the young girl never exposed her arms.

One Sunday the three of them went to the beach, and still the new nanny did not take off her long-sleeve pullover. Kell was beginning to wonder why. He thought it was odd that she didn't appear to have any desire for swimming and twigged that there was something going on. That evening Kell went out, leaving the girl to look after Rhett. She had her own bedroom upstairs in the house, and when Kell arrived home a little later than usual, all seemed well on the home front. But at one o'clock in the morning he heard the shower start, and muffled noises coming from the bathroom, so he got out of bed, went down the passageway, and listened outside the bathroom. He could hear that there were two people inside so he opened the door, and there to his surprise was a man, a stranger, holding up the nanny in the shower. She was unconscious.

'She had taken a drug overdose, and he was her dealer,' Kell says. 'I grabbed him by the neck and dragged him down the stairs, threw him out the front door, his clothes after him. I told him I didn't want to see him again. The next morning, I told the girl she'd have to go, but I took her to my doctor first. He gave her a lecture, placed her on a methadone programme, and we found her a home to go to, a nice family who knew she was a heroin addict, and they took her in and looked after her. She was clean for years, but eventually took up with heroin again and died from an overdose.'

The next nanny was stubborn and strong-willed, and seemed to have designs on Kelland. One Sunday evening, returning from a barbecue at a neighbour's home, he was confronted by the drunken nanny, who let it be known that she wasn't too happy about Kell not inviting her to accompany him that afternoon.

'I came home from another barbie not long afterwards, and she's lying back on the lounge, bottle of brandy in hand, drunk as a skunk, even more upset, only this time she threatens me. So I locked Rhett in his room and locked my room that night, and I got up at six o'clock the next morning and told her to pack her bags and get out. I told her if she didn't get out I'd call the police.'

Meanwhile, Kell's business in Maitland was struggling and he considered selling his home. He telephoned Pat in Los Angeles, thinking she may want to keep the house, but she didn't, so he sold it, paid off his business debts, and moved into a rented home in Frenchs Forest. His neighbours at the back, in the next street, were the Farriss family.

A year had gone by since Michael and his mother had left, and Kell thought it time for Michael to return. He called up Pat and told her that he'd had enough and wanted Michael to return immediately. 'I bought an Air New Zealand ticket for Michael in Sydney and sent it over to Pat, and told her to send him back. I picked him up from the airport and I was so thrilled to have him back in Sydney. Michael appeared very tense and mixed up about his mother when he returned, and he was clearly glad to be back.'

Not long after Michael's return, Kelland had to go to Hong Kong on a business trip. Before he went he hired another live-in nanny. The next morning the new girl rang the front bell and when Kell opened the door 'there was an absolute vision standing there'. She was about twenty-five years old, and she was 'a beautiful, slim, gorgeous-looking doll. The boys just loved her. After a couple of days it was obvious she was not a great housekeeper, or cook. In fact she was hopeless, but the boys loved her and she loved the boys, they were great company for each other. My mind was put to rest and I left for my short trip to Hong Kong.

'When I returned, the place was like a slophouse, dishes piled high, speakers all over the place. There had been a party going on and my home was a wreck and I was really annoyed. I told her how I felt about her housekeeping, went to my room, thought about it, decided to forgive her, and went back to tell her, but she said, "Eat your heart out."

'The next morning I was regretful that she was leaving, so I went to her and asked her to stay. I just wanted my boys to be happy. She said no, today was the day she had to leave. And she walked out the door, just like that.'

Kell reckons this is the time the boys started on pot— true enough in Rhett's case. 'I think Michael had already started smoking pot in Hollywood,' Rhett says, 'but she definitely started me smoking pot. But Michael and she had an affair, I think. I'm pretty sure she taught him about sex because I don't think he'd had sex before that. It wasn't just sex she taught him, but Tantric sex, so Michael said.'

Tantric sex is the method that pop star Sting would crow about some twenty years later. If Michael Hutchence was taught Tantric sex at the age of fifteen by a woman ten years his senior, his future sexual activities would have had to pass a pretty stringent test for him to be happy and satisfied. It would stand to reason, in fact, that he would have been forever searching for something new, something exciting on the sexual front.

Kell had already filed for divorce and was waiting for twelve months' separation to go by so that the divorce would go through automatically. Only two days to go, out of the blue, he got a call from Patricia. 'I'm on tomorrow's flight,' she told him.

'The twelve-month period was just forty-eight hours away, and I told her she just was not staying with me. "I'm about to have twelve months' separation from you and an automatic divorce and that's what I want," I told her.'

But Pat insisted she wanted to see the boys and was coming back.

'Not with me you're not,' Kell responded, adding, 'I'm booking you into the Belrose Motel and you can stay there.'

'Just before Mum returned,' Rhett recalls, 'she'd had an accident on the set of a movie called *Dynamite Women*, and she put her back out somehow. So when we went to pick her up from the airport she rolled off on a wheelchair.'

Kelland says he knew she was in some kind of trouble just by looking at her—not the story behind the wheelchair, but the look on her face—and he just didn't want to deal with her. So he went to the motel and let Pat stay in his home with her boys, rather than go through further drama on the eve of his divorce.

On his return from Hollywood a few months earlier Michael had once again enrolled in Davidson High School, where he reacquainted himself with Andrew Farriss. The musical partnership was about to begin.

four

The Farriss Brothers, Doctor Dolphin, Guinness, the Nullarbor and Manila

> I'm drunk
> Can't see my glass
> Not worried
> Chair dancing man
> Sex talk eats you alive
> We go making friends til we're satisfied
>
> 'Golden Playpen'
> *Shabooh Shoobah* 1982
> MICHAEL HUTCHENCE
> AND KIRK PENGILLY

The Farriss brothers were born in Perth, Western Australia; the eldest, Tim, on 16 August 1957, Andrew on 29 March 1959, and Jon on 10 August 1961. 'When Jon, Andrew and I were little kids we always pretended we were in a band,' Tim Farriss told me. 'Andrew would play make-believe piano, and I grabbed a tennis racket as though it were a guitar. Jon played cushions. He was always going to be a drummer, it was preordained. We used to mime records and dream of being in a real band.

'In 1966 Mum and Dad wanted to visit England, to see Mum's sister Wendy. She had a friend who was really good friends with Rolf Harris, and after we arrived in the UK Wendy invited us along to see a taping of the famous Rolf Harris children's show. We were lucky enough to meet Cilla Black and George Harrison. Andrew, Jon and I all looked at each other and said, Yep, this is for us, this is what we want to do. He's a great bloke, Rolf, and he never, ever forgot us. In fact a few years ago, when he heard that Mum was dying of cancer, he asked for a photo of her, I'll never forget it. I was really impressed with Rolf Harris. At one stage I wanted to call my son Rol. Get it? Rol Farriss.'

In 1971 Dennis and Jill Farriss uprooted their family and left the west coast for Sydney, where Dennis took up an appointment as Australian manager of a major insurance company. After a stint in the Koala Motel in the North Shore suburb of Manly, the family finally moved into a home not far from the Hutchences.

The roots of the INXS family tree can be traced to seeds sown by Tim Farriss and his mate Kirk Pengilly, two young, self-motivated, strong-willed and not so naive lads who emerged from Sydney's middle-class northern suburbs during the early seventies. 'Tim and Kirk were buddies from school,' Michael Hutchence would recall in his 1988 interview with America's *Spin* magazine. Hutchence featured on the front cover of the February issue, and inside was a four-page article on America's newest sensation, INXS, headed 'Beyond Thunderdome'. 'Tim and Kirk were like the older guys, the ones who sold us the drugs,' according to Michael. 'They had women we couldn't talk to because we were too shy.'

'Yeah, that's how I remember it,' Tim Farriss told me,

referring to Hutchence's recollections. 'Michael was very timid and shy of Kirk and I. He and Andrew used to come and watch us rehearse when we were in our band, Guinness. Basically it all started with Kirk and I. We used to play in church halls, weddings, parties, anywhere we could plug in our amps. My young brother Jon was the original drummer when he was only ten. Kirk and I used to have every Tuesday afternoon off from sports. We wanted to be band guys, not sport guys, and we ended up playing in the school band.'

In the 1988 *Spin* article Tim said that his school was having a hard time disciplining the kids, and the powers that be ended up hiring a militant guy to bring them into line. 'He was really heavy-looking,' Tim said, 'and he looked like this Marine sergeant with reflecting sunglasses, Marine crewcut and all, a big man, the heaviest son of a bitch you could imagine, and he'd come to school and just scream—every kid in school was petrified of this guy. One day he signalled for Kirk and I to go to his office, and we thought, Oh no, here it comes. He made us all line up, all the naughty guys waiting to see him, and all these kids are coming out crying and stuff. He left Kirk and I 'til last, so when we went in we were nervous as shit. He slams the door and has this look on his face, he takes off his glasses and says, "I hear you guys play in a band. Well, my wife runs the committee for the local primary school and they have a big fête coming up and we want to know if you guys will play at it." So we said, Sure, we'll do it, and from then on we got away with murder!'

Kirk and Tim ended up playing at the sixth-form farewell in 1974. 'Kirk wore his mother's terry-towelling pink bikini and the flowered rubber bathing cap, glasses and all, with a lily-white body and Juliette Prowse legs. I carried a foam surfboard and wore board shorts and mask and snorkel and flippers, and a guitar around my neck. We wrote this song about the teachers and it brought the house down.'

Michael, having just returned to Sydney from his unhappy twelve-month sojourn in Hollywood, quickly reacquainted himself with Andrew Farriss. 'I used to hang out with Andrew, who had bands and things over the years,' Michael stated in the *Spin* article, 'and I always used to watch him play. Andrew was the singer, the front guy in all these bands. I really started when he didn't feel like singing anymore. He just gave me the microphone one day and said, "Do you know this song? Just sing while we try out this drummer." He was going through some really bad drummers, which is why we ended up with little Jonny. He came and tried out and was really very good.'

The band was Doctor Dolphin. Jon Farriss played with both of his brothers' bands at various stages; it was inevitable that he would be the drummer for INXS when they eventually evolved.

So in the beginning it was Kirk and Tim leading the way, with school chums Andrew and Michael looking on, being inspired but attempting their own take on playing rock music. Doctor Dolphin was a non-performance outfit and did not play publicly at all. 'We got into snobby music,' Hutchence recalled. 'We wouldn't listen to anything that was rock'n'roll music for about a year. We really did get elitist for a while, we wouldn't go to the beach, we listened to jazz. In fact we had this experimental music circle for a while.'

Rhett Hutchence has fond memories of his brother's first band. 'I don't know what it was about him, and I don't know whether or not I am biased because I am his brother, but I thought Doctor Dolphin were a good band. They were all talented musicians. Michael's voice wasn't all that good in the beginning, you know, but he was a natural front man. In the end he had a beautiful singing voice, it just evolved into his own style.'

But at fifteen, Michael Hutchence saw himself more as a potential movie actor or poet. In 1988, at the age of twenty-eight, Michael claimed that in his mind he was 'musical' at the age of fifteen. 'But words-wise, I used to write poetry and crap,' he said. 'I didn't have the rock star mentality, I had the "serious young artist" mentality. I was actually more into poets and things like that, and that attitude and that scene. Ferlinghetti, Bukowski . . . I thought it was pretty interesting so I started reading a lot of the stuff.'

Rhett at this stage was even less sure of where his future lay. 'Usually what my parents thought I would be good at was something I just didn't want to do. My mum once told me I would be a good car salesman, but I haven't been a car salesman. They would see me do something once and think that's what I was going to do. I never had any interest in being an actor. Music I left to Michael. I was interested in drumming at one stage, but Jon Farriss was just the best and he was my yardstick and I never thought I could be as good as him. Michael brought the world of music to me—what my family thought I would be good at put me off for life. If they told me I would have been a great drug addict, I would have been okay.'

Doctor Dolphin used to rehearse in the house of a friend named Glen, whose father was head of the local bank. Glen's father soon grew tired of the strange smoke smells and screams and music wafting up from the downstairs room, and Doctor Dolphin lost their rehearsal room. They moved to the Hutchence garage. Garry Gary Beers was the bass player. 'I think Andrew met Garry at the beach,' Michael recalled years later. 'I think Garry and Tim were dire enemies in high school, but we all got together.'

'I was a bit of a joke to those guys,' Beers remembered. 'But I did have a car and a licence. It was a real shag-wagon, even though I was a virgin. I was eighteen or nineteen before I got laid, but there was Michael, already fucking everyone in sight at fifteen or sixteen.'

'I had been recovering from bone surgery and looking at Andrew's friends—his mates who were in the band—and Michael,' Tim recalled. 'They were lolling around in the back pool and having a good time. I lay on a fold-up bed in front of the window. I had bone spurs taken off my left leg and right shoulder.' Tim used the time to think about the future, forming The Farriss Brothers in his mind.

When Jon was sixteen, Tim decided to put his theory into practice. He and Kirk combined the best elements of both bands and the briefly named The Vegetables were born, with Jon providing the beat. Then, on Tim's twentieth birthday, in August 1977, the band made its debut as The Farriss Brothers, the six members of whom were to stay together for almost twenty-one years, only death tearing them apart. The band members were: Tim Farriss on guitar; Garry Gary Beers on bass; Kirk Pengilly on saxophone, guitar and vocals; Andrew Farriss on keyboard and guitars; Michael Hutchence doing lead vocals; and Jon Farriss on drums and keyboard.

By the end of that year they were on their way to Perth. In an interview with the UK magazine *Q* in 1988, Michael claimed that Kirk had a dubious means of earning money back then. 'He had this really straight car with Christian books scattered all over the back seat. He had a guitar case in the back, a good Christian acoustic guitar, and it would just be stuffed full of dope. He'd open it up and do business out of the back of the car. And the cops would never touch him, because they didn't want to get into a conversation about God.'

This has been one of the most consistently retold stories about the early Farriss Brothers days, but according to Tim the story is pure fantasy. 'A friend of ours had a van, and he was a Christian, and that was when it was just Kirk and I, but it is bullshit about selling dope, total fantasy. Wish it was true. Kirk and Garry had a Hi-Ace van which we carried our gear around in. Garry bought his before we went to Perth and filled it with gear and put it on a truck.'

But it was a good story, one that has become a legendary INXS tale, doing the rounds in publicity stories for years, each storyteller changing minor details to make it a classic Chinese whisper.

It takes three or four days to cross the expansive Nullarbor Plain. 'It was sort of very three-musketeers, six-musketeers kind of trip,' according to Michael. 'We stopped about midnight in the desert, and we'd been smoking dope all the way because it kept us going, and Kirk got me out because we didn't know which way we were going. All we could see were these little kangaroos' eyes, little eyeballs bouncing everywhere. And Kirk says, "Right, I think we'll have something to eat". Kirk's very pristine and perfect about everything. And he pulls out this wok. He has all these Tupperware containers lined up with diced vegetables—this is so Kirk—and he cooks this Chinese meal. I thought, This is so weird. I didn't really know him that well! So we had this Chinese meal in the middle of the desert with kangaroos staring at us.'

Perth in the late seventies was not a vibrant music scene. Since the sixties it had become one giant beer barn for miners from the expansive northern mining towns. The workers would come to Perth after working non-stop, twelve-hour shifts underground, three months at a stretch, and maraud the multitude of 'nightclubs'. They spent a fortune on booze and sex, and the bands were simply background fodder. If bands did not have a repertoire of Top Forty cover songs, they simply didn't get a gig. Any Perth act worth their salt during the sixties and seventies high-tailed it out of there as soon as they could afford the petrol money or the train tickets.

'It's this bizarre scene where guys make a lot of money playing in big pubs, perfectly playing the hits on the radio at the time,' Michael remembered. 'We got to Perth and got this big house. It's really cheap to live there, really beautiful climate. We were on the dole, of course, plus we made about twenty-five bucks each week playing.'

Tim Farriss was the acknowledged team captain, manager, coach. He was ably assisted by Kirk, with whom he would collect the money at the end of each gig, but Tim was the main man, pushing the band, getting them work, devising promotional stunts. Tim and Kirk were the ones to whom they all turned when they needed stability, and as the years rolled by, Tim's role remained unchanged. Tim was the level-headed one who nurtured the band whenever its members went through troughs, whenever their morale needed boosting. He was the first to marry—he wed his teenage sweetheart, Buffy—the first to have children.

The idea of being in Perth was to rehearse every day, to write songs, to move closer to their goal of success on a grand scale, a goal which soon became global success. After spending almost a year in Perth, the band decided to return to Sydney, but first Tim arranged some gigs in the northern mining towns so that they could return home with money in their pockets. They were showing the signs that all great bands display early in their careers, a penchant for hard work, an obsession with being independent, self-reliant and self-supporting. Any band that has made it to world ranks and stayed there, as INXS did, has this obsessive desire to succeed at their core.

On reaching their first mining town, way up north near Port Hedland, The Farriss Brothers must have felt like they had landed on Mars. Michael, perhaps in an exaggerating mood, recalled in 1988, 'They have this central area with six pods coming off and there's red dust everywhere. They have dust locks; it's like nowhere else. You have to walk into a room and whoosh! All the dust gets blown off you, and you go to a dust-free area. And they have wet canteens and dry canteens, one to get pissed in and the other to eat in, which not that many people do. The people there are all escaped convicts, or people that just did time, desperadoes. We played there New Year's Eve one year. It was one of the most horrifying experiences of my life.'

'The whole experience of going to Perth was pretty awesome, really,' Kirk Pengilly said in an American magazine interview. 'Most of us left jobs, security, girlfriends, everything. When we got there and started going to mining towns, we were doing it all ourselves. It was more of a personal adventure for the band.'

'The only reason why anybody would be there was to

mine,' Jon Farriss recalled. 'Every oddball and crazy weirdo was there, either running away from something, or they'd gotta get back five thousand dollars or be killed, or they'd just escaped from prison, or the guy's a ridiculous alcoholic, or some woman is so butch she wants to drive a big truck and wear a hard-hat and has drinking competitions with the Scottish—that's what was happening when we were there. It was a 24-hour-a-day operation. Another guy, the only way he'd introduce himself wasn't to shake hands but to take a bite out of your shoe. He wouldn't stop until he'd taken an actual bite out of the shoe.'

Another story about those early Perth days that has also done the rounds many, many times is the one that has Michael receiving a birthday present of a girl on a leash. Again, Tim discounts the story. 'I can't remember that one,' he told me, 'unless I was non-compus. If I knew anything about that I'd tell you. In the early days in Perth, Mike and I were not close. Mike would only carry his microphone. I was always on his case to help carry the gear from gigs, to stop talking to chicks and come and help out with the gear. He used to have a beautiful girlfriend and anything could have been possible, but I never knew about the birthday present or the leash.'

Rhett, who dropped in to Perth on his way to Manila to join his father, did know about the girl and the leash. 'The band was in Perth and they hadn't been there very long and I went over on the way to the Philippines to go and live with my dad. I knew I wouldn't be able to see Michael again for a while, so I went over. The band had this house and they were all living in it. It was a real band sort of a house. You'd walk in and there'd be girls' underpants hanging from a light in the living room and the house was a mess. A few groupies hanging around, I think. There were dishes piled up, typical young guys living in a house together. Michael had a girlfriend at the time, Amanda I think it was. She was the girl that somebody gave Michael on a leash. Somebody gave him this girl on a leash and said, This is for you, and there was a girl attached to it. She was right into poetry and I think they were kinda both good for each other. I stayed for two weeks, then joined Dad in the Philippines.'

• • •

Prior to The Farriss Brothers leaving for Perth, Kell made a difficult but monumental decision. He'd been asked to go to the Philippines and take charge of a large leather factory. 'I decided I had to get my own life together. I had to get out of the situation with Pat,' Kell told me. 'I hated to leave my sons, it tore my heart out, but I felt I had to do something for myself for a change. I told Pat we were going to finally be divorced. I told her I'd look after the boys and her up to a point, but that she'd have to be a full-time mother for the boys. Michael was about to take off for Perth with the Farriss boys anyway, and Rhett was still at school.

'I was very worried about Michael. He'd given up school, left home, was leaving for Perth, and I just thought there were too many temptations out there. Nobody was supervising him. I always used to sit down with Michael and try to encourage him with his drawing and his poetry. I wanted Mike to matriculate and then go to university, but he persuaded me that music was his thing. I told him to try it for a year but if it didn't work out to go back to school. We would occasionally be in touch when he was in Perth. I'd call him on the phone, he'd sometimes want some money.

He was always wanting to buy new equipment. But he seemed happy and that was the main thing.'

Not long after he arrived in Manila in 1976, his work based in Bataan, at the top of Manila Bay, Kell's divorce to Patricia came through, and after sixteen years the Hutchence family split apart permanently.

Rhett, fourteen years old and still in Sydney, was understandably giving Patricia a hard time. 'Rhett was really putting on a bad performance with his mother,' Kell said.

'Even though she came back from Hollywood and we lived together for a while, it just wasn't working out,' Rhett told me. 'I just couldn't come to grips with what had happened. I don't think you leave a twelve-year-old like that. I think it's the responsibility of everybody in the family to make sure I was looked after. In a way I guess at the time I thought it was also Michael's responsibility, not that he had much of a say or could do much at his age. Ultimately, though, I thought it was my mum's responsibility to look after me. She thought Michael would be easier to deal with, and she couldn't take both of us so she thought leaving me with Dad was the solution. She also had a failed marriage and that is something to consider too. She tried to make it up to me for years by trying to buy me things, you know, or she'd send me a hundred dollars in the mail, that sort of thing. Michael and I used to call ourselves the Prince and the Pauper, we were arm in arm all the time up until he left for Los Angeles and then we kinda lost contact for a while. When Michael left for Perth with The Farriss Brothers, leaving me for the second time—I often wonder whether or not I felt abandoned by him again. I don't really know.'

On the subject of his son's band, Kelland said, 'I thought they should have changed their name from The Farriss

Brothers, it sounded like a butcher's shop. I was helping out by lending Mike fifty bucks here and there, or buying some new amplifier for him and the band. But anyway, I left Australia for the Philippines to set up a leather goods factory in Bataan. I'll never forget arriving in Manila. It was the wet season and I arrived in Manila like a refugee.'

Once Kell had left, Pat and Rhett still didn't get on. 'I told Rhett to jump on a plane and get himself up to Manila,' said Kell, 'but I made him promise me that he would go to school. It was pretty wild in Bataan, at the Hill Tops Hotel in particular. There were a lot of Japanese factories in those days and Ford Australia ran a big pressing plant. The guys were all pretty wild and were always leaving their wives and running off with Filipino women. There was never-ending drama. The bureaucratic fumbling system closed us down slowly but surely—we were also getting shot at by guerillas on the drive from Manila to Bataan and the trade unions did the rest by imposing stupid rules and regulations. There was a lot of action going on though, plenty of women all over the place, drinking, parties, a wild, wild atmosphere.'

It didn't take long for Rhett to fit in at the Hill Tops Hotel where Kell was living. Kell remembers with great fondness what Rhett did for his fifty-second birthday celebrations. 'Rhett had arranged for the piano player to play "Happy Birthday" as I walked into the lounge that night. He'd also organised a huge birthday cake for me. I was so proud of him.'

Rhett enrolled at the International School, where Kell reckons he had to attend the principal's office on an average of twice a week. 'Rhett was and still is extremely bright and intelligent but he just never studied, he just walked into a class and just did it. But he mucked around too much.'

'Yeah, I wasn't at school for academic reasons—purely social,' Rhett recalls. 'I got an undergraduation, then got thrown out of school. The headmaster gave me an early graduation, which meant that I didn't have to go to the ceremony, I didn't have to go for the last two weeks of school. I got my diploma, and as long as I didn't return to school he was happy.' According to Kell, Rhett was dismissed because he was smoking pot. Rhett left Manila in 1980, returning to Sydney and a job in a furniture shop.

'On my return to Sydney, I originally moved in to live with Michael and his girlfriend, Vicky Kerridge. In actual fact they tolerated my daily joint consumption. However, when I started letting off small explosives and blowing the air-conditioners out of their walls, they took offence. They didn't even mind the fake bomb hoaxes I called in. From when I left Sydney for the Philippines,' Rhett told me, 'I never spoke to Mother for seven years.'

Meanwhile, The Farriss Brothers had finished with the red dust bowls of West Australian mining towns and had returned to the thriving Sydney rock'n'roll scene. It was all happening. The huge halls in suburban Sydney were being filled to their sweat-dripping rafters with hard-core, four-on-the-floor pub rock music. Bands such as The Angels, Midnight Oil and Cold Chisel, along with their astute management, had completely changed the face of Australian music. The precedent set in the late sixties and early seventies, primarily by Billy Thorpe and the Aztecs and a slew of blues-based rock bands, had taken hold, forging a unique Australian sound. The mantle had been taken a step further by AC/DC, now on the verge of becoming international superstars after tirelessly and relentlessly touring the UK and the US. Punk rock music had bludgeoned the UK music scene to death, forging its own new era of music, and it spread its coat-tails Down Under. There's no doubt that INXS, as they were soon to be called, took the function of punk but not the form.

'In our early days of playing music, pre-The Farriss Brothers, Kirk and I tried to sponge everything we could from early Oz rockers, and we were inspired by acts such as La De Das, Billy Thorpe, and Blackfeather,' Tim told me. 'Whatever was going on, we were right into it.' But by the turn of the decade, The Farriss Brothers were being influenced by the aftermath of the punk and new wave explosion, doing covers of songs from bands like Graham Parker and the Rumour, and Elvis Costello and the Attractions. 'We did covers just to get by, because agents told us we had to. We all shared a house in Newport when we first came back from Perth while we were still The Farriss Brothers,' Tim said. 'All we did was write songs and party hard. Our whole dilemma was that in the atmosphere of Australian music at that time, it wasn't cool to move on stage, or be boisterous. The trend was to be sullen, have an attitude, and not move or look as though you were having a good time. Bands used to pretend they were having a bad time, and that was impossible for us to do because we were having a ball and we didn't see why we should change that just to suit a boring trend.'

'I have some tapes that a fan sent me from America from that time, live from the Alley Cat Wine Bar in North Sydney in June 1979. It blew me away. This fan at the time had two mikes wired up inside his sleeves and stood up with his arms held wide and recorded the gig. The songs we did were amazing, stuff like "Slip My Disco" by The Tubes,

"Love Is The Drug" by Bryan Ferry, "Watching The Detectives" from Elvis Costello.' Eclectic, to say the least.

Without doubt the three Farriss brothers were becoming not only a driving influence on Michael's creativity, but also an integral part of his life in the form of a substitute family, one that gave him the stability that was lacking in his own. He would later recall that the Farrisses were like the perfect television family. 'They're really wholesome,' he said, 'their father listens to Sergio Mendes records all the time. They always had percussion instruments on the floor and stuff.' Dennis and Jill Farriss treated the outwardly shy Michael like a member of the family.

Michael's closeness to Tim, Andrew, Jon and their parents didn't take away the love he had for his mother, his brother and his father. He would remain close to them on a certain, some would say superficial, level, but in time he told some close friends of the disdain he felt for the crumbling of his own family. In time, the deeply scarred feelings he had for his mother and half-sister Tina, would be known to just a few. He loved them, but in many ways they just did not know him at all. He would continue to have strong feelings for Rhett and his father. He knew how troubled Rhett remained. And he knew how hard Kelland had tried to keep the family together. He would continually be torn between his mother's take on family life and his father's take. Like us all, Michael was a product of where he came from, and he appears to have spent the rest of his life trying to reach the middle ground.

Kylie Minogue has commented on Michael's relationship with his family: 'If I described my family, it's all very easy and great and good relations, but it was always, there was always something that was a bit . . . odd about Michael's family, or unresolved. I know Michael cared so much for Rhett and would get very worried about him. But would sometimes be infuriated by him. But that's typical of siblings, you know, I could say the same with my brother and sister. But it was deeper than just being in the situation that they both were in as siblings.'

In the early days the band used to do all their own promotion, as well as book their own gigs. One night, while he was placing leaflets underneath windscreen wipers of cars at the Newport Arms Hotel, Tim was approached by Gary Morris, manager of Midnight Oil. 'He asked me who I was and what band I was doing the leaflets for, and he was impressed so we started talking and he was interested in the band. Eventually, he became our manager.'

The first thing Morris wanted to do was change the name of the band. Midnight Oil roadie Colin Lee Hong thought the name INXS was the way to go. 'Gary had a slightly different concept,' Tim explained. 'He wanted us to be seriously inaccessible.' Of course, the name eventually became a tag for the band's desire for an excessive lifestyle.

'Gary had this vision of us becoming supermen, standing up for good things like love, hope and liberty, all under the name of God,' Michael explained years later. The band's agent at that time was Chris Murphy, a tenacious, single-minded, ambitious young man who loved the band and saw clearly their sense of purpose, their spirit and strength.

Murphy was a smooth talker who could sell ice to the Eskimos. He was just the man INXS needed to help them realise their dream of world domination. These were six serious musicians, and their aim was to conquer the world and do it as fast as they could. Murphy was just as ambitious, and when he realised what they wanted he knew he could take them there. He loved the band and the band loved him. A bond was forged and he became their manager. The partnership between an artist and a manager is like a marriage. Dreams are dreamt, ambitions and plans are made for the future, total trust is placed in each other, mutual goals are set. Until 1990, when the marriage started to crack at the seams, it was a relationship that took both parties to the pinnacle of success.

When the band's world dreams came to fruition, many said it was Murphy who made the band, that without him they would not have made the record deals they did, would not have made it through the quagmire that is necessary to even get into the rock rat race, that they simply would not have been as successful as they had become—that Chris Murphy made INXS. But others say the band was ambitious and aware enough to have made it without Murphy, that they would have simply got someone else to manage them and that it was INXS who made Murphy. For now, in 1980, INXS were ready to bring a brand new unique form of rock music to Australia and to the world.

five

Thrusting clenched fists, wiggling arses: INXS and Australian music

> Hey, here's the story
> Forget about your trouble in life
> Don't you know it's not easy
> When you gotta walk upon that line
> That's why—you need
> That's why—this is what you need
> I'll give you what you need
>
> 'What You Need'
> *Listen Like Thieves* 1985
> MICHAEL HUTCHENCE AND
> ANDREW FARRISS

There's no doubt that Chris Murphy's clever management of INXS made him one of the most successful rock'n'roll managers of recent times, certainly one of the most famous and controversial. But the list of Australian managers who believed in their bands and worked tirelessly to promote them internationally is long and goes back more than three decades. Australian managers have played a major role in opening up the international arena for home-grown talent, often placing themselves in debt as they chased success for themselves and for the acts in which they had such faith. It was Australian managers, sometimes with an ego as big as their dreams, who forged the way for Australian bands, attempting to take them to audiences on the other side of the world.

Not all succeeded. Due mainly to international inexperience, Mike Vaughan, manager of The Easybeats, was not able to capitalise on their worldwide smash hit, 'Friday On My Mind'. But some did succeed. George Young, guitarist, leader and, alongside Harry Vanda, co-songwriter for The Easybeats, had two younger brothers, Malcolm and Angus, who became the rhythm guitarist and lead guitarist in AC/DC. The band steamrolled world rock crowds in the eighties under the management of Michael Browning. Adelaide-born Robert Stigwood, who managed The Beatles for a while when their manager Brian Epstein committed suicide, went on to direct the career of The Bee Gees, who remain among the most successful pop groups and songwriters of all time. The three Gibb brothers lived in Queensland during the early sixties, and spent their apprenticeship years in the enormous RSL clubs that were littered across the sprawling suburbs of Sydney. Stigwood then moved into producing movies and stage shows, including two of the biggest, *Grease* and *Evita*.

One of the key managers who opened the way for the Australian international rock invasion of the eighties was the flamboyant, charming, astute and deadly persuasive Roger Davies, who managed Sherbet. Unfortunately, the timing, when the band moved to Los Angeles for a year in the mid-seventies, was not right and success in the States eluded them. Davies, though, went on to revive the flagging careers of Olivia Newton-John and Tina Turner, and he later managed Mick Jagger's solo career and Janet Jackson. Davies never hid his secrets or his contacts from his fellow countrymen; he was always open to other Australians who wanted to learn. He introduced Australian managers to lawyers, promoters, industry hard-hitters, and unwittingly began a trend followed by dozens of Australian managers, including Chris Murphy, with whom he shared contacts and advice.

Former bass player for The Master's Apprentices, Glenn Wheatley, had also moved into management by the mid-seventies, and he picked up a mainstream group featuring singer Glen Shorrock, a stalwart of Australian rock entertainers since his sixties band The Twilights first had success. Bass player for The Zoot, Beeb Birtles, also featured in the group, alongside Graham Goble, a former Adelaide musician. The band was Little River Band, a country-rock outfit modelled on the harmonies of Crosby, Stills, Nash and Young, and the smooth, West Coast sound of The Eagles. Little River Band had a clean, almost sanitised sound, but their harmonies were faultless, and world-class. They were also brilliant songwriters, Goble producing songs that became middle-of-the-road pop classics. During the height of the band's success, they had four Top Twenty American hits and several European hits, eventually selling twenty million albums. It was Wheatley who headed them in the right direction, touring the band at least a dozen times across America, all paid for on his American Express credit card. Wheatley, too, passed on his knowledge to many Australian managers who followed. He let them stay in his Marina del Rey apartment, gave his advice and introduced them to American record label personnel and lawyers, the ones who made the decisions.

During the seventies Australian music was starting to

stumble upon its own identity. Bands like Skyhooks were writing songs about urban Australia, about ordinary Australian teenagers who took drugs, had sex, and were, well, like any other teenagers. Australian music was beginning to evolve its own individuality; the schizoid outlook of not feeling able to fit into English or American music dissipated; local artists and songwriters had some belief in themselves, in their own past, their own history, their own musical heritage, however limited it might have been in an international sense. Australian bands began to write about Australia without being self-conscious, the music becoming a hybrid of British pop, rock and blues alongside American country rock, southern boogie rock, and pure pop. The British have always been able to take the elements of original American music, give it a twist, mix it with a dose of British eccentricity and burlesque pantomime, and throw it back at the Americans. The Americans love it every time. A little less confident on world stages, Australians have soaked up the influences of both countries' music, and, as inhibitions have been shed, a unique Australian sound and attitude have been the result.

In the seventies and eighties the conduit for this Australian rock hybrid, the apprentice's gauntlet, was the gruelling live-music circuit. It was tough, rough, relentless, poorly paying, but essential. For Australian artists in the late sixties and early seventies, the industry cash for musicians consisted of speed, acid, pot and sex. For the artists, even big-name chart-topping artists, there was no such thing as real cash money. It has often been said that the live pub circuit in Australia is the best in the world, indeed the only constant one in the world. But this is a home-grown fallacy. Europe, the United Kingdom and the United States have always had, and still have, lucrative, viable, well-organised live circuits. London alone has one of the best and most diverse in the world. It wasn't so much the circuit that was different in Australia as the nature of the venues, the nature of the crowds, the large distances that had to be travelled between gigs, and the relative infancy of the Australian music industry. Acts in America and England could rely on hit records to take them to their audiences, whereas to survive in Australia, there was no choice but to tour.

The American and European music movers and shakers were touring big-name international bands constantly; open-air rock festivals were happening like clockwork; there were ticket offices, bookkeepers, auditors, accountants, lawyers, all part of a multi-million-dollar business. Australians, separated from the rest of the world, could garner experience with international bands for only two or three weeks at a time. The main touring season was summer. The overseas touring crews were on a grand scale, with promoters, managers, public relations people, and others, and Australians in the industry had to learn the ropes quickly or be replaced by international workers. They learned quickly. Some went to America and became successful there; others infiltrated the global arena elsewhere, taking on the internationals with a brash bravado and something with which the Americans in particular became enamoured—a young, rough-edged naivety.

By 1978 punk, both American and English, had arrived and the message, if not an identical style of music, took hold: anarchy. This was when the beer barns erupted all over Australia, drawing increasingly larger crowds to hear a new generation of Australian bands who played it rough, loud and raunchy. A slew of bands erupted out of the suburbs, with blistering lyrics, screaming guitars and a thundering thudding beat, among them The Angels, Midnight Oil and Cold Chisel. The music of all three of these big drawcards was fast, raucous and brutal. Fans in the audience clenched their fists and thrust them in the air in time with the thudding bass beat. The music scene was one big party, male-dominated, aggressive, and its new bands and their loyal followers were generating a lot of cash.

It was this as much as anything which changed the business side of the Australian industry, ensuring that in the future acts like INXS could not only survive but could make money. Up until then, bands had made virtually no profit. The monopolised music industry was heavy-handedly run by virtually one organisation and its affiliated companies, Mushroom Records. Their spin-off agencies booked the bands they managed, published and recorded the music they wrote, and indirectly ran the venues at which they performed. It was more or less a closed shop, and if you didn't fall in line you suffered. The promoters, the agents, the managers, and everyone down the line made money, leaving little for the people who actually created the music, the musicians. Mushroom's approach did make a contribution to the overall vitality of the industry, and in some isolated cases for the acts themselves, but it did nothing for many Australian artists trying to gain global success.

'If you didn't work with the main two or three agencies in those days, you didn't work,' says Rod Willis, the manager of Cold Chisel, perhaps the most legendary band in Australia's music history. Chisel would always be an Australian band, so Australian in fact that they never really made much of a dent elsewhere in the world. 'Bands would sometimes have to go through a few agencies before getting to the venue to play, thus losing almost half their money to agents, promoters and managers.'

Willis had been based in London during the late sixties and early seventies. On his return to Australia, at the same time as he started managing Cold Chisel, he met up with John Woodruff, manager of The Angels, and Ray Hearn, manager of Flowers. Sick of the low money their bands were getting, the trio decided to form their own agency, Dirty Pool. 'We took the office manager from the Solo Premiere Agency, Jenny Elliot, and the main booker, Richard McDonald, both of whom shared our vision. We decided to turn the entire situation on its ear and start booking our acts directly into big venues, based on a guarantee and a percentage,' Willis recalls. 'Nobody had attempted this before because nobody had an act strong enough to pull it off. We were lucky, we had The Angels, who were at that time fast becoming the biggest live draw band in the land, and Cold Chisel who were fast closing the gap. We also had Flowers, Iva Davies' band, who later changed their name to Icehouse. Icehouse were not as big as their stable mates, but they had a niche university following, amongst the first of the Aussie new wave bands.'

If some promoter didn't like the idea, refusing to take a booking, the bands would play at a nearby venue and blow the resistance away by attracting the crowd from the original venue. Next time around, the promoter would book the band, making less money than he had before. Dirty Pool instigated marketing and promotion of bands for the first time. Their acts would only perform in city areas once every two months, instead of every week as they had done previously. They would criss-cross the expansive Sydney suburbs, and in between times travel interstate. In less than a year,

Dirty Pool and its roster of artists were the most powerful in the land. The agency began to expand and eventually took aboard Mental as Anything, Divinyls and INXS.

• • •

In this atmosphere of hard-rocking, macho music INXS flew against the trend, forging their own style which was a far cry from pub rock. Despite their love of Australian music, or quite possibly because of it, INXS stood apart from the pack right from their beginnings.

'Growing up with Oils [Midnight Oil], Angels, Chisel, the pressure was on to be total rock in those days,' Kirk Pengilly told me in London in August 1997, during the band's last major interview before the death of Michael Hutchence. 'But the Sydney radio station Double J was great in those days, it would play Rufus then Deep Purple then Jackson Five. They had variety, it was all mixed up. Australia was a hybrid of many kinds of music, but we loved funk music.'

'I think "One Thing" was the first time we actually got that style, that groove,' Hutchence told me. 'It was the first time we actually had that beautiful space.' But in essence, that quirky cross-pollination between diminished but evolving analogue keyboard, new wave, funk, pub rock, punk and traditional rock was well in evidence prior to 1983, when 'One Thing' was taken from the band's third album, *Shabooh Shoobah*. Andrew Farriss certainly saw the style earlier. 'The song that I can say was the first signature INXS fusion of funk and rock is "Underneath The Colours" in 1981. The way that song was styled, the way the riffs phrased, the way Michael sings the song, it was very similar to what we did five to six years later.'

Chris Murphy, on taking the managerial reins of INXS handed to him by Midnight Oil's manager Gary Morris in 1980, fell instantly in love with the band, their natural hard-working ethic and their desire for success. He wanted to succeed overseas as much as they did. The outlook of Australian musicians was very international at this time, with bands as diverse as AC/DC and Little River Band already international hit-makers. Any serious band was looking outside of Australia—it just wasn't cool to admit it. John Woodruff, manager of The Angels, had signed his band to an overseas recording contract two years before, in 1978. Rod Willis, too, had already signed an overseas deal for Cold Chisel. Midnight Oil, Men at Work, Mental as Anything, Divinyls, and others had their sights set in the same direction. Icehouse were signed by London-based Chrysalis Records in 1981. The really ambitious acts already had international success mapped out. Anybody who knew what they were doing could see the tremendous opportunity for Australian acts overseas—some before they had even gained any kind of substantial success on home turf. There was also a handful of alternative Australian acts who were looking at the European market rather than the obvious American one, Europe being more conducive to their style of music.

One of these acts was Nick Cave, whose previous band Boys Next Door imploded, changed their name to Birthday Party, and moved to England. In just three years, Nick Cave's Birthday Party became underground legends, still today garnering praise for their unique, wild, unpredictable shows, and their rich, dark, emotion-drenched operatic rock music. In 1983, with some changes, the band became Nick Cave and the Bad Seeds. Although their record sales are not astronomical, Nick Cave and the Bad Seeds hold a unique position on the world's contemporary music stage. Cave has global legendary status without corporate industry constraints, playing and singing what he wants, when he wants. He was one of Michael Hutchence's biggest influences. A part of Michael Hutchence aspired to the status, the credibility, the poetry, the intellectualism, the darkness and the spirit of Nick Cave, the edge he wouldn't have as lead vocalist for INXS. In time, he and Cave would become friends.

As the move overseas for Australian bands began, Chris Murphy signed INXS to the independent Australian label Deluxe Records, owned by Michael Browning, who had steered AC/DC to initial success. AC/DC had begun its journey to conquer world rock audiences in 1975. The concept was to tour constantly, country to country, city to city, no breaks, no holidays, just touring and recording. The band toured non-stop for almost five years, building such a huge, intimate fan base that when the band eventually broke, longevity for the band was ensured. Sadly, lead singer Bon Scott didn't live long enough to see the fruits of his sacrifices. He died of misadventure, the result of a massive, depressed drinking binge in London, brought on by the ceaseless touring and a broken heart following the break-up of a relationship. But AC/DC have since become one of the most successful bands in rock's history, in territory first charted for them by Michael Browning. Although he eventually parted ways with the band, it was Browning who negotiated their record contract, who knocked on the right doors, who did all the self-degrading schmoozing and cruising and bruising. Soon after his time with AC/DC, Browning started Deluxe Records.

The first INXS single on Deluxe was released in May 1980: 'Simple Simon' and 'We Are The Vegetables'. 'A double-A side,' Tim Farriss recalled. 'I was proud of that first single, but especially so because I'd co-written "The Vegetables"'. The band's first album, *INXS*, was then recorded under the guidance of Duncan McGuire, former bass player for Doug Parkinson in Focus, a band once managed by Browning. INXS would perform live gigs around Sydney, then proceed to the recording studio and record with McGuire until dawn. When 'Just Keep Walking', the band's first single from their debut album, squeezed into the Australian Top Forty in November 1980, INXS had begun in earnest its long, hard road to the top.

A year before, when he was nineteen, Michael had met a beautiful young, strong, dark-haired schoolgirl called Michele Bennett. The two became an item, eventually falling in love. Their friendship and romance blossomed during the most formative period of Michael's career, in many ways the most formative time of his life, a time when he went from being a gangly, shy suburban teenager, to outwardly shy international sex-rock god.

For the next two years, Michele and Michael were inseparable, Michele sharing the rock'n'roll lifestyle. She was privy to Michael's every thought, his every emotion, his every dalliance, desire, ambition, as well as his deepest secrets. They became soul mates, and would remain that way until the morning he died. Nobody knew Michael in quite the same way as did Michele Bennett.

Prior to the recording of the band's third album, *Shabooh Shoobah*, INXS took a short break after constant touring. During a 1985 Australian *Penthouse* interview, Hutchence talked about how the break provided him with an opportunity to explore the intricacies and complexities of his relationship with Michele Bennett. 'You go through stages of gaining maturity,' Hutchence said. 'That was one of the most important times for me. I learned that learning to share myself with another person actually made me a more complete person.' Michele was his closest, intimate partner during this period, his constant companion as he literally went from rags to riches, from anonymity to global fame. The changes the couple endured as lovers from their teens to adulthood were enormous. Eventually, success for INXS would prove to be a contributing factor to the couple's break-up just as INXS became one of the biggest bands in the world.

Hutchence's long-time friend Lian Lunson, now based in Los Angeles as a filmmaker, also met him around this time. 'The first time I met Michael was briefly in Melbourne, and then I moved to Sydney and lived in Cammeray. Jon Farriss and his brother Andrew shared a flat just about two doors down from me,' she remembers. 'Jon and I and Nick Conroy were friends, and one day they brought Michael over to my house. Michael had known Michele for some time, I know that she was with him the night we met in Melbourne and I think that was about a year before. He was very much in love with her. He talked about her a lot and was completely besotted with this young girl. I remember thinking what a romantic he was and that she must be very special. Anyway, he and I became fast friends. Before I met Michele I was constantly thinking how lucky she was, to have this beautiful person love her so much.

'Michael bought a Citroën car when he was in Melbourne and brought Michele up to Sydney to live with him. They arrived late in the night and the very next day he brought her over to meet me. He had not exaggerated. She was one of the most beautiful girls I had ever seen. He was so proud of her and they were an incredible couple.'

Lian Lunson, along with Michele and a few other friends—Greg Perano, Nick Conroy, Jon Farriss and eventually the director Richard Lowenstein—became a close-knit group. It stayed that way through colourful, mainly fun times for most of Michael's life, until his final two years when his phone calls became less frequent and he became more distant from his mates outside the band.

'We pretty much did everything together,' Lian told me, 'and our friendship seemed to weather everything. Michael had a sense of humour that was very similar to mine, and our friendship blossomed. There wasn't much we wouldn't discuss, you know he talked to me about everything and I talked to him about everything. Michael had an incredible sense of humour and a boundless sense of adventure. He adored women. I don't think his life was complicated then. His life was certainly not one that held any dark secrets. He was a lot like his dad, a very loveable guy. Michael was an incredible bright light, he didn't like to hurt anybody, he didn't like confrontation at all. In those early years he was as happy and healthy as I ever saw him.

'With the lifestyle he ended up living, it changed in time, with all the other relationships and all that went with them. But he was really happy with Michele. I don't think at any time during their relationship or after it ended did I think of one without the other. And I don't think they did, either.

'It wasn't just Michael who finished it. She was unhappy as well. She had been a model, she is incredibly smart and she just didn't find the modelling world and the lifestyle that went with it very fulfilling anymore. Eventually she started a set job where she worked nine to five and her lifestyle began to change. She could no longer stay out with him until three in the morning, and she had to get up early to go to work, and so their lives slowly drifted apart. But they remained soul mates, always great friends and complete soul mates.'

Michael had met Greg Perano in 1980. Perano was the founding member of Hunters and Collectors, a very hip inner-city Melbourne band whose infectious rhythmic style of rock music was a standout in its day. Perano and Hutchence would become very close friends, with Perano sharing many of Michael's manic adventures and much of his life in general. Perano was one of Michael's most intimate mates, one of his closest confidantes.

'Michael was a huge fan of Hunters and Collectors,' Perano told me. 'When we first started to tour Sydney, I began to notice this lanky, thin, somewhat awkward-looking guy with unruly hair dangling over his face always hanging at the front of the stage. Every night he'd be there and when his band went to Melbourne, there he'd be again, up in front of the stage, in the first row of the audience, moving in time with the music. Then he started to drag the rest of the band along with him, so I asked some friends who he was, and they told me he was the lead singer of this band called INXS. One day he came to the Jump Club in Melbourne, and as I came off stage after our set, Vivian Lees, the manager of Hunters and Collectors, told me there was this guy who wanted to meet me. Vivien introduced me to Michael and Michele.'

From that point on, Perano and Hutchence shared good times and bad times, and Perano would often make up the third person on evenings out with Michael's girlfriends, particularly Kylie Minogue and Helena Christensen. They went to parties, had many adventures and numerous, deep emotional conversations, in many parts of the world. When Perano left his band, the friendship with Hutchence became closer.

'We connected with what was going on in the world, and on a musical level I think he originally liked the edge that Hunters had in our music. We developed a strong friendship, Michael and I, and there were always strange elements, almost like mental telepathy sometimes. We shared the same passion for music, for reading, for women, it was a complete friendship, you know? We rarely argued. Throughout our entire friendship, he'd phone from all over the world and we wouldn't miss a beat. He'd fly in a couple of times a year as the band became more famous. We'd spend a lot of time together, and we'd listen to music, play each other different stuff we were into at the time, we'd go out to places, we'd walk, we'd talk.'

Greg Perano suffered years of deep depression and insecurity and Hutchence stood by him, helped him through in the early days of their relationship. In later years it was Hutchence who suffered the depression, often turning to Perano for support. Perano was one of the few people that Michael continued to confide in during the final years—particularly with regard to his personal relationship with Paula Yates.

• • •

In the early 1980s I was myself managing a band—a full-tilt new wave outfit called Divinyls, featuring the amazing talents of guitar player Mark McEntee and vocalist extraordinaire Christina Amphlett. In 1982/83 we toured across

Australia with INXS for an intense twelve-month period. We stayed at the same motels, shared the same dressing rooms, smoked the same joints, drank from the same liquor jars. Influenced by the more astute of my contemporaries, I travelled to London, Los Angeles and New York, a recording deal for Divinyls being my goal. In those days, Australian record companies gave a very small budget for albums recorded by Australian bands, their narrow vision looking at recouping recording costs only from within Australia. They would not put any effort, money or muscle into selling or breaking the band overseas, even though most Australian record companies were owned by overseas companies. The Divinyls and I decided that instead of signing to an Australian label, thus receiving less cash and diminishing the band's chances of success overseas, we'd sign directly to an overseas company.

Divinyls were certainly not a big headline band in Australia at the time, but they were rising fast, a notch lower than INXS on the status totem pole, 'the next big thing' tag being attached to both bands. Our thinking was that if the band were going to slog it out on the Australian live circuit, then they may as well slog it out on the American live circuit with an American or English company giving the financial support. After months of negotiations, and being deeply in debt, I decided upon the English-based Chrysalis Records, who also had a Los Angeles office, and who at the time of signing was in the throes of moving their main American office to New York. Icehouse were already signed to Chrysalis and had enjoyed moderate European success with their first international album, *Icehouse*.

The American music industry at the time when many Australian bands were moving into it was rampant with cocaine. So widespread was the availability of it that you could not speak with anyone in the business without a line being chopped out on the boardroom table, or an agent or promoter tilting their coke vial towards your nose. Cocaine was a way of life in the American music industry, a necessary part of the deal, an incentive, available twenty-four hours a day in any quantity to anyone with the cash. It was $US50 per gram, very cheap by Australian prices.

When Chris Murphy first came to coke-soaked America, he called me at my New York office and we arranged to go out for dinner. Murphy was visibly shocked at the aggression of New Yorkers, their abrasive manner and their forthright attitude to life, but, like us all, he was excited. Ironically, Murphy eventually gained a universal reputation for being aggressive and rude himself. But as any good New Yorker will tell you, they're not really aggressive, it's just the way of New York life.

Australian music was fast becoming the flavour of the month again, just as it had been half a decade earlier. As Men at Work rose to the top of American charts, Chris Murphy was negotiating a record deal for INXS with Atco. The label loved INXS, signed the band and began a long-term marketing plan to break them into the United States. Apart from the cunning charm that most Australian managers seemed to have at that time, their incredible live marketing knowledge learned back home also stood them in good stead. There was also another key element that Australians possessed, and that was the art of video making. Although Americans had been making promotional music clips for artists and movies since the forties, at the time the eighties new-wave, post-punk revolution began, video-clip making was not part of the mainstream music industry in the United States. There just weren't the outlets for them to be shown. In Australia, though, promotional videos had become an essential marketing ploy, and television channels had been consistently programming rock video shows since the beginning of the 1970s.

Then, on 1 August 1981, Music Television, or MTV as it became known, soared onto the American cable airwaves, its first video being, appropriately, 'Video Killed The Radio Star' by The Buggles. The response was overwhelming and everyone joined in the advertising slogan, 'I want my MTV!' Desperate to fill twenty-four hours a day of music, the channel soon found bands from Australia and England who not only had well-honed videos, but good story lines, a good look, and, in the case of the first Australian act they championed, Men at Work, a sense of humour. After a few months of being on air, the fledgling channel hammered Men at Work's debut American single, 'Who Can It Be Now?', and stuck with it as the song very slowly gained momentum around the United States. It took almost a year, but eventually the song entered the US Billboard charts, on 7 August 1982. It hit number one and stayed in the charts for four months. The group immediately released the classic 'Down Under' which zoomed into the charts in November of that year, staying there almost five months, a month at number one. Men at Work have since sold in excess of fifteen million albums worldwide. Their album *Business as Usual* held down the number one slot in the US for sixteen weeks and was only knocked off by Michael Jackson's *Thriller*. The thunder from Down Under had begun.

Seeing the potential of Men at Work, and realising that many Australian bands with good videos were beginning to make their presence felt in the world's largest rock market, MTV began programming selected Australian videos. Icehouse, The Angels, Mental as Anything and Divinyls were amongst the first chosen few. But it was INXS and the sexually charged Michael Hutchence who grabbed the attention of the country's mainstream MTV generation. Their sound was different, their music a cross between rock and funk—you could dance to it—their look was unique. They combined many elements of rock music and presented them in a way that was set apart from most of their contemporaries, not just in Australia but in America too.

'INXS were definitely different,' says Australian music journalist and editor, Scott Howlett. 'Gel had arrived, and INXS looked as if they liked the idea, with Hutchence the main culprit, lathering it through his hair. In their first videos the clothes they were wearing were more effeminate than their contemporaries, and the way Hutchence danced awkwardly was very modern, and his style was the eventual source of impersonations. Many young male rock fans considered them a bit of a girls' band, but one you could certainly take your girlfriend to. The fact that they could play live was an added bonus. INXS were a very good band and they also had youth on their side.'

INXS's second album, *Underneath the Colours*, was released in 1981 in Australia, and while the single from the album, 'Stay Young', was a radio hit, the album was only a moderate seller. Anthony O'Grady, long-time Australian journalist and founder of the Australian rock magazine *Ram*, believes *Underneath the Colours* to be one of the few great Australian pub rock albums. 'It possessed sensibility and anger, flash and pomp,' he says. 'It was the fiery, melancholic comedown of the next generation. It was concerned with questions of adulthood, responsibility, direction, and the value of relationships. Only a few of the questions raised were answered, most left forebodingly open.'

The band certainly presented a sharp, dance-oriented stage performance, Tim Farriss, Kirk Pengilly and Hutchence particularly visibly exciting. The fey Hutchence charm, the outward shyness and the soft, sexy voice, though in their infancy, were already potent. Hutchence assumed a slightly camp, slightly effeminate look in his pose, sultry and sullen. He wore leather trousers and soon scored comparisons with Mick Jagger and Jim Morrison. He had the awkwardness of both, the charisma of both, but his style was totally unique, absolutely fresh. His un-Australian accent, together with his slight lisp, added to the mystique. Hutchence was far and away the most individual and charismatic lead singer in Australia at the time, totally original with his unruly hair, his own rag-tag style.

'I've always been that way, even when we were playing the Bilgola Bop,' Hutchence told me. 'There used to be this guy, for instance, who is now a friend, who used to come along with scissors and try and cut off my fringe because it wasn't fashionably short. I've always had the balls to be myself and live my life the way I want, okay? Which, by the way, is a very Australian thing to do.'

By the time Chris Murphy was in New York to settle INXS's recording deal, the band had become a major drawcard on the Australian live circuit. The man who has often been described as the seventh member of INXS, Gary Grant, became the group's tour manager, living, working and touring with them. Later made a partner in the management business owned by Murphy, it was Grant who would lead the management front guard on the ground, the man who had to deal with the six maverick young musicians and their whims, fancies and idiosyncrasies. Their Australian success now guaranteed, girls, drugs and parties all on tap, INXS were moving into a fast, furious lifestyle, pretty much the norm for successful rock'n'roll bands.

'We were working seven gigs a week,' Gary Grant told me. 'Picking up $3000–$5000 per gig was normal. At $7 a ticket, this was good money and good crowds. The venues were all overcrowded, 1500–2000 people cram-packed into venues licensed for only 500–1000. I remember going back to my place one night and having to count $21 000 in cash, our takings for the week.'

Touring Australia was relentless, exhausting, and could be soul-destroying. It's a surreal world, a world unto itself, a bubble filled with entertainers, musicians, technicians, engineers, lighting crews and sound crews, travelling from city to city, town to town, day after day, all with a law unto themselves, their own time schedule to keep. It was also fun, a non-stop party the beginning and the end of which were blurred by lack of sleep and hangovers. Drugs and alcohol were just as integral as the timing of the next meal.

'Even though we were making good money,' Grant told me, 'the band was frugal, saving for their move into America. INXS was run very tightly. Murphy did a great job on that side of things. The band was involved and total democracy ruled. INXS were six individuals whose chemistry combined to make them an amazing outfit. Murphy was a great jockey, but he was riding a fucking serious thoroughbred. You put the same jockey on a nag and he may not be able to make it win. I saw him ride a few of those nags and they didn't win any races. I started with them in 1981 when "Stay Young" was released. They used to do the run up to

Newcastle to play at the Ambassador. I don't know how many millions of miles we did. That was the beauty of starting with them then and being part of the entity. We'd all pitch in and buy fish and chips at the beginning, and when they hit the big time we'd argue about what restaurant we would eat at in Paris. I was there in 1981 when we were doing 250 shows a year. That went from 1981 until through to the end of *Kick*, when they went off the road for a while.'

INXS would often open shows for hard rockers Midnight Oil and Cold Chisel, finding themselves the brunt of hostility from the mainly male audience. The band endured the backlash, brilliant live performances being their saving grace.

'I had no faith in what we were doing,' Andrew Farriss recalled during an American *Rolling Stone* interview in 1988. 'I never saw the thing lasting at that stage.' 'We were so unprofessional,' added Hutchence, 'but the strength was there that was necessary to carry it off.'

Hutchence was passionate about Australia. He loved it, but in the band's early days he also knew the disadvantages of being based there. 'The first Australians were British outcasts, and pub rock was the sound of a country that started off as shit,' he said. 'It takes a lot to get a thousand red-eyed, drugged, been-surfing-all-day-in-the-sun people interested. "Fuck you" is one of the prime exchanges between pub rockers and their audience.'

• • •

The influence of producer Mark Opitz on Australian music can not be overstated. He worked with The Angels, Cold Chisel, Divinyls, AC/DC, and is one of the most experienced and successful Australian record producers, having

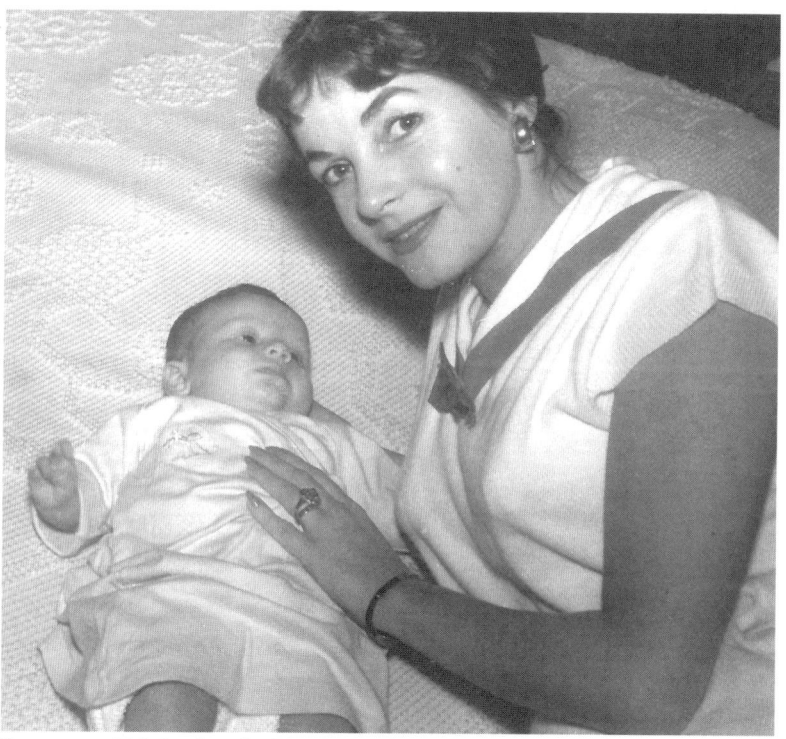

Patricia and Michael at the Hutchence family home in Howell Avenue, Lane Cove, April 1960 (KELL HUTCHENCE FAMILY PHOTO COLLECTION)

Games with Kelland at the Hutchence home in Kowloon Tong, Hong Kong. Michael is on the far left and Rhett is standing on the balcony
(KELL HUTCHENCE FAMILY PHOTO COLLECTION)

Michael and Rhett at the Frenchs Forest house, early 1974 (KELL HUTCHENCE FAMILY PHOTO COLLECTION)

Michele Bennett and Michael (Lian Lunson)

Richard Lowenstein and Michael, circa 1987
(photographer unknown)

been at the forefront for almost two decades. 'We made some of our first albums with Mark Opitz,' Hutchence told *Spin* magazine in 1988, a year after the band's big US breakthrough. 'He really talked to us, taught us to explore ourselves, to rationalise what we were about, and made us realise we had a foundation of funk and rock'n'roll. We loved rock'n'roll but we hated the stupidity of it. Somehow we found some even ground. We did "The One Thing" and I thought, This is finally us.' After releasing their third album, *Shabooh Shoobah*, INXS took off for their first US tour.

Gary Grant recalls fondly his first night in New York with Hutchence. 'I remember the first time we were in New York, Michael and I were cannabis smokers. We got a nickel bag and he smoked a mean joint and we decided to go for a walk and weren't sure of the area, so the next thing we were on 42nd Street with all the freaks and we got lost, eventually making our way back to the hotel. It was like, wowooooh, let's do that again, let's go have another look. We were young and so excited about it all. We sat up and talked all night. Michael was a great conversationalist, you know, he would talk for hours and hours, and talk about anything.'

The band's first American show was in 1983 at a dive in San Diego. Then came a tour support with Adam and the Ants, The Stray Cats, then a support for The Go-Go's.

During this tour, INXS performed at New York's Beacon Theatre and the legendary Nile Rogers appeared backstage after the show. Rogers and his band Chic had recreated funk pop, Rogers being at the forefront of an entire new music genre. He quickly recognised that INXS had at the heart of their music an empathy and feel for funk. 'He had the same attitude as us and he really made us loosen up,' Hutchence said. He and Andrew Farriss had written a song called 'Brand New Day' which eventually became 'Original Sin', a blistering, loping funk rocker that truly stamped the INXS sound. Rogers produced the track and it was included on the band's fourth album, *The Swing* in 1984. The single went to number one in France and was their first number one in Australia, but was banned in many southern American states because of its lyrical content pertaining to inter-racial issues.

'Stations that played it there actually used to receive bomb threats,' Hutchence told Australian *Penthouse* magazine in 1985. 'If they disagreed with the song that strongly, at least it shows they listened to it carefully,' he said, adding, 'I hope that's what it means, anyway.'

The inaugural INXS American tour ended at the US Festival in southern California, America's second biggest ever concert, featuring the world's most important acts performing in front of 150 000 punters stretched as far as the eye could see. The opening act was Divinyls, followed by INXS, who completely floored the crowd, earning the band an encore. Following the US Festival, Grant didn't immediately return to Australia but stayed on in the United States. Chris Murphy had told him to remain there.

'Chris was right,' Grant said. 'Just don't come home, he told me. So many Australian managers would go over there and have their meetings for two weeks and then go home and think it's all done. We worked in the record company offices every single day at the Rockefeller Centre.' Grant stayed based in New York, becoming the band's personal manager, and eventually Murphy set up a permanent base there too. The band's US lawyer, Bill Leibowitz, was also based there, and he recruited Martha Troup, a savvy New

York woman who soon became part of INXS's American management team. She is now INXS's worldwide manager. She and Michael enjoyed a close business relationship and were also very good friends. Martha Troup was one of the last two people Michael Hutchence telephoned on the morning of his death. The other was Michele Bennett.

It was 1984, and while INXS hadn't yet completely broken into the American market, everyone knew they were well on the way to doing so. The band returned from their first American tour to a sell-out Australian tour, virtually without a break. *The Swing* rocketed straight into number one spot in their home country. They soon left for Europe where they performed their first show in Düsseldorf, Germany, then flew straight to London for their debut UK show at the Astoria on 26 May. The band still wasn't in the superstar stratosphere of global stardom, but the pace was getting furious nevertheless. By the end of the year, 'Original Sin' had reached number one in Argentina. *The Swing* album was still in the Australian charts a year later. INXS were on a roll.

They returned to Sydney in March 1985 to record their fifth album, *Listen Like Thieves*, at Rhinoceros Studios under the guidance of Chris Thomas, probably the most successful producer in the world at that time. 'He came to our show in LA and said, "That's the best show I've seen in my life!"' Hutchence recalled Thomas saying in the backstage dressing rooms. '"But your records don't sound like you, I'm sure I can make you sound like you." Chris had produced every band that had an influence on our music: Sex Pistols, Pretenders, Roxy Music. Who else could we use?'

Chris Thomas was a legend in his own right. He was tall, English, loved a drink, could produce a mean rock'n'roll record, loved the rock'n'roll lifestyle, and, like most people in the music industry, sported a considerable ego. He was about to work with six strong-willed Australians who could hold their own. To say that the liaison became heated would be a massive understatement. INXS were proud of their sound, their roots and their direction, they were young, they were adamant. Thomas had been around since The Beatles' *White Album*, having also mixed Pink Floyd's classic *Dark Side of the Moon*. He had strong ideas about the way things should be done. There are many tales of clashes between INXS and Thomas, including one where Thomas, having stormed out of the studios after an argument with one of the band members, had to be crash-tackled by engineers and dragged into a pub to calm him down.

INXS were feeling pretty cocky, their well-planned goal of world domination within their grasp. Michael and Andrew, especially, were taking no prisoners. The explosive atmosphere worked a creative treat, however, because the resulting album became the band's most successful to date. It hovered outside the US Top Ten, with the resulting single, 'What You Need', becoming their first American Top Five hit.

The *Listen Like Thieves* album took INXS into mainstream America and shored up their chances for European success, including the elusive United Kingdom. The band was vindicated, its stance of sticking to its guns by staying outside the mainstream of Australian music proving to be the one thing that took them close to the top of the mountain. They still weren't there, but they were superstars waiting to happen. It was inevitable. Their lives were changing forever—their lifestyles, their personal lives, their bank balances, their freedom, or lack of it. It would take just one more album for INXS to become, for a short time, the biggest band in the world.

One of the most satisfying things for INXS at this time was knowing that their imminent world success would come as a result of their own belief in their unique brand of rock'n'roll: white boys writing, playing and performing funk-rock chic that bridged the gap between funk, pop, rock, and new wave. Their sound was later to influence many American mainstream bands of the nineties. Hutchence put it very eloquently to me in London in August 1997, following the band's final London concert: 'Instead of punters thrusting their fists into the air in a four-four motion as they did, we encouraged them to wiggle their arses in a rotating motion.'

But just as INXS were about to reach the pinnacle of success, there was a little matter of a solo career for Michael. His solo aspirations caused a lot of heartache in the INXS camp, and rifts—most noticeably with manager Chris Murphy. It was something that Michael Hutchence would brood about for years to come.

six

Dogs in Space, Max Q

> Rooms for the memory
> Rooms for the memory
>
> 'Rooms for the Memory'
> *Dogs in Space* soundtrack 1985
> OLLIE OLSEN

Michael Hutchence made his movie debut in Richard Lowenstein's film, *Dogs in Space*, a harrowing look at the late-seventies underground scene in Melbourne as experienced by a group of young people living in a shared suburban house. *Dogs in Space* might well have been but a blip in the twenty-year career of INXS, but it had, and still has, a life of its own. It was a pivotal experience for Michael Hutchence, giving him a feel for the world of acting and the confidence to believe that one day he would have a career outside of his beloved INXS. It was his first real chance to do something creative outside the constraints of the band, thus challenging Chris Murphy's autocratic and possessive approach to its management. The movie was also the starting point for an extremely close friendship between Michael and director Richard Lowenstein, and it spawned

Michael's first solo release, the single 'Rooms For The Memory', taken from the soundtrack of the film. The recording of the song forged yet another important creative friendship for Hutchence with Ollie Olsen, the song's producer, who later produced Hutchence's first album outside of INXS.

In *Dogs in Space* Hutchence portrayed the real-life character of Sam Sejavka, the leader of a punk band. While the film had many subplots, one of the main threads throughout was Sejavka's struggle to deal with heroin addiction. The movie was not a box-office success but became a cult classic around the world, and is still talked about in awe by aficionados. It remains one of the few films that tried to make sense of the drug-drenched alternative lifestyles in Australia during the seventies.

The film also indirectly led to a working relationship between Lowenstein and INXS, which would eventually result in some of the band's most effective and memorable video clips—a total of fourteen, plus a 48-minute concept video of the band.

Richard Lowenstein graduated from the Swinburne Film and Television school, now part of the Victoria College of the Arts, in 1979. In his final year he came to prominence with a short film he wrote and directed, a half-hour dramatised documentary called *Evictions*, which won him an award at the 1980 Melbourne Film Festival. Lowenstein went on to direct the brilliant and controversial *Strikebound*, a movie that gained world attention, taking him to film festivals around the world. He completed the movie in October 1983, at the age of twenty-four. He then directed video clips for such luminaries as U2, Crowded House, Tim Finn, and Hothouse Flowers. Never one to hide his political views, Lowenstein also directed a commercial for the 1990 election campaign of the Sandinista government of Nicaragua.

Two weeks before the 1984 Cannes Film Festival, Lowenstein got a phone call from Gary Grant, who was with MMA, INXS's management. INXS had seen his breakthrough video for Melbourne band Hunters and Collectors' song 'Talking To A Stranger', and they just loved the style of it. They wanted Lowenstein to direct a clip for them. Lowenstein told Grant that he'd never heard any of INXS's records and he couldn't do the video because he was leaving for Cannes in four days' time. 'But we're ready now,' Grant said impatiently. 'Just grab your camera and catch the next plane for Queensland and you can finish the rest in London after Cannes.'

'I can't just hop on a plane tomorrow,' Lowenstein retorted, 'and besides, I won't be able to finish it because I'll be in Cannes.'

'Well, we have to be in Nice in a couple of weeks anyway so why don't we finish it there, or maybe in London or something like that?' Grant responded.

'It was this sort of cheerful naivety that I couldn't really say no to,' says Lowenstein, 'so my partner Lyn-Maree Milburn, who was also a camera operator and animator, together with Troy Davies, who did styling and wardrobe, and I left for Queensland the next day. I grabbed my old hand-wound Bolex camera, hopped onto a plane and arrived in Mackay in north Queensland. We were all totally pale and dressed in black, the children of Nick Cave, The Cure and Joy Division, we'd practically never seen sunlight, and we're peering out of the window of our motel room going, Oooh, it looks very bright, doesn't it?'

When Gary Grant came to the motel room to take the Melbourne trio to meet the band, Richard Lowenstein was wondering whether or not they'd made the right decision. 'Gary led us over the road to another motel where there were these six guys in shorts and Hawaiian shirts, with suntans and girlfriends, sunglasses and everything, all reclining on banana lounges by the pool. We're all squinting at the sunlight like possums who had never seen the light of day, when one of them, the most effusive, gets up and lopes over towards us, holding out his hand with a seductive puppy-dog grin and a disarmingly direct gaze. He said his name was Michael. Michele Bennett was there, and she already knew Troy and yelled out his name. The others held up their Pina Coladas and said, "How's it going?" We sort of looked at each other going, "Get us out of here." Within days we were snorkel-diving off boats on the Great Barrier Reef with these guys.'

Within the next few days, everyone had bonded. Lowenstein had particularly taken to Hutchence and Michele Bennett, forming an attachment that would last until Michael's death and beyond. Bennett and Lowenstein are still extremely close friends. Troy Davies and Lynn-Maree also became close friends of Michael and Michele.

The song INXS wanted Lowenstein to do a video for was 'Burn For You', a textured, rhythmic song with atmosphere, perfect for a Lowenstein clip. The band was in the middle of a tour of north Queensland, taking in tropical coastal towns like Mackay, Townsville and Cairns, and the video eventually took on the character of the tour, according to Lowenstein. 'We had subtitles in front of each town and did it like a little running mini-documentary of the tour,' he said. 'And because we ended up filming the last chorus of the song in London, it sort of became the progression from Mackay, Townsville, then London with a population of fifteen million or something.'

From the tropical coast of Australia the group then flew to Nice, on the lower tip of France. 'Because the band was actually playing in Nice when I was in Cannes,' Lowenstein continued, 'I took a few people from Cannes to the INXS show and met up with Michael, who came back to Cannes after the show. He and I did an all-nighter, where we sort of stayed up all night focusing on some poor young French girl.

'I would often pick up a lot of his mannerisms and sometimes that involved both of us focusing all our attentions on the same girl, as was the case in this particular instance. It wasn't really about sex, although it was sexually based, but about flirting, the thrill of the flirt and not knowing where it would end. There was never any hint of anyone going to bed with this girl. She was the daughter of a publicist, she was a French girl and she was about fifteen and had been having trouble with the boys at school, and we just both concentrated on her totally all night. She was an INXS fan but was too cool to let us know. She told us how the boys at school hassled her for sex. We said we'd stay up and go with her to school and beat up the guys that were hassling her. Eventually we all got tired and ended up falling asleep on her mother's couch, while her mother was asleep in the bedroom.'

It was at breakfast on the morning after Michael and Richard's all-night French bonding that the seeds of *Dogs in Space* magically appeared. 'We went to the girl's school the following morning and looked through the fence and growled at a few boys and told them to keep their hands off her. I had a ten o'clock breakfast meeting at the incredibly expensive Carlton Hotel in Cannes with a well-known, quite conservative, matronly Australian film producer of the era. So I invited Michael to come along and get a free ten-dollar orange juice and have some fun.

'We kind of loped in there and were both totally wasted by this time, so we sat down and Michael immediately fell asleep at the table and I'm starting to pitch this intense political thriller I'd been working on. This great work of political passion that had been going on for years and I'm telling her the story and she's totally unimpressed, nodding, Yeah, yeah. Michael is asleep, head on his arms on the table, and I'm pitching away and I'm getting a really bad response from this woman. So I stop and go, "Well, I've got this other film I'm working on." I hadn't discussed this with anyone or even thought about it at all, but I started the pitch. "It's a rags to more rags story about a bunch of punks and hippies living in this big house in Melbourne with a punk band and everyone living in this house, and Michael is going to be in it." And then perfectly on cue, Michael lifts his head up and says, "Yeah I am." We then ad-libbed this non-existent script for about ten minutes, which wasn't bad seeing as how we'd never discussed it. Then Michael puts his head down again and promptly goes back to sleep. The producer's face came alive and she said, "Now that sounds like something I'd be interested in. Send me the script and we'll talk." I hadn't written it, I hadn't even thought about it.'

After the meeting Lowenstein had to leave, so he bid farewell to Hutchence, who was lying spread-eagled on the pavement, face upwards on the front steps of the Australian Film Commission, staring into the sunlight, waiting for the INXS tour bus to pick him up for the next leg of the tour.

Lowenstein went to London, meeting up with Troy and Lynn-Maree, to finish the 'Burn For You' clip, and then became involved in another INXS video, this time for 'Dancing On The Jetty'.

By November of that year, 1984, Lowenstein had begun to develop the idea from the morning meeting in Cannes, an idea that had actually been going through his head for a few years: a chronicle of events that had taken place in a large student house full of mismatched people in which he had lived during the late seventies. He enthusiastically wrote a treatment, and the more people he showed it to, the more excitement and encouragement he was shown. 'The characters stood out on the page. I started to get pangs of nostalgia,' he said. One of the central storylines was a young girl who turned up on the front doorstep of the house and became intertwined in the variety of subcultures therein.

By February 1985 Lowenstein had a first draft of the script, which had become a busy flow of humorous and dramatic episodes, vaguely strung together. He started to shop it around, trying to raise money—from Film Victoria, the Australian Film Commission, Burrowes-Dixon Production Company, Fred Schepisi, Peter Beilby and Robert Le Tet of Entertainment Media, Alan Finney from Roadshow, Coote and Carrol, Terry Hayes from Kennedy Miller, and Hill-Samuel in Hollywood. Mostly they baulked, wanting to change the script, the title, scenes in the movie, some demanding a guarantee of Hutchence's involvement. It took almost a year before the money was finalised, and the movie seemed in doubt on many occasions.

For Lowenstein it was a year packed with disappointment, disillusionment, another movie, more videos for INXS while the band itself headed full-tilt into the big league.

This made Lowenstein's task of securing Hutchence more difficult, for the more successful the band became, the more powerful and difficult its management became. But the bottom line was that Michael Hutchence really, really wanted to play the lead role in *Dogs in Space*. Nothing was going to stop him. As the commercial success he had worked so hard and so long for loomed in America, he was paradoxically strongly attracted to the opportunity of acting the lead role in a film about his beloved cool Melbourne—the city that housed a subculture which embodied an important part of his desire for credibility. Melbourne was the home of Nick Cave and a host of alternative bands in the Australian post-punk movement. In the mid to late eighties, critics in the UK, along with many in Australia, had unfairly crucified almost every INXS album released, even though they were selling millions in the US; the contribution INXS were making to a new music style was consistently overlooked. At the same time, Nick Cave's band The Birthday Party were being propelled to a godlike status in the British press, and it was that sort of credibility that Hutchence craved.

Late one April evening in 1985, in the midst of his frantic mining for film cash, Lowenstein was rewriting the script for *Dogs* in front of the television. It was 2 am and he was watching a rock movie called *Stardust*, starring David Essex and Keith Moon, who was smashing away on his drums and acting his normal loony self. The phone rang.

'Is that Richard?' a voice on a crackling line asked.

Richard said that it was.

'This is Pete Townsend,' came the response, as Moon was still crashing away on his drum kit. 'I've just seen your movie *Strikebound* and was very impressed,' went on the founder of The Who. 'I won't send you the script because I need to explain it to you in person. I'll fly you to London, we'll talk about the script, then we'll both catch the Concord to New York to sell it to the record company executives. The film is called *White City*.'

Lowenstein placed the phone back on the receiver. In *Stardust*, David Essex was about to take a lot of drugs.

On his way to London, Lowenstein, with his producer Glenys Rowe in tow, dropped into the offices of INXS's management, MMA. 'I decided to go and see Michael's management, meet the lions in their den, so to speak,' Richard said. 'It was an enlightening experience. They blustered and bullshitted and carried on about how many millions they could raise for us at the snap of a finger if only we'd come to them in the first place. Glenys and I nodded knowingly. All we really wanted from them was a letter saying that Michael was interested in doing the film. They then suggested having INXS as the main band in the film. Then they asked me what I was doing wasting my time with Pete Townsend. I smiled and metaphorically patted them on the head. It was something they would probably never understand. Glenys was in a state of catatonic shock. Compared to the emancipation of females in the film industry, the music industry was in the dark ages. These people appeared to have no comprehension of music. Thankfully, the band members have more sense than their management.'

Townsend and Lowenstein were supposed to be going to New York to sell *White City*, but the record executives were at a conference in Hawaii, so the pair sat down in a hotel room and began rewriting the script. Glenys Rowe had gone back to Australia and was trying to fund *Dogs in Space*, but having no luck. There was no way the money would be raised from film financiers before June, so Glenys was nervously trying to raise it independently, hustling investors, and seeing brokers, underwriters, lawyers and anyone else she could think of who might want to invest in a film about heroin and alternative lifestyles in Melbourne. Townsend then asked Lowenstein to help out with the musical side of his movie and was remarkably open to his ideas. 'I got brass and backing singers, everything a filmmaker wants,' says Lowenstein.

Meanwhile, Chris Thomas was in Sydney producing the INXS album, *Listen Like Thieves*. He asked Townsend to book some studio time in London for the band to put some finishing touches to it, complaining to Lowenstein that every studio he spoke to was owed money by the band's management company and wouldn't take the booking. Lowenstein flew back to Melbourne to finish the script for *White City*, and completed it in May 1985. Amazingly, by June the Townsend movie, shot in London, was completed. Lowenstein returned to Sydney to continue working on the script for *Dogs in Space* and the new INXS video, 'What You Need'.

It seemed that *Dogs in Space* might never get off the ground because of a lack of finance. 'It looked highly unlikely that we would get the money before June of '86,' Lowenstein said, 'plus INXS were touring Australia and Europe until January, and then America. This meant that the only time Michael would be available for shooting the movie would be in January. It was obvious that if we couldn't get the money in the next few months, *Dogs* would have to be dropped.'

By September 1986 Richard Lowenstein had completed the video for what would become INXS's breakthrough single, 'What You Need'. He took the finished product to Chris Murphy who responded by saying, 'My daughter will really like it. She likes colouring in.' Lowenstein was flabbergasted. 'Sometimes I wonder why we bother,' he reflected. But the band was ecstatic with the video, which went into high rotation on American MTV. The song eventually went to number four in the charts, finally breaking the band into the biggest record market in the world—but it didn't help finance *Dogs in Space*.

As the year came to its end, the film's finance finally started to look like a reality, but with INXS's star continuing to rise, the demands on Michael's time grew. INXS had played to 30 000 people in Argentina, before returning to Australia and performing to 10 000 at a 'Rocking the Royals' concert in Melbourne, where Prince Charles and Princess Di were special guests. While the band was in Melbourne a meeting was scheduled between Chris Murphy and prospective film financier Geoff Burrowes. Murphy didn't turn up, and a subsequent meeting had to be arranged for the following morning.

'The bullshit was flying back and forth across the table so thick and so fast,' Lowenstein recalled. 'It seemed more of an exercise in who could hype the other, in how big INXS were in America, and then, finally, a serious discussion about where and when Michael was going to be available. We finally resolved to make it all legal and get our lawyers to contact theirs and see what we could sort out.'

Five days before Christmas, with the film supposed to start shooting in five weeks, the money was still not in place. Lowenstein was frantic. At one stage he announced that the movie would be cancelled, but negotiations continued. Contracts could not be signed, crews could not be finalised, people were working on the hope that the film would go ahead. Some of the best technicians were slipping out of Lowenstein's grasp because he was unable to confirm that the film was definitely happening.

Other problems were mounting. The owners of the house that was to be the main setting of the movie suddenly demanded $20 000 for filming rights. On 29 December Gary Grant phoned to say that the band had been scheduled for a concert in Vancouver, Canada on 20 February, two weeks into the scheduled shooting dates. One of the Sydney actors who had been cast for *Dogs* died of a brain haemorrhage in the shower. A young boy from Melbourne who had been given a major role was found hanging from the ceiling of his rented room in a self-made noose. The film looked to be in dire straits. Then Lowenstein received a telex from Chris Murphy in which he stated that due to a conversation he had with Lowenstein and the dubiousness of the funding situation, he had rescheduled the INXS US tour. It would now be impossible to have Michael on 24 February, so unless the film was moved back to 6 March the whole deal was off. This change of heart from Murphy cost the film an extra $50 000.

Meanwhile, INXS were going from strength to strength in America with their single 'What You Need'. The word from the US was that it was Richard Lowenstein's video that had grabbed everyone's attention, contributing to an increase in live bookings, and thus, ironically, placing Hutchence's availability for the movie in further jeopardy. Lowenstein then received another telex from Murphy: 'The good news is that "What You Need" went to 23 with a bullet here in the Billboard charts. The problem is that Atlantic Records now urgently need a video to "Listen Like

Thieves", which will be the next single. When could you shoot a video for this track? Please advise.'

Lowenstein agreed to shoot the video, and, miraculously, funding finally came through for *Dogs in Space*. The film was saved. Hutchence was suddenly made available, and on 3 March shooting began.

Richard Lowenstein was very impressed with Michael Hutchence as an actor and truly believed it could be his future vocation. 'Michael was doing incredibly well at portraying the character of Sam. I kept getting very strange feelings of déjà vu as I caught glimpses of him out of the corner of my eye. He was doing it so well I was scared no-one would realise that the self-conscious posing was part of the character. I think this is the character most people would like to imagine Michael to have, and won't want to believe otherwise.

'In the sex scenes, I looked at the ceiling and told them to do what came naturally. I think it might've come a bit too naturally. We had to tape up Michael's erection with black gaffer-tape so that Saskia, the girl he makes love to, wouldn't get injured by it.'

Michael left immediately after the filming finished, on 26 April, for what turned out to be an eight-month tour of America with INXS. The band members were now becoming bona-fide rock stars. The final cut and edit of *Dogs in Space* was not completed until the end of 1987, and when it was finally finished the Australian Censorship Board had doubts as to whether it should be seen by a general audience. The board was of the opinion that the film glamorised the drug culture, making it appear trendy and attractive, and it objected to what it described as 'coarse, abusive or sexually explicit language'. The movie was finally given an R certificate, thus isolating the audience at which it was partially aimed—teenagers.

Hutchence returned at the end of 1987 to introduce the movie at several Sydney and Melbourne previews, then promptly left for Hong Kong to try to obtain residency. According to Lowenstein, Hutchence appeared down about the film. 'He seemed very depressed whenever I spoke to him. He thought he was too prominent on the poster, and that there was not enough of him in the promo for the song. He seemed very worried about the possibility of being crucified critically for his first attempt at acting. I was unable to console him as I had no idea how the critics would respond, especially the mainstream critics.'

But they need not have worried, the critics praised Michael's performance and the movie was also highly acclaimed.

• • •

As the filming of *Dogs in Space* began, Ollie Olsen had been called in by Lowenstein to oversee the musical soundtrack. 'Ollie was the lead singer and songwriter of an infamous Melbourne, late-seventies cult electro-punk-disco band, Whirlywirld, and he took over my office in order to co-ordinate all the little bands for the movie,' recalls Lowenstein. 'He wrote his name on the door and wrote Musical Director underneath it. A small price to pay for enthusiasm. At last I found someone I could trust creatively, and someone who understood the sort of music I was talking about for the film.'

Olsen was regarded by some as the uncrowned king of the new edge in the Melbourne music scene. He steered clear of the mainstream commercial scene, electing instead to experiment with his music. He was not in the slightest interested in becoming part of the pop merry-go-round, and was therefore the obvious choice to produce the music for the movie. He also proved to be an ideal choice for Hutchence in his bid for street credibility.

'The first time I met Michael was on the set of *Dogs in Space*,' remembers Olsen. 'He sang a song of mine in the movie, 'Rooms For The Memory'. Following the release of the song, which enjoyed only moderate success, we'd catch up whenever he was in town. In late 1988 I was working in a record store and Michael was in town, so he asked me to come over to his hotel during my lunch hour. I took him over a couple of tracks I'd been working on because I'd heard he was working on a solo album. He liked the ideas of the songs.'

Hutchence not only liked the ideas of the songs, he liked the idea of doing something outside the perimeters of INXS. The irony was that he chose a time when INXS were just realising their dream of success. The band was not only rocketing up the American charts, but had broken through in the UK as well and were solidly placed in Europe. At this critical moment in the band's career, a moment that required solidarity and a unified sense of purpose, Hutchence chose to explore his desire for street credibility. It was as if, as INXS became commercially successful, he craved non-commercial independence.

'The thing I found so interesting about Michael was that he was fascinated by the alternative scene and the underground scene, and the artistic scene,' says Olsen. 'That's why he did the Max Q thing. I think he was a person who was kind of caught up on this rollercoaster of fame and there was a part of him that perhaps was on a more spiritual level.

'Not long after Michael heard my songs, he phoned me up at the record store and wanted me to come and record some demo songs. He flew me and some of my musician friends up to Sydney, where we recorded a couple of tracks at Rhinoceros Studios. We recorded "Buckethead" and "Way Of The World".' The musicians were all old friends of Olsen's. Like INXS, they had known each other from school days, when they'd started playing music together. A few weeks later, following these original two recordings, Olsen received another call from Hutchence, this time asking him if he had a passport. He didn't. 'I asked him why I needed a passport,' Olsen remembers, 'and he said that he wanted me to come to Los Angeles the following week because he wanted to do an album with me.' Hutchence had dropped the idea of doing a solo album and had decided to work with Olsen.

Olsen was excited about the prospect of going to the United States. 'I'd never been to America before, so it was a great opportunity. I got my passport and went to LA and we stayed at this Malibu house on stilts—a real kind of *Baywatch* scenario. I was spun out by the whole thing. Michael and I spent two weeks together, getting into each other's heads and coming up with ideas. It was the first time he and I had spent any real time together outside his hotel rooms. It was classic with Michael, you always had to meet him in his hotel rooms. He and I got on incredibly well during that two weeks and we found we had a lot in common. And we both figured we could make a good record.

'My musical knowledge was a lot wider than Michael's. I'm into all kinds of music, avant-garde, classical, thrash, you name it. But our meeting point was our mutual love of acid and house music, which was purely an underground movement at that stage, mainly in New York and London. It was early days for both music forms, and we found we were both into it big time. It was not then the phenomenon it eventually became, it hadn't hit Australia, and even internationally it was still an underground thing. We were also both into dance music and black music and stuff like that. What was interesting was that we found we were also both into Barry White, and I felt we should have strings on our record like he used strings. So we hatched the Max Q thing in LA. He initiated the project because he had the bread to do it.'

According to Rhett Hutchence, Michael was so keen to get the recording off the ground that he mortgaged his home in Paddington, Sydney, to finance it.

It wasn't all work and no play for Olsen and Hutchence during their Los Angeles meeting. This being Olsen's first trip to the city, he wanted to see the sights. Walking along LA's famous Venice Beach one steamy Saturday afternoon, amidst the brash, buzzing, animal noises of people pumping up muscles, they heard a song blaring out from a radio. 'I go to Michael, "Which one of your songs is this one?" and he says he didn't know,' recalls Olsen. 'And then the vocals came on and it was that song from Fine Young Cannibals, "She Drives Me Crazy". You know, the one with that memorable riff. To me it sounded so much like INXS, it was extraordinary, and we just pissed ourselves laughing because he never realised just how much the song sounded like an INXS riff. I really thought it was an INXS song, and he couldn't remember if it was or wasn't.'

A couple of months later, Olsen and Hutchence went to New York to do some publicity on the Max Q album and were special guest presenters at the American Music Awards. 'It was quite bizarre, really, only two months earlier I had been working in a record store and here I was giving an award away in New York with superstar Hutch,' Olsen recalled. 'Backstage are some of my heroes like George Clinton and Lou Reed, it was just bizarre. But the funny thing is, we were giving the award for the best single or something, I don't know, and as we open the envelope, the song comes on, and it was the Fine Young Cannibals song that we'd heard in Venice Beach—the one with the INXS riff!'

Hutchence had finished doing the *Kick* tour with INXS and was at the peak of his pop career, on the brink of superstardom, with the world at his feet. The album solidly established INXS as one of the very biggest bands in the world. 'It was an amazing experience just hanging around with him under those circumstances,' reckons Olsen. 'He made me see a lot of things about the rock star thing that really put me off. I just could not have dealt with all the shit that Michael had to deal with. See, I'm not really a rock musician. I'm a dabbler in all forms of music. My whole thing is, I just want to make music. I'm more interested in the actual process of making music rather than performing it. The whole process of touring and being a big star and all that stuff, it completely detracts from what is really important about music, which is much bigger than the music industry. I'm talking about art. It's a deeply spiritual thing that sort of transcends popularity.'

Following the Los Angeles jaunt, Olsen returned to a mini-studio in Melbourne and in just a few short weeks put the fruits of the pair's creative liaison together. He programmed the majority of the album on a computer and sang on all the songs. 'I kept sending Michael tapes and he'd send me back faxes of his ideas. Some of the words on the album actually came from little letters he'd written me and I turned them into lyrics. I put the album together in rough form and sang it all, and he added all his bits and pieces later.'

A few weeks later Michael and Ollie joined forces in Sydney to start making the album. 'I brought all the musicians I wanted to play on the album from Melbourne up to Sydney, we went into Rhinoceros Studios and took about four weeks to record the album. Then Michael and I went to New York to mix it.'

Two of the original house music names at the time were Frankie Knuckles and Todd Terry, the latter of whom was an absolute hero of Ollie Olsen's, and Olsen was adamant that Terry mix the album. 'He was a real god to me at that time, still is—God of House Music,' says Olsen. 'Basically it was Frankie Knuckles and Todd Terry, they're the two legends of that entire genre. Michael's management, and Michael to a certain degree, were not into Todd being involved, but I was really interested in getting a completely different perspective on the record, like somebody from a different world coming in and working on it. I think it was quite successful from that perspective.' There is no doubt that the Max Q album was distinctly different from anything else that was around at the time.

Compared to organising something for INXS, the Max Q recording was relatively smooth, and Olsen thought that Michael found the ease with which the project came together quite strange. 'He kind of stepped out of one band that had been together for a long while, and straight into another that had been going for a long while, only they were my friends, not his. I mean, my mates and I had been together playing music since school, just like the Farriss brothers, but we just played different music, that's all. Most of the people in Max Q were friends of mine, not Michael's. There was this incredibly strong musical relationship between us all. There was a whole infrastructure. It was easy to slip into. My friends are all extremely laid-back, and Michael loved that.'

Michael also loved Ollie Olsen. 'He's definitely the master of another universe,' said Hutchence some two years after the project. 'His approach to life and his values are so high and noble, it's inspiring.'

The other musicians in Max Q were Gus Till, Arnie Hanna and Michael Sheridan on guitar, Bill McDonald on bass, and John Murphy on drums. Olsen produced, worked computers, midis, tape loops, wrote most of the songs, and provided some backup vocals. Gus now lives in England doing trance music. Michael Sheridan studies music and plays with Olsen on various musical projects. Arnie Hanna is studying hardcore computer music at Canberra University, and John Murphy has been touring internationally with an industrial band called Death in June.

Once the album was completed, Chris Murphy was concerned about using Hutchence to promote it and he told Olsen, 'We gotta kind of make Michael like he's not there.' Ollie reckons from that point onwards he could see what was coming. 'The guys and I were disappointed that it wasn't pushed outside of Australia. It was a great opportunity for us. We benefited in the short term, but in the long term the project itself didn't. When I did the Max Q album, I was thirty years old and I had already developed an incredible distaste for the recording industry. I was very weary of the business side of things. I had more anarchistic values and style and I just did not trust these people from the start of the project. When Max Q came up, I was in this band called No, and we were basically doing super-hardcore gigs like thrash dance stuff. I wasn't part of the pop scene at all. I was a complete outsider and I walked into this situation with that in mind. When Michael's management started to show signs of ruffling the project I wasn't surprised. At the start it was exciting, flash hotels and all that stuff, but we kind of watched it disappear very, very rapidly.

'There was definitely friction happening between Michael, Chris Murphy, some of the band, and I think Michael was getting quite upset by it all. I remember having a meeting with Chris Murphy and Michael one time, and Chris was throwing us a bone by offering this situation where he would organise a live Max Q show in Melbourne and Sydney, just one-off shows. Michael was into it, but when I went to the other guys, it was kind of like, We'll have to rehearse for it, who knows for how long, we would have had to put the rest of our lives on hold for the time being, and we didn't know for how long. It all seemed very exciting and all that kind of stuff, but we weren't really going anywhere with it, because Michael had INXS who were becoming bigger and bigger by the day. To us it seemed completely pointless. If it wasn't going to be followed through properly, what was the point?'

Chris Murphy discouraged record companies around the world from associating Hutchence closely with the Max Q album, and would not permit him to promote it. He talked the talk with Hutchence inferring that it would be far cooler if people found out of their own accord that Max Q was indeed Michael Hutchence. INXS were now near their peak with the huge success of the *Kick* album, and a successful solo project from Hutchence would have propelled him to superstar status. Murphy did not think so. His job was to manage INXS. If he thought Michael's solo project would damage INXS, no doubt he had to take the side of the band. But when the album failed commercially, Hutchence felt thwarted.

The Max Q album represented a large personal and creative investment for Hutchence, it was a vehicle for him to express himself outside INXS, and Murphy's actions hurt him very deeply. Hutchence loved INXS and would not have left the band but the Max Q album was the final straw for the fading relationship between Hutchence and Murphy. Hutchence felt betrayed by Murphy. Eventually, Hutchence fired Murphy as his personal manager although he waited a few years.

Murphy was deeply offended when Michael sacked him, but Michael just didn't care anymore. As far as he was concerned Murphy didn't give a damn about Michael's personal career. Michael felt he was sold out for the benefit of the band.

At precisely the same time as the Max Q album was recorded, bands like The Happy Mondays and Stone Roses were beginning to make an impact on the fluid English music scene. The tracks on Max Q were certainly comparable in terms of being new, exciting and different, and had the album been released and promoted in the UK, there seems little doubt that it would have been at the forefront of what was happening musically at the time.

Michael's long-time friend Greg Perano is aware INXS's management was concerned that if the Max Q project became too successful it would take Michael away from the band. 'They wanted it to be a faceless record. It was an excellent record,' says Perano. 'It could have been absolutely huge. It was incredibly exciting for him and it was exciting music. And the computer-generated videos that came out with the songs were so far ahead of their time. It was on a par with what was going on overseas. It was exciting for Michael, but it also created resentment with the management. If his management had only said, Okay Michael, go for it, create a solo career, he would have brought that back to the band and improved them and maybe complemented some of their ideas, and maybe it could have happened the other way, too, if they went out and had solo careers of some kind. But Michael went along with the band because he wanted the rest of the band not to feel insecure. He knew there was a sense of insecurity there.

'I think Michael's heart lay in creating his own music.' That's what he felt. And making the film as well, because it was a new challenge to him. You had to take risks and learn something all over again. I think that's where the future lay for him. Michael was always trying to find out what else was going on in music all over the world. He would always be calling on new influences. He was always looking for new material and new trends, and it was Andrew who could articulate it all in INXS. Andrew could see that it was a special formula, he and Michael writing songs. As far as the music was concerned, it was a perfect combination. The formula had been set. With Ollie Olsen, it was another formula with someone else articulating. I dropped into the recording sessions for Max Q sometimes, and it was so refreshing because he had this group of relatively unknown people—to him—all together, and everyone was going along with just the music, without ulterior motives as to who was going to be listening to the music. Michael was like a sixteen-year-old kid again.'

Hutchence has said that the Max Q experience was when he felt he had finally become a musician. 'Prior to Max Q I didn't think I was my own person in a creative sense. I'd never been able to pick and choose what I wanted to do or where I wanted to go. I found it incredibly liberating,' he said in 1991. 'I felt Max Q was the best thing I'd ever done, not just for me, but for INXS.' There's no doubt the experience restored his own faith in himself as an artist, in his ability to stand on his own. The irony is that, although he called the shots for scheduling and financing for much of the project, it was actually Ollie Olsen who wrote most of the album, who gathered the musicians.

Greg Perano, being himself a musician, thinks that Hutchence took INXS 'a lot further than they would have gone if they'd had someone else out front. A bit like Bon Scott with AC/DC, really.' Perano feels that if Michael had been allowed to do his thing, it would have enhanced the band, not harmed it.

Richard Lowenstein agrees, but thinks there was more to the Max Q episode. 'I know that Michael had very split ambitions, like he was very frustrated that he couldn't actively go out there and promote the album. I think he was led into an area where it really backfired, plus there was the fact that Chris Murphy refused to publicise that album, or let Michael publicise that album. It really upset him, because he was in his ideal world. He wanted to continue with INXS because he really did like being in the band, and being part of the band—not only being a member of the family, but the actual popularity of INXS was intoxicating. And he had that identification with the band members. I don't really think that he ever thought, or wanted to say, That's it, it's all over, let's split up the band. That's why he was finding it so hard to go into new areas. I think in his ideal world, like he lived the rest of his life, he wanted his cake and wanted to eat it too. He wanted to have the stability of a solid relationship or long-term relationship, even if it was only a year or a couple of years, at the same time as being free enough to go and explore. I think with Max Q he was just having an affair. It was like being married and having an affair, he wanted them both to happen at the same time. If Max Q had been a huge success I don't think it would have reflected badly on INXS at all. There were a lot of insecurities in not only band members but management, and it would have been just fantastic if both the INXS and Max Q albums did not coincide.

'But Michael could be very easily influenced, and with a smooth talker like Chris Murphy he could be talked out of anything. And sometimes talked into anything. I don't think he really had that much faith in the fact that they were both able to happen at the same time, so when for example he wasn't allowed to do a front cover for Max Q for magazines, he didn't just go, Fuck it, I'm going to do it, you know, I'm going to ring up Chris and say I'm going to do it. Or ring up the magazine and say, I'm here let's do it. He would be indecisive. Chris Murphy would talk to him for hours, convincing him that the world-domination plan was still in place. Michael would end up being talked out of something, but he would resent it. He would bow to Chris's point of view, but there'd be a build-up of resentment because he'd let himself be talked out of doing something that he really wanted to do. I think beneath all the rock-star hype, Michael was incredibly insecure.' This notion was reiterated by almost everyone who knew Michael.

INXS wrapped up their *Kick* tour and almost self-destructed due to the internal pressures created by stardom and constant touring. The majority of the attention INXS now received was focused on Michael, and in many ways Max Q was his saving grace. It could be seen as his anti-rock-star phase; he seemed to be going against what had made him so popular. The music of Max Q, with its fusion of techno, electronica, massive guitars and screaming vocals, would gain world appeal a decade later through the likes of British bands such as The Chemical Brothers, Prodigy, and Underworld. But Hutchence had already been there with Ollie Olsen. Kirk Pengilly would later comment that when he heard Max Q he felt insanely jealous and likened the feeling to a lover having an affair with someone else.

Hutchence seemed to be in two minds about his worldwide popularity with INXS, loving the chance to indulge his every desire yet loathing the circus atmosphere that had engulfed the band. He chopped off his hair and began wearing Buddy Holly-style glasses. He said at the time that the cutting of his hair was simply a protest against the long-haired heavy-metal bands of the day. He appeared to do everything possible to try and make himself unattractive. His image had become a burden to him and he wanted to shed it. The Max Q project probably alienated many INXS fans, but for others it was a welcome change for the man at the front of the band. In many ways, Hutchence became the ghost of the year. He disappeared from public view, he travelled extensively, changed his image, distanced himself from the public perception of his persona.

By all accounts, this period should have been his happiest,

and in many ways it was—but the signs are that this period was also the beginning of a long soul-searching for Michael Hutchence. He had reached a pinnacle with INXS, and almost as soon as he reached it he seemed personally unsatisfied. He might well have found a freedom with Ollie Olsen and Max Q, but while the music was fresh and unlike anything he had been singing, it still was not really his music. He co-wrote four of the songs, and the rest were Ollie Olsen's compositions, so on the songwriting score he was worse off than in INXS where he co-wrote most of the songs with Andrew Farriss. And it was Olsen who made most of the musical and production decisions, albeit with a large input from Hutchence, so that it was more an Olsen recording than a Hutchence one. Not having to worry about commercial success, and being able to experiment with sounds was exhilarating, however, and he did achieve his sought-after credibility. Hutchence had also done Olsen a great favour in asking him to do the recording, and he liked to play on that sometimes.

'But then I would retort, "Yeah, but you're singing my songs", which is fair,' Olsen says. 'We both helped each other out, and I think ultimately that it was a great collaboration. I also happen to think I got some of the best vocals out of him that he's ever done.'

The aftermath of the Max Q album left a pretty bitter taste in a lot of people's mouths, according to Olsen. 'I remember when I saw Michael at Wembley Stadium a couple of years after the album and we hooked up after the show. It wasn't quite as crazy as normal, and Michael and I were talking and he said something really nice to me and we had this kind of cosmic experience. It's pretty hard to explain, but it was kind of like this energy that we both felt that was between us, and it sort of departed and it seemed like the passing of something. Things were intense between Michael and me. Obviously, when you write songs with somebody, you have a relationship with them that is on an interesting level. We wrote songs together and discussed very large issues. I like big issues and we had reasons to discuss big issues. We discussed things through at a high level. I certainly think he had a sense of universal consciousness. The guy had done a lot of acid and all that kind of stuff and he had had extraordinary experiences, and extraordinary events had happened to him in his life, so I have absolutely no doubt in my mind that he had, to some degree, confronted a deeper nature within himself, and the deeper reasons for life itself. The point is that our relationship was big and open and very deep, but at one point after Max Q it just sort of shut. And I think it was never really resolved until that night of our shared cosmic experience after the Wembley concert.

'The thing is that a lot of other people benefited from the Max Q collaboration in ways that Michael would not have dreamed of. Not just the guys in the band, they were all on their own directions anyway, they enjoyed the experience and have benefited, but they are also very good at what they do. But I mean, I have been able to start a new record label and been able to help young artists and stuff. Mainly electronic artists, who are really creative, and I think that is fantastic and Michael would have loved that. He did love it, he knew about it.'

Like so many of Michael's friends, Olsen had tried to make contact during Hutchence's final couple of years but found him more difficult than ever to reach. 'Personally, I think this was one of his big failures,' emphasises Olsen.

'His friendships often fell down, I felt that he didn't follow through with people. It's very important to have a network of people that you can actually talk to, and for a person who is in a position like Michael was in, it is particularly so. I was living with him in New York when he was at the height of his fame and I just observed people around him. I think he was socially surrounded by sycophants. I think Michael was perpetually living in fear of being taken for a ride by people who were just hanging out for his money and all that went with it. I think he was really terrified of that sort of thing. It happened all the time to him, and it was very hard to make friends in that situation. The people that were in New York couldn't give a rat's arse who I was—they didn't know or care. And I saw how he dealt with them and stuff. But when he was away from all of that and he was actually in a room with somebody he trusted, like myself, he was an extremely different person. I think it is important that if you are in that sort of situation to have some kind of base, like a strong group of friends or family that you can talk to and have some kind of honest relationship with, outside of the ridiculous relationship plays and dramas that he was involved with.

'The last couple of years, I just had this nagging feeling with Michael and I kept phoning his home in England or France and I never got through to anybody. Either it would ring out or somebody would come on the phone, not identify themselves and say he was away. I tried to ring him many times, and deep down inside myself I worried. When I finally contacted him I was relieved because he had just become a dad and he sounded quite happy, actually.'

seven

Kicking arse 1986–1992, saving arse 1992–1997

> So how do you feel?
> I'm lonely
> What do you think?
> Can't think at all
> Whatcha gonna do?
> Gonna live my life
>
> 'Need You Tonight'
> *Kick* 1987
> MICHAEL HUTCHENCE AND
> ANDREW FARRISS

INXS's most successful album, *Kick*, ended up selling nine million copies around the world. It stayed in the British charts for two years and spawned five hit singles, all of which are played still on radio stations from Iceland to Tasmania. *Kick* was the album that catapulted INXS into rock superstardom, and the earnings from it turned each member of the band into multi-millionaires. The years that followed this success were fast, furious and formidable, testing the band's depth of friendship and resolve, and cementing

Hutchence's status as a sex god, a role he alternately relished and loathed.

Perceptively produced by Englishman Chris Thomas, *Kick* was the first time the band's unique sound was captured on tape. There had been hints and promises of it in previous songs on previous albums, and the band had always been fun- and dance-oriented, having done club and dance mixes since *Shabooh Shoobah*. But *Kick* was when it all fell into place. Whether or not it was because of the continual tension and sometimes bitter clashes between producer Chris Thomas and the band during the recording, the reality was that *Kick* was INXS's finest commercial recording. It was undoubtedly a masterpiece, but like many great rock-'n'roll albums it was born partly out of frustration and emerging differences within the band.

INXS had been on a rapid rise in the US since their 1986 album *Listen Like Thieves*. *Rolling Stone* magazine was a supporter, enthusiastic about the band's sound: 'INXS rocks with passion and seals the deal with a backbeat that'll blackmail your feet,' one critic enthused. The rhythm section of Jon Farriss and Garry Gary Beers was fierce. The steady, block-rocking beat was as important to the sound of the band as the guitar chops, the saxophone, the riffs, the keyboards and the vocals. It was the rhythm section that provided the balance, the foundation around which the rest of the band could move, both musically and physically. Farriss and Beers had an extraordinary connection when they played, sometimes needing only to eye each other on stage to vary the skip of their thunder funk and lift the groove; they seemed to read each other's musical thoughts. Jon Farriss and Beers were the linchpin for the sound of INXS.

In March 1986 *Listen Like Thieves* was certified a gold

record in the US. 'What You Need', a sexy, definitive funk-rock song taken from the album became the band's first Top Ten single, eventually hitting the US Top Five. Even America's non-music magazines got into the act, with *Newsweek*'s Cathleen McGuigan announcing that INXS had 'a hard-driving, irresistibly danceable sound and a sexy, live-for-the-moment attitude—tempered with just a dash of social consciousness'. She concluded that the band possessed 'all the right ingredients for late 'eighties success'. To get there, the band simply had to keep applying the pressure—more record releases, more touring, more consolidation. When you're on a roll, you're on a roll, and in the world of rock, once it begins you just keep rolling—and that's exactly what happened to INXS.

Having set up a solid base in Australia and the US, and having made their presence felt in Europe and the UK, the band capitalised on their first American hit single with a world tour, If You Got It, Shake It, beginning in May 1986. In June the elusive market of London, and consequently the rest of the UK, finally fell under their spell when the band played a sell-out concert at the Royal Albert Hall. The UK had probably been their toughest market, the English media at that time being more interested in what clothing, eyeliner and haircuts bands were into than in the music they were playing.

Then, just before the release of *Kick*, they mounted a huge concert tour of Australia called Australian Made. The tour featured other Australian heavyweights at the time, including Jimmy Barnes, Divinyls, and Mental as Anything. It was a triumphant success, and there was an unspoken feeling that it foretold the band's future international superstardom. But even that didn't stop some critics.

'They're a funny bunch, Australians,' Hutchence sighed in 1988. 'They react to success strangely and they assume, because you haven't been back there for two years, that you've kind of turned your back on them. You're either the prodigal sons or a bunch of ship-deserting rats. When you're there it's, Why doncha get your ass over to England and show them bloody Poms a thing or two, mate! Then when you get back it's, Where the hell ya bin? You can't bloody win.'

Earnings from international record sales continued to pour in, and Chris Murphy pointed the band in the direction of real-estate investments and, investing in the Australian movie *Crocodile Dundee*. The movie became a global hit bringing its star, former Sydney Harbour Bridge painter Paul Hogan, worldwide fame. Murphy also pushed his partner Gary Grant sideways. Grant, after putting in so many years on the road to help the band build a solid base, was suddenly sidelined to the role of Australian manager. Some band members did not like the idea. Others felt Grant had overstepped his station. There is no question though, that the man who had put in the groundwork on the road, and who was the seventh member, was on his way out.

INXS was individually and collectively beginning to fray at the edges from the incessant touring. 'The band was frazzled,' Gary Grant told me, 'and they came close to splitting up just before *Kick*.' Its members were beginning to live up to the last part of their name—excess. There was excessive drug and alcohol use; excessive partying, with too many waking hours and not enough sleeping hours; the excessive boredom of being constantly on the road—all the excesses that are synonymous with rock'n'roll success.

If you're in a rock'n'roll band and you have the money,

you can get whatever you want, twenty-four hours a day. You don't have to go search for it, it will come to you.

But it is also true that the band started to become more involved with the business side of their affairs, taking part in meetings with their New York lawyer, Bill Leibowitz, making collective business decisions, trying to decipher the financial complications of million-dollar success on a global scale. This alone would be enough to drive most to distraction. Combined with this was the pressure of writing and producing the next record while still on the road. Andrew Farriss, in particular, began to resent the notion of touring. He was one of the rocks of the band in terms of sobriety; his brother Tim was the rock of inspiration, solidarity and dedication, and now a proud father of a son, James.

In October 1987 INXS commenced their Calling All Nations tour in the US, three days before *Kick* was released. The tour started at small theatres and colleges with capacities of 2000–4000 seats, but as more hit singles were released and momentum gathered they moved to larger venues, and ended up performing in stadiums before 30 000 people. The band toured America until the end of November and immediately returned to the UK for a December tour.

Just two months after its release, *Kick* had soared to the top of charts all over the world, and the debut single, the haunting, funky 'Need You Tonight', became INXS's first American number one hit single. Their back catalogue immediately began selling like wildfire, *Swing* and *Shabooh Shoobah* also going gold. In March the second single from *Kick*, 'Devil Inside', was released, reaching number two, and in the same month the band sold out three shows at New

York's prestigious Radio City Music Hall. By May the third *Kick* single, 'New Sensation', had also reached the US top three. INXS were the hottest ticket in town, selling out three arena shows, in Madison Square Gardens, Meadowland Arena and Nassau Coliseum. The ballad 'Never Tear Us Apart' became the album's fourth single, reaching number four in the charts. In September INXS moved on to spread the word in Japan, then returned to Australia for a tumultuous, record-breaking homecoming tour. The press might have continued to miss the point but the fans got it big time. That year the band also swept the American MTV Music Awards, leaving with seven awards.

This was INXS's finest hour, when they truly were on top of the world. But they had paid a high personal price. Fatigued, emotionally drained, absolutely partied out, but very, very rich, the band could at last afford to take a long break, and take stock of what had happened. After touring and recording together for more than a decade, they now led a radically different lifestyle. No longer a struggling rock band, they were millionaire rock stars mixing with the rock elite. Their options were limitless. Everything was on offer, and everyone wanted a piece of the action.

Around this time INXS and U2 were seen by some as the two biggest rock bands in the world, and U2's singer Bono and Hutchence became the very best of friends.

'I might have met Mike in '82,' Bono told me, 'but I remember meeting him properly in 1988. Mike Hamlin introduced us when he was producing the movie *Rattle and Hum*. Michael and I were exploring the late-night watering holes of Los Angeles where the community shrinks after midnight and makes it, particularly for Irish people, easier to deal with, because everyone else is getting up at six o'clock in the morning and jogging into the corporations. So if you stay out late, it's just a smaller community. LA really came into its own at that time, and I remember there was a load of French-speaking types creating really experimental, innovative clubs. There was amazing stuff going on at the time in downtown LA. I met Michael at a place called World War III.

'We were just talking and he was very shy, and I thought, Oh, he's doing the shy thing, okay, I've done that too. That's the first device of all showmen, it's a common trait. Anybody who stands out in front of 50 000 is not shy. They may be insecure, they may be complex, but they're certainly not shy. But we all use it. It's a great one—"Oh look, he's quite shy!" After a while I delightfully found out he was far from shy. Michael had this beautiful joy and exuberance for life. We were checking each other out, I suppose. We ended up very drunk and playing Tom Waites songs on the piano in the Sunset Marquee Hotel at about six o'clock in the morning to the night porter, and the shyness sort of melted away on all our parts—the faux shyness, that is. Edge was playing piano. We started off playing a song of ours, "Wild Irish Rose", which is a kind of Tom Waites rip-off. Michael sat down and starting tinkling away.'

The trio jammed on, and as in all drunken sunrise jam sessions the words were not right, nor the tunes, but they gave it their best shot. From then on, Michael and Bono shared many close moments and exploits, from LA to France, right around the globe, right up until Michael died. A mutual admiration society grew between the two bands.

'I remember being conscious of INXS. U2 were in our own world, I have to say—I can't quite tell you what that world was, but we were off in it. We were lost in our music and our own zone. We were not hugely aware of what was going on around us—not in terms of stature or the world, but in terms of our music. I remember thinking that INXS were like T-Rex or something and I've always been a huge fan of T-Rex and Marc Bolan. Michael had some of that Bolan presence. I didn't see them as a rock band, and it turns out they didn't see themselves that way, either. In the end they were sort of working on this white funk thing—that's where they were coming from—and I saw Michael as this great relevant pop star, more attractive than the '70s rock star cliché, and I thought that was such a modern thing to be. INXS had this certain lightness of touch that made them what they were, and that's what was interesting about them. And of course Michael was an extraordinary singer. It really struck me what he was doing as a singer, and it annoys me that he was so underrated by himself. It was his tone, and his phrasing was impeccable. He pioneered close microphone singing almost whispering, which was innovative at the time.

'There was a thing that INXS carried with them, which was a badge, which was that they'd come up through the pubs and clubs, and I think we had that too. We wore that like a badge too. It was like when new bands came along and had records played, or when they were flavour of the week, or had great airplay, INXS and we knew they kinda didn't have that organic thing that we both had.

'Both INXS and U2 stayed together, both from the same era, since the beginning and they stood the test of time'.

As Michael began expanding as a singer and a star, so did the demons begin expanding in his head. He started to suffer from lack of privacy, his fame was becoming claustrophobic. 'I think it's really hard to keep a sense of yourself,' he said, 'because everybody takes a piece. You start to think heavy, you start manipulating.' He was the one who fronted up to the media for interviews, he was the man on the spot to collect awards, his gypsy life becoming even more global. He travelled, rather than putting down roots like his fellow band members. His and Andrew Farriss's lifestyles couldn't have been more different. Andrew was a family man, Michael a wandering, partying cavalier.

The band's break ended up lasting for eighteen months. The six of them had had enough of each other. They had grown up together, lived together, travelled together, shared intimacies that would remain forever. They were a family. They could not hide from each other.

'When you start off in bands at age sixteen and stay together until you're twenty-six you know who each other is, as opposed to who you're pretending to be,' Bono reckons. 'They actually know. And maybe there's times when you actually want to get away from that, because you might feel you've shed skin, like a snake, and all they see is a trail of them and not the new you. I think Michael always had aspects of that—he always wanted to discover a new side of himself. But he also needed the band to turn around and tell him who he was. Almost like a family. And everyone knows how tough on each other families can actually be.'

INXS's members embarked on solo projects. Andrew Farriss produced Jenny Morris's second solo album *Shiver*, which went triple platinum in Australia. Garry Gary Beers co-produced Melbourne band Absent Friends, alongside Sean Kelly. Tim Farriss ventured into film-making and big-game fishing, combined the two and made a documentary called *Fish in Space*. Jon Farriss and Kirk Pengilly contributed to the music. Tim then bought a fishing boat called

King Kong and went fishing. Beers bought a large farm and built a 24-track recording studio. Other farms, mansions and properties were bought, houses were renovated. Chris Murphy, now a multi-millionaire himself, expanded his company MMA Management and signed more acts. He created a publishing company, MMA Music, and a new independent label, RooArt; he set up offices in New York and London and delegated areas of INXS's management to others. The attention he gave to his own businesses, coupled with the end of his hands-on approach to managing INXS, widened the rift between Murphy and Hutchence, and eventually the band. The fallout would be a management–artist split in the mid-nineties, but there was more success to come before that took place.

During the break Hutchence, apart from his involvement with Max Q, sang solo on a collaboration CD, picked up awards for the band, and went to Italy to act in *Frankenstein Unbound*, a horror film directed by the legendary Roger Corman. Hutchence played the poet Percy Shelley in the film. It wasn't a starring role but it was an important one, giving him the opportunity to work alongside John Hurt, Raul Julia, Bridget Fonda, Catherine Rabett and Jason Patric, and confirming just how much he wanted to keep acting. 'The thing I learned was that there were no rules,' Hutchence said of the experience. 'You just have to go out and do it.'

Following a suggestion from his business adviser Gordon Fisher, Hutchence moved his base to Hong Kong for tax reasons, and he and Jon Farriss rented a luxurious apartment together. Because Hong Kong was now his place of residence, Hutchence could live only six months at a time in Australia. It was in Hong Kong at this time that he wooed

Kylie Minogue and bought his beloved home in the south of France.

'We were taking a holiday where we went through the south of France and we were looking at different houses for him to buy and eventually he ended up with the place he had until his death,' Kylie remembers. 'I stayed there with him the first time he had it. We had Christmas dinner there and I had to cook the roast and was very nervous. I was trying to learn French from a book so that I could go down the street and buy all the right things. But during that time we just really lived it up. It was like a gastronomic journey of the south of France and Italy and we'd have different wines for each course and we'd spend a fortune on food. Some people might do one thing like that in their lifetime and I just remember feeling that it was so wonderful. It was like a fairytale to be doing all of those things.'

At the tail end of 1989 the band regrouped to record their seventh album, called X to mark their tenth anniversary of recording. Taking production honours for the third consecutive album was Chris Thomas. As it turned out, the group didn't have enough songs so Thomas dispatched Michael and Andrew to Hong Kong to write some more material. To consolidate their position, it was imperative that the next album be a success. Andrew and Chris Thomas, both headstrong individuals, locked horns on the recording of X, which would be the final INXS album for Thomas. Once recording was completed, Andrew went on tour with Jenny Morris, leaving the mixing to Hutchence and Thomas in London.

In August 1990 the X album's first single, 'Suicide Blonde', was released, and eventually hit the Top Ten around the world. INXS were getting even hotter, and in

September put in a blistering performance in Los Angeles at the MTV Music Awards. Three weeks later, the album was released and went on to become double platinum, selling four million in the United States and reaching the number one slot in the United Kingdom. In October INXS began their first five-star luxury tour of the world. They had struggled enough, they could now afford it, and they went the whole hog. For the X Factor tour, they had an entourage of fifty-three, including hairstylists and wardrobe attendants. They had French champagne on tap, stayed at the best hotels, chartered jets to hop along the east coast of America for each night's sell-out show. They knew they had to be brilliant, and they were. Their performances were the very best of their career. When their tour moved on to Europe, Tim Farriss moved his family into a house overlooking the Thames in Chelsea and used it as a base to commute to gigs.

They were so hot that by November they had sold out four Wembley Arena shows in London. Just seven months later, in July 1991, INXS hit the jackpot, the pinnacle of stadium-rock success, by selling out London's Wembley Stadium, performing in front of 72 000 people. In terms of live performances, this was INXS's zenith. They recorded the concert for a live album, filmed it, and broadcast it live to radio stations across the United Kingdom. The band received a second Grammy nomination for Best Performance by a Group for the single 'Suicide Blonde', the first being for Best International Group. Then, with a thousand gun-toting guards in front of the stage, INXS performed before 50 000 people in Mexico, and headlined Rock in Rio, in Brazil, performing to 100 000 people, before taking the circus to Argentina.

In January 1992 the band was again invited to perform live at the American Music Awards, and then on New York's famous *Saturday Night Live* television show, just prior to performing yet another sell-out concert at Madison Square Gardens. They could do no wrong, and at that year's UK British Phonograph Industry Awards won the Best International Band and Best International Male awards. In March tickets went on sale for their Australian tour, with a record-breaking 22 000 tickets being sold in just twenty minutes. INXS were awarded Best International Band at that year's inaugural Australian Music Awards.

But the chemistry of the band had changed. While they had indisputably reached their peak, the balance had shifted. When the band regrouped to record *X*, there had been an undeniable rift between Michael, the band, and management. The band had gone back to their roots, management had not met the challenge, and Michael had gone forward to another world. Things would never be quite the same again.

• • •

As INXS's fame had increased, the gap between Hutchence and the rest of the band widened. During their eighteen-month break the other members had burst out of their restrictive bubble and developed as individuals. But Michael remained in the bubble, with the media increasing their pressure on him as the charismatic front man. He was the main man as far as they were concerned. 'We tried to fight it for a while,' Garry Gary Beers said at the time, but it was to no avail. Privately, band members began to have fears about Michael's ability to handle the pressure; his behaviour was starting to become erratic, singular and isolated. 'I couldn't cope, so I retreated,' Hutchence told *Q* magazine in 1992.

Michael began to have strong feelings of resentment towards long-time manager Chris Murphy. He was still smarting from the Max Q project and now felt isolated from the rest of the band; he distanced himself, forming his own inner sanctum of drug buddies, party buddies and questionable other buddies. When you're lonely, famous, vulnerable and rich, buddies flock from everywhere. Hutchence was beginning to spend more time in London, more time on his own. Ecstasy was rife, sexual opportunities were rife, any drug was available, and this man who attracted the universe pushed life to the limit. His relationship with Murphy deteriorated further over an incident with *Rolling Stone* magazine, who wanted to feature a solo Hutchence on the front cover. Chris Murphy said no. *Rolling Stone*, extremely powerful in America at that time, featured many singers from bands on the front cover, without the other members. If they could do it with Mick Jagger, they asked, why couldn't they do it with Michael Hutchence?

'Murphy was protective of the band,' INXS's New York lawyer Bill Leibowitz recalls. 'He would say that he represented six people, not just one person. Of course there is logic in that, and there is a logic in the huge investment that had been made in INXS as a group. Murphy would argue that by focusing on what was best for INXS he was also protecting Michael because if he got a swollen head and left the band the odds were that he would not be as successful as INXS, so that both Michael and INXS would be critically damaged, creating a setback in their career. This was Murphy's rationale.'

Chris Murphy called *Rolling Stone*'s bluff and lost. The magazine wasn't going to bend. Neither Hutchence nor INXS appeared on the front cover. With the rest of the band, who felt that Murphy was earning too much money, Hutchence forced Murphy into renegotiating their contract with them.

Murphy had become an impersonal manager rather than a personal manager, daily directions being delegated to underlings in his organisation. The band felt they were the ones out there on the road doing the blood, sweat and tears for success, while Murphy was back at the office. Band members could not get hold of Murphy on the telephone, and he was increasingly ignoring Hutchence. Sometimes weeks would go in between his speaking to band members. His underlings effectively became the day-to-day management, passing on messages to Murphy. When the band forced him to renegotiate his contract with them, dropping his percentage, he had no choice. He had to succumb to the band's pressure or the band would walk.

Hutchence let Murphy know in a very personal manner his feelings of mistrust for him and the rift between the singer and the manager never healed.

According to Bill Leibowitz, 'The relationship between an artist and a manager is like a marriage. There are good marriages and bad marriages. A managerial relationship, like marriage, must be grounded in trust and mutual respect. When cracks appear, the strength of the marriage depends on how those cracks are sealed—if they can be sealed.'

Success and money and fame might give you more choices, but the irony is that the greater the choices, the less the focus, and the more dissipated you become. Michael Hutchence was now in a world of his own; his interviews meandered off into personal views of the world, politics, sex, drugs, travel. They were his way of breaking out, but the band felt his behaviour was out of place while he was also promoting their career. Michael was testing the band's limit, and so concerned were they eventually that they insisted someone accompany him at all times in interviews. Michael increased his social drug use during this period—Ecstasy, cocaine, heroin, uppers, downers, alcohol. Some of his friends say that he did not do drugs to 'kill the pain or kill himself', but to experience his mind, to have more fun. 'Michael was never out of control,' says Martha Troup. 'Very rarely. No matter what you hear. Yeah, he lived life on the edge, but you could always have a conversation with him.'

Michael was intoxicated by the club culture and went anonymously to clubs after shows rather than joining the post-gig party with an entourage and a million hangers-on. 'Clubbing keeps me in touch with what's happening,' he said. 'The thought that I am doing this as a career revolts me. I know that sounds perverse, but I'm a perverse person. I don't see my behaviour as being all that abnormal. By the standards of most people or even the rest of the band, sure I'm a bit different. I haven't found my own true love and settled down. I think it's wonderful that they have, of course, but it's not the way my life is.'

Fame is a strange drug. It's intoxicating, highly addictive and can be destructive. One of its negatives is that it can fan the fires of paranoia. As Michael moved from Kylie to Helena Christensen, the reason for his original fame seemed forgotten by the media, and possibly even himself. 'There's a really evil, insidious part to being famous,' Hutchence said at the time. 'The media have this really weird ability to mess with your personal life, all in the interests of selling a few newspapers. I think it's boring. Who the fuck cares?'

'Fame a contributing factor? I don't think fame is that difficult,' Bono said, pondering Michael's demeanour in the years prior to his death. 'One thing Michael was not was a whingeing rock star. He and I would be travelling at speed on some motorway in France or Los Angeles on a big one, having a laugh and a shout, and we'd be thinking, Isn't this great that we can do what we can do, that we are so blessed. So spoilt. He wasn't a whinger. My conversations with him were with someone who was sound. It's really important to get across that the guy had a certain "taking care of business" attitude about himself, as well as being gentle and fun and smart. He wasn't just this dizzy chick. He wasn't that. He had a bit of Kell in there. Sound, you know what I mean? That was the mannish side of Michael.'

In March 1992, amidst great personal distractions, INXS's ninth album *Welcome to Wherever You Are* was released. During the recording, Garry Gary Beers was preoccupied with the birth of his child; Tim was out of action due to Reiter's disease, a genetic, physically incapacitating illness; Kirk and his wife Deni Hines were in the throes of divorce; Michael was reportedly often as not insecure and out of it. The album had some fine moments but it was, like the band, disjointed. Its production was supposed to be a joint effort, the band's first break from Chris Thomas in three albums, but in reality it was Andrew's and Mark Opitz's album. It contained some good songs, such as 'Taste It' and the plush, orchestra-ladened 'Baby Don't Cry', and 'All Around', but rock music was going through a generational change. Grunge and all its fashion accessories was taking over, and superstar bands from the eighties like INXS had to reassess.

Chris Murphy decided that a free charity concert should be held at Sydney's Centennial Park in late March of that year, the profits of which would help a local AIDS organisation and a heart foundation. The Concert For Life, while it might have been conceived in goodwill, ended up being a public-relations disaster for INXS, and effectively crushed their standing on home soil. The concert was seen as a shrewd exercise in promotional exploitation, with extravagant lighting systems for INXS, extravagant film crews to shoot promotional videos for INXS, extravagant accommodation bills, and a massive shortfall in profits due to the costs. The Concert For Life did for INXS what ice did for the *Titanic*.

Other bands on the bill, such as Crowded House, felt used because instead of everyone being given equal billing the event was used for promotional purposes by INXS, and the blow-out in costs meant less money for the charities. The crowd was around 10 000 short of expectations. It was a fiasco and it was INXS and Gary Grant who had to take the flack from the media. Chris Murphy had made many enemies on the way up, and there were a lot of people waiting for him on the way down. The band refused to speak with the media when challenged, and suffered as a result. Andrew Farriss almost immediately moved his family and himself to London.

Michael was at this time living with Helena Christensen in France. On some fronts he appeared content, but he was creatively frustrated with INXS and wanted to boot it in a new direction. He was becoming more and more difficult to get along with, harder to reason with. It was a difficult time for INXS. Once you've hit the big time and a new generation makes new demands, it is sometimes hard to reverse the evolution. The band had reached a level of stagnancy and something radical had to happen for it to move back into the potent force it once had been. It needed direction, and the direction just was not there anymore.

Their next album, *Full Moon, Dirty Hearts*, was released in November 1993 and was only moderately successful, although it showed signs of the direction in which the band might have gone. It contained the blistering, brilliant track 'The Gift', and an absolutely classic duet with Michael and blues legend Ray Charles, 'Please (You Got That?)'. The album was accompanied by a stripped-down pub and club tour, and it was during this tour that Michael was given something else to worry about.

Rhett Hutchence had landed himself in trouble with a couple of heavy-handed heroin dealers in New York City. He owed them money, and when he couldn't come up with it he was abducted and taken downtown to the meat market district, where he was locked in a storage room and held for ransom, the idea being that Michael would pay. Rhett tried to escape by writing a note and throwing it out the window. Unfortunately, one of his captors found the note and as he returned to punish Rhett for his escape attempt, Rhett lunged at him with a screwdriver. A meat packer happened to observe the incident and phoned the police, who arrived on the scene and charged Rhett with attempted murder.

Michael was contacted, and after getting in touch with New York criminal lawyers bailed Rhett out of jail. After guaranteeing he would leave the country, Rhett was set free and the charge was dropped. His kidnappers were known to the police, and that had worked in Rhett's favour—that and the amount of money his brother paid to free him. Understandably, this incident exasperated Michael, and he put Rhett on notice.

Around the same time, Michael and Helena visited Johnny Depp's club in LA, The Viper Room. 'The most beautiful women in the world were there that night,' Jason Donovan recalls. 'Michael was with Helena, and Kate Moss was there, and all these models, and they were all at the front of the stage, and all of a sudden Michael and Johnny get up and start singing that old rock classic "Gloria". I was doing a lot of cocaine at the time, and all of a sudden I blacked out and fell unconscious. Michael got me out of that whole situation. He just stopped the band and jumped offstage, Helena called the ambulance, and Michael helped get me onto the stretcher. He tried to stop the press getting a picture of me. He was just such a great friend that night. He and Helena saved me.'

Despite being sidetracked by the sensational events going on around him, not the least of which was the beginning of his tragic love affair with Paula Yates, Hutchence still managed to keep up his work ethic. In 1994 he recorded 'Under My Thumb' for a compilation tribute to The Rolling Stones, his backing band the London Symphony Orchestra. In the same year he recorded 'Baby Let's Play House' with NRBQ for another compilation tribute, this time to Elvis Presley. In June 1995 he took lead vocals on the song 'The Passenger' for the *Batman Forever* soundtrack, and a year later recorded 'Spill The Wine' for the *Barb Wire* movie soundtrack. In October 1996 Michael sang on 'The King Is Gone' for The Heads' *No Talking, Just Head* album.

By 1997, Michael was irrevocably involved with Paula Yates, and for the first time ever was not able to simply get up and walk away from a confronting situation. It is amazing therefore that he managed to hook up with Andrew Farriss to co-write what would be INXS's final album. He was simultaneously fighting Bob Geldof and defending Paula Yates, yet he also took on his third acting role, in a film called *Limp*, and began the finishing touches to his solo album.

Limp was never meant to be a Hollywood blockbuster but it certainly had an eerie plot. Filmed in the year of Michael's death, it tells the story of a jaded record company man, played by Hutchence, who suggests to a young musician that he kill himself in order to ensure a place in rock immortality. In the script Hutchence's character says, 'Cobain was close. But only because he killed himself. It was brilliant on his part. Otherwise he would've just been another flavour of the day. Give me one good reason you shouldn't kill yourself.'

The film's co-star, Robby Sutton, reckons that Hutchence threw himself into the part. 'What he said was shocking, but how he said it was even more shocking. It was with belief, from the pit of his stomach.' Writer and director Duane Lavold said that Hutchence did not fit the stereotype of a depressed ageing rocker. He hung around with the cast and crew, bursting into eighties songs whenever the mood struck him. 'He put his ego aside and worked sixteen-hour days almost for free,' says Lavold. 'We didn't have any star wagons for him.'

'Michael wasn't looking for the big motion picture,' says Martha Troup. 'He knew he had to work his way up in acting, and he was committed.'

Hutchence's solo music work was also approaching its final stages. From 1994 he'd been secretly working with Tim

Simenon from Bomb the Bass, having recorded half an album's worth of material. He then switched to working with former Gang of Four guitar player Andy Gill, writing and recording songs with him at various studios. In February 1996 Hutchence announced that he was working with Black Grape collaborator Danny Saber, who described Hutchence's music as 'pure genius, better than anything Noel Gallagher could touch'. Andy Gill told me that the Hutchence material was 'kind of cinematic with a wide quality to it. There's a dark feel to it. There are eight or nine finished tracks, and Paula certainly wants it released. These songs were from Michael's heart and they explain just how he was feeling, especially towards Geldof. Bob was the one person who consistently upset Michael.'

In January 1998 it came to light that there were some twenty-five songs in various stages of completion. Martha Troup said that Michael wanted it to be a big deal. 'It meant a lot to him, this solo album, just like being in INXS meant a lot to him. He loved his music.' Sadly, the legal wrangle now taking place over Hutchence's estate has put a hold on the release of the solo recordings.

Given the emotional and personal weights on Michael's mind, yet such a prolific work output, I asked him during his final year about the future of INXS. 'Look, INXS are just one of those bands that are on many levels at once,' he told me. 'I don't look back, I only look forward. You know that I've always thought that my "unabashed sexuality" has held back serious critical praise for the band, at times. That's INXS; everything we are, we are not, and everything we are not, we are, but at least we have fully explored all the possibilities of enticing love and hate and waving the flag for Australia.' I asked him if he felt cheated by the Australian

x Dear Greg — wipe that bloody smile off your face!! Love Mike & Kylie x

Greg Perano, Kylie Minogue and Michael, Kings Cross, Sydney—1990
(Greg Perano)

Patricia and Michael, Surfers Paradise (Thommy Campion, Icon Images)

Helena Christensen and Michael, Paris, 1991 (GREG PERANO)

Kell, Michael and Tiger Lily at Kell's Bellevue Hill home, September 1996
(KELL HUTCHENCE FAMILY PHOTO COLLECTION)

Michael, Paula and Tiger Lily in Sydney, September 1996—
the day police raided Michael and Paula's London home
(PETER CARRETTE, ICON IMAGES)

Michael, Paula, Tiger Lily, Pixie Geldof, Emma Cohen and 'Bogart', at Tiger Lily's first barbecue, Sydney, 1997 (GREG PERANO)

Michael and photographer Richard Simpkin, a long-time fan. Kelland Hutchence took this photo on 20 November—it was to be the last photo taken of Michael (RICHARD SIMPKIN)

public and media, in light of his international success, and he replied, 'I've always prided myself on being oblivious to the sensationalism, but it's the innocents that get hurt.' With reference to the tall-poppy syndrome that had plagued INXS for much of the nineties, he told me that he had always been good at cutting himself down before anyone else could do it for him.

INXS had sold more than thirty million albums, won two American Grammy awards and five MTV awards, and yet they still had not got the critical and media respect they deserved in their home country. 'I'm not looking for adulation or medals,' Michael told me prior to his death, 'but respect will come in the end because it should. What we're looking for is just the tiniest touch of understanding, real understanding. This naive presumption that someone like me hasn't got a clue about what's going on, hasn't read a book or hung with the devil, met God . . . You know, it's a big life—make a difference, lads. We've been diplomats for Australia, we're always mentioning Australia, we're always plugging Australian bands.' He was trying to hide his bitterness.

Michael Hutchence was a complicated man at the end of 1997, very deep, and very troubled about certain aspects of his life—aspects that were darker than most people would imagine, and certainly darker than he let on. His life was a paradox. On the one hand he wanted the rock'n'roll madness and mayhem, on the other he wanted nothing more than to settle down and lead a normal lifestyle, family and all. But the rock'n'roll industry is a drug, a magnet attracting the rich, the famous, the poor, the unknown, the infamous, the misplaced, the freaks. It's a bubble world, a travelling circus where so many secrets are kept by the ringside players that often as not we don't hear the real stories until the characters are dead. Despite its exotic attractions, the fact is that rock'n'roll is the loneliest vocation in the world, its schizophrenic core and its army of sycophants all contributing to the corrosive effect on anyone who gets addicted.

eight

The cavalier sex god, Kylie, Helena, Paula

> Cry baby cry when you gotta get it out
> I'll be your shoulder
> You can tell me all
> Don't keep it in ya
> Well that's the reason why I'm here
> Are you ready for a new sensation

'New Sensation'
Kick 1987
MICHAEL HUTCHENCE AND ANDREW FARRISS

Michael Hutchence was a chameleon. The more famous he became, the more personalities he developed. The more personalities he delved into, the more emotionally lost he appeared to become. Some would say he was a free spirit, others that his soul was trapped. He seemed to be on an endless search for adventure and excitement. He also seemed to have an obsession with purging himself from his past, and an endless desire to find romantic stability: a partner with whom he could atone for the dysfunction of his own family. He wanted the impossible: a woman who would be substitute mother; a wild, reckless uninhibited lover; a connoisseur of life; a dreamer; a woman with a career; a deep friend with a sharply honed intelligence; a soul mate; mother of his children; an emancipated, perfect companion.

In this incessant search his personality and star status placed him at the front of the queue. Moreover, he possessed a warm, magnetic and loving personality that endeared him to most during his short life. So irresistible was this man's attraction, so intimate and personalised was his attention to people he met, that literally hundreds claim to have been his friend, but there were probably only a handful of people who really knew Hutchence. Some knew his party antics, others his fears, still others his dreams, a few his darkest side. Most of his acquaintances, male and female, speak of his charisma, his grace, his seductiveness, his way with people, his flirtations with women that inevitably led to more intimate dalliances; some speak of epic debauchery. Many, many women were drawn to him and it was not always just a sexual attraction. Hutchence had the ability to make people, particularly women, feel comfortable, at ease, the centre of his world.

Michael's sexual reputation preceded him everywhere he went round the globe, every city, every town, every after-hours club, every dark dingy bar. Even if he didn't want it, he got it. The sexual aspect of his life and the legendary status it acquired rank alongside his beautiful poetry, his generosity and sense of humour, his unique singing style, and his penchant for social drugs and escaping problems is how he is remembered. The life of Michael Hutchence was more than partially dedicated to the pursuit of sexual pleasures, sexual liberty and experimentation, to the magic and the enigma of women.

Lian Lunson remembers Hutchence before he was a star, before his reputation began to precede him. Even then he was seen as a standout in the crowd. 'Before he was a star, women still loved him,' Lunson says. 'He was incredible, he had an incredible suss about him, and would look at a person, particularly women, and just make them feel like they were the only person in the world for that brief time that he talked to them. He just exuded this sexuality and sensitivity and intelligence—you know, women would go crazy. There are not a lot of men around like him, really, he was quite exceptional like that. And beautiful, he was a gorgeous-looking man. His sense of humour was the added bonus.'

Whether in a platonic or a sexual sense, Hutchence was quite definitively a woman's man first and foremost, even though he appealed to both sexes, straight or gay. INXS American fan club president, Mary Woodsmary, from the Bay Area in San Francisco, once had a party at which she had the *Live Baby Live* concert from Wembley playing. 'Not only were my female friends glued to the television with their tongues hanging out,' she said, 'but a group of gay male friends pulled up chairs smack in front of the screen, watching sexy Michael do his thing, totally enthralled, not moving an inch for the duration of the entire show. Michael had that kind of effect on people, gay and straight. He was magnetic.'

'Guys like Michael, who have the temperament of Michael, always have a woman somewhere who they don't have sex with,' says Martha Troup. 'They need the intimate friendship of a woman and they just simply love them.' Troup became Michael's closest confidante in his final years, and it was not just him they talked about. 'Michael would make me talk to him about my own life, he knew everything about my life and I knew everything about his. We'd talk about everything. He was proud of himself in respect of sex.'

Says Greg Perano, 'He was an incredibly handsome guy. He was a character and people were instantly attracted to him.' Richard Lowenstein recalls a party in the late eighties following the Countdown Awards, hosted by the TV pop programme that ruled the Australian airwaves for that decade. 'Michael was talking to one girl very effectively, and he had another girl who was leaning behind him resting her face on his leather jacket, licking the leather on the back of the jacket. Michele Bennett was there, too. I remember thinking that it's just incredible how he does it. He had this feline feminine sort of quality without being effeminate, which appealed to both men and women. I was quite aware of his attractiveness and I am very appreciative of that quality, particularly in men. It was always stimulating to be around. The way he would look you directly in the eye. Bono does the same thing, he stares at you directly in the eye so you are the only thing that exists.'

'Michael loved women,' says Bono. 'He believed in women and it was very important that women believed in him.'

Richard Lowenstein says Hutchence was totally enchanted by women. 'There's a great difference between loving women and desiring women. Michael was truly a lover of women. He loved their character, their smell, their femininity, their sensuality, their sexuality, their dress sense, their way of being. He just loved them and he loved them even when sex was out of the picture. He loved being the knight in shining armour, which probably led to his downfall in the end,' Lowenstein said.

The first and longest lasting platonic female bonding

Michael Hutchence had was with Hiraani Campbell, who is now happily married with two children and lives in one of Sydney's picturesque North Shore beachfront suburbs. The same age as Michael, she and he played together as children, and Michael named his daughter, Heavenly Hiraani Tiger Lily, after her. 'We had a bond, Michael and I,' Hiraani told me, 'and so did Rhett and I. These two little boys would come over to our place with their parents and the three of us would go and play on Clontarf beach. They were happy family times. Michael was my age so there was an immediate bond. Our families had barbecues—they were exotic, fun nights. I remember people getting together, lunches, drinks, lazing in the sun, surfing, the beach, all the fun of Australia in the sixties. We used to do the hula. My mother is Polynesian and the parties always had Polynesian music playing. Michael loved the percussion.'

When the Hutchence family moved to Hong Kong to live, Hiraani and her mother and father went to visit them there. She and Michael were ten years old and she can remember life being very different for the Hutchence boys in Hong Kong. 'When they returned, things were still the same here but different for them.' The pair remained close friends throughout his life. 'When Mike left home I went to his house for parties and things. I had a life and a boyfriend, later my husband, and often we wouldn't stay too long. We weren't part of the music industry. I used to say to Michael that it was impossible to talk to him under those circumstances because there were crowds of people at parties and things and we didn't know any of them. I feel a bit like an extended sister, and we understood a lot of things and learned a lot of things together. He never changed towards me, ever, but we were poles apart. I was pursuing life, love and a family, and he was the rock'n'roller, but it never made any difference. I didn't live in his world, and the fact that I could still be a friend was great. I am sure there were other people with whom he was closer later on in life. But we always had an intimate relationship in terms of sharing our experiences. I watched him as he started his rock'n'roll journey and kept in touch over the years, and basically he never changed towards me. Our relationship remained exactly the same as it always had been. He was never self-conscious or shy with me, because our friendship went back so far.

'It's almost theatrical, the way he had to live his life. He was a performer, he was a star. I remember asking him one night if he needed a bodyguard. "Oh no," he used to say, "that's part of the fun of it all." He was generally quite relaxed about it all, it seemed, and didn't necessarily want to draw focus on himself. He just wanted to cruise and live life. He was a bit of a chameleon and showed different faces to different people. I only knew a few of his faces and they were all relaxed and down to earth.'

Hiraani remained close with all of Michael's family, especially both parents. 'Patricia is a woman I love and admire greatly, as I do Kell,' Hiraani says. 'I have always been close to all of them, regardless of whether they've been together or had rifts or whatever else, and I have maintained a relationship with each of them on an individual level. I have no qualms about talking to any of the family at any time about anything. I have never been dragged in to any family problems. I looked up to Patricia, I thought she was quite amazing.'

After Michael split with Michele Bennett, he began a romance with a girl called Rosanna, who was commonly known as Jonny. Hutchence met Jonny in America and they had an intense, outlandish, at times tempestuous affair that would last for a little more than two years. For about a year the couple were inseparable. 'I spent some time with Jonny and Michael in 1989,' Ollie Olsen said. 'One time I remember we were on our way to New York to mix the Max Q album, and I met Michael and Jonny in Tahiti. When I eventually hooked up with Mike after arriving, these people asked the three of us if we wanted to go shark feeding in the morning. We were at a restaurant and really drunk and stuff, and we said, Yeah, why not? Next day they picked us up really early in the morning—we had these terrific hangovers—and took us out to the reefs, whereupon they immediately jumped into the water and tied a rope between one rock and another. The water was fairly shallow, about five feet, I guess, and then they told us to jump in the water and hold onto the rope. It was quite a tourist thing, you know, but we were completely unaware of what was going on, we had these bulging hangovers. They proceeded to throw fish guts in the water, and the little fish came and then the big fish came, and Michael and Jonny were talking to me with snorkels in their mouths and I was thinking, When are we going to mix this album? And then the sharks came and we were absolutely shitting ourselves, there were about ten sharks, all about five feet long, a foot away from our faces. It was just unbelievable.

'But the whole thing was that it was a great lesson in life, because after that Michael, Jonny and I went to New York and I realised it was the same thing, you know, sharks and all that. I found myself walking down by myself in very dangerous streets where people were going crazy and stuff. It taught us a large lesson in life, and I'll forever be grateful to Michael for that experience, amongst millions of others I shared with him.'

Michael enjoyed outdoor activities, physical, adrenaline-pumping experiences. When time allowed he indulged in paragliding and hang-gliding. His time with Jonny was intense, close, and constant and eventually he started to feel a little hemmed in. Jonny had become dependent on him and was not developing interests of her own outside Michael's life. The more Michael tried to grab some space, the more possessive Jonny became. When he wanted to move on, finish the relationship, Michael displayed a trait that had become part of his trademark when finishing a romance. He found it difficult to actually call it quits, did not seem to know what to do or say, did not want confrontation. Martha Troup recalls that the only way Michael knew how to end it with Jonny was to sneak into another hotel in New York so she wouldn't know where he was.

'With women, Michael's big thing was that he actually loved them too much,' Lian Lunson says. 'He found it difficult to sit down with a girl and say, This is not working, let's try and address the problem. He wasn't capable of that really. He never was.'

• • •

One evening around midnight in 1988, Kylie Minogue walked into a sleazy little bar called Benny's in a back street of Sydney's Kings Cross district. Benny's is the kind of bar that exists in any big city, the one you go to when the others are closed at the tail end of the night; it wasn't exactly the kind of bar in which you'd expect to see the former soap idol. Kylie was with her boyfriend at the time, Jason Donovan, also a former soap star, and surrounded by security men.

'It was a party after the Countdown Awards,' Kylie told me, remembering her first meeting with Hutchence. 'I was so young really, about nineteen or twenty, and I remember being overly protected by some bodyguards—they must have thought I was too innocent to be in a place like that, or might get harassed or something. I remember feeling a bit odd there because I could hardly have a good time, this bar wasn't something I was used to, and I felt a bit too crowded, pushed into a corner. Anyway, Michael sort of stumbled by, I don't know if he was... he was probably really drunk. And I think his first words to me ever were, "I don't know what we should do first, have lunch or have sex."' Kylie laughs, adding, 'That was entirely shocking to me—then'.

Jason Donovan has a slightly different recollection of events. 'Terry Blamey, her manager, was with her that night. Terry was causing major problems for me in the sense that I was twenty-one, I was jealous, I was in love with Kylie, and Terry was this shadow behind me all the time. I can remember not wanting Kylie out of my sight, I saw Michael go by and I had my back to Michael and Kylie when they first met, and at the back of my ear I heard Michael whisper, "Do we go out to dinner, or should we just get married?"'

Whether he suggested sex or marriage, Hutchence left an impression on the twenty-year-old Minogue. 'I couldn't make any words come out of my mouth, I was too taken aback,' Kylie laughs again. 'I do remember that I kept thinking about him. I couldn't understand... I was just... I couldn't imagine why he would pay someone like me attention. I'm absolutely sincere, I was like, My God, I'm so uncool and here I am, and I'm just a little thing, and he's Michael Hutchence and fancy saying anything like that to me!' Kylie remembers thinking she'd probably never see him again. 'But, you know, it was shocking and amusing... and tantalising... and humorous. And in a way, that was Michael.'

Kylie and Michael didn't meet again for another year, when she attended an INXS concert at the Sydney Entertainment Centre in 1989. 'I remember being in the audience and I thought that he looked at me. But then of course later on I became all too aware that he was very shortsighted and couldn't see a God-damn thing, so there was no way that he saw me in the audience. It didn't matter, it made me feel good just thinking about it! And then I was backstage afterwards and I can't remember who, but somebody said, "Michael would like to meet you". And again I thought, Oh, okay. And I went and met him and we had a little chat and then a bunch of people went back up to his hotel room. And to set the picture, you've probably been to those things so you know what I mean, but there's rock'n'roll type music people sitting around doing various things. I was just this kinda straight person at this rock'n'roll party. So straight. And he and I were sitting on the bed, which was all in the same room as everything else was happening. He was asking if he could get me a drink, and I kept saying, "Oh no, no, it's okay, I'm fine, thank you." He kept asking, "Can I get you a drink," and I guess that he managed to... successfully and sweetly... er... get me to have a drink in the end. It was a Bailey's on ice because it didn't taste like alcohol. Not that I hadn't had a drink before then, you know, I was probably more racy when I was about sixteen than I was then. But anyway, we were sitting there having a chat and talking about whatever. And I think his girlfriend Jonny was jealous at the time because he was talking to me. She is an absolutely adorable girl.'

One of the things that Kylie and Michael spoke about on his bed at the post-concert party was homoeopathic drops for the throat, popular with some singers. Some time afterwards, Kylie was about to embark on her first live concert tour, and the initial stop was Hong Kong. She asked a mutual friend to contact Michele Bennett, who was about to produce the next video for INXS, and have her find out from Michael the name of the doctor who gave him the drops. Michele gave Kylie Michael's phone number in Hong Kong, where he was living with Jon Farriss.

'So I called him up for the name of the doctor, and I also told him I was going to be in Hong Kong the next day,' says Kylie. 'He said, "Can I take you out to dinner? Can I take you out on a date?" I said, "sure that will be nice". What I didn't know was that he'd been informed that I was coming and he had delayed filming of the video so he could stay in Hong Kong to take me on the date.' Next evening, having arrived in Hong Kong, Kylie waited for Michael to pick her up for their first date. 'He was hours late to pick me up, not ten or fifteen minutes or an hour, but two or three hours late. At that time I was with my manager, my assistant, my mother, my dancers, everyone who was involved in the production of the tour. They were all going out elsewhere, and I guess they felt they had to stay with me until I was picked up. So when Michael arrives three hours late, he had these stony faces from my entourage in front of him thinking, You better improve from here on or you'll have to deal with us. Michael and I went out, we must have stayed out talking in the streets of Hong Kong till four or five in the morning. We just hit it off amazingly well. But I wouldn't let him kiss me, which probably drove him crazy. I just thought, You can't kiss me. He'd gone from having women that would just throw themselves at him, and not being able to kiss me gave him a bit of a shock. We spent a few days together, and I remember we were on a junk in Hong Kong and he had his bags with him and really didn't want to go, but had to go and work. I did my show in Hong Kong and then went to Japan. Shortly afterwards he flew to Japan to meet me. He started sending flowers and there were constant telephone calls and we started going out then. I just remember him treating me so well. And he did throughout our entire relationship.'

The fairytale love affair between Minogue and Hutchence boosted both their careers and was something very special in both their lives. He was the teacher, she the eager pupil. He handed on some life experiences, she provided some much-needed freshness and calmness—for a while. An innocent former soap star, sugar-sweet, and the rugged pop star with a legendary sexual reputation. On the surface an unlikely match, but in reality the Hutchence–Minogue alliance was pure magic. Minogue was suddenly seen to have lost her innocence, to have got down and dirty, emerging from her wide-eyed days as a teenage soap queen into a sultry, solid singer who was sexually awakening before everybody's eyes on the front pages of the newspapers. Kylie played it up to the hilt, wearing blonde wigs and miniskirts. Hutchence's sexual reputation was even further enhanced, but at the same time he was seen in a different light by the media and the public, who began to view him as tabloid fodder. Although he was accustomed to media attention, it had hitherto been primarily for his music, his lyrics, his wild offstage antics and associated rumours. Now there began an intense interest in his personal life. In short, Kylie and Michael were a cool couple—the coolest couple around.

This was the beginning of what would become Hutchence's battle with the paparazzi and the tabloids. The intense intrusion picked up steam later on when he hooked up with Helena Christensen and it turned into a frenzy when he was landed by Paula Yates. Hutchence and Minogue could not go anywhere without the prying eyes of the media. No matter how many measures they took to preserve their privacy, they just couldn't escape the infringement on their lives.

'At the time I was twenty-one, a time when I was turning from a girl to a young woman and really eager to learn about the world,' Kylie said. 'He was a great teacher, but I think I taught him some things as well without knowing it at the time. To come from the lifestyle he had lived up to that point and then to be going out with a girl who really, in a sense, had experienced so much of an irregular lifestyle—because of the beginnings of my career in *Neighbours*—but who in a worldly sense hadn't experienced that much. The most famous quote about what I learned from him I didn't really say, and that was "I discovered sex."' She laughs. 'But I guess I did. It was like I had blinkers on before. He was totally charismatic, and intelligent, witty, funny, and filthy. He was like all kinds of extremes. He was poetic, romantic and good old-fashioned rock'n'roll as well. And I think he was probably attractive to men as well as women. But what was amazing with him, I remember, was that he really let me be myself. He just loved me. Unconditionally, and it was consistent until the end.'

Hutchence was very supportive of Minogue and he helped and encouraged her with her image and live performances, always paying attention to her career, happy to see her succeed. 'I remember doing a warm-up gig in a small club in Melbourne and we called ourselves The Singing Budgies. And Michael was so adorable, because of course I was nervous, it was a secret gig, it was a really small gig, and he ran out with about five people, back from the front of the stage and he was so proud of me. It was gorgeous. He was yelling and screaming and putting his arms in the air and it was great. Truly great. You know, there he was, Michael Hutchence. He didn't need all of the attention. He could take a back seat and was so proud when I would shine. Whether it would be on stage or whether it would be in a private situation at a dinner with friends, he'd just kind of look over and be really proud.'

A large cornerstone of the liaison between Kylie and Michael was sexuality, and the chemistry did not end when the relationship ended. 'There was just this electric, sexual energy between us. Even after we finished, people would say, Oh my God, you two. We could be on opposite sides of the room, and it was just like . . . I could see his eyes, I can still see them right now.'

Apart from some of the finer points of sex, Hutchence also introduced Minogue to partying and drugs. 'Yeah. Actually just Ecstasy I have to say, just Ecstasy,' Kylie coyly recalled. Like most of Michael's friends, Kylie grows protective of Michael Hutchence once the conversation delves too deeply in some directions. 'I'd never known him to take more serious drugs when he was with me,' she said.

Kylie eventually met Michele Bennett and could see there was something special between her and Michael. 'To have been with Michele for that amount of time in his early years—it was evident that she was really special to him, a very important part of his life. And I guess that a lot of people have that kind of person from their earlier years that will be there forever. They know you from the beginning before you kinda took off on your own in the big bad world. For me that would be a couple of my girlfriends, I'd say, or if Michael was still here I would always be thinking of him as someone that had a unique understanding of me. I lived in this world and then Michael introduced me to the galaxy. He never tried to change me. He just wanted me to be, and experience.'

Kylie also experienced Michael's avoidance of confrontation. Even with Kylie, he had difficulty breaking up honestly. Martha Troup comments, 'Michael had a pattern with women. When he wanted to break up with them, I don't know what the chemistry was, but he wouldn't want to hurt them and tell them it was over. He would just move on until he met someone else that he wanted to be with.' He had been carrying on a telephone affair with Helena Christensen for the final three months of his relationship with Kylie, and the end was not clear-cut or decisive but a downward slide, leaving Kylie bewildered.

'Things between us were consistent until the end, but I couldn't even tell you what was going through his mind then; it was one of those situations where you're not too sure why you broke up, but you did,' Kylie said.

Rhett remembers being in New York with Michael when the couple split. 'I don't think he had actually met Helena by then, he was just having a phone relationship with her. I was with him in New York, he was on the phone. I was in the room and he was talking to somebody and was really excited. And he said, "Rhett, I want you to talk to Helena," and he gave me the phone and I just had a few words. That was the first time I talked to Helena. She was in Miami or somewhere like that. He was still having a thing with Kylie at the time.'

Kylie was in Australia when Michael phoned her. She was preparing for a concert tour. 'We broke up on the phone when I was in Australia about to do another tour,' Kylie told me. 'I flew to Manhattan so that we could talk. He was very strange at that point and I just remember him being somewhere that I'd never seen him before—I'm sure you probably have correlating stories from other people at that time—I saw him on the floor in his hotel room just very distressed and I don't know what he'd been taking or what he'd really been going through, but he was not together, to say the least. That was the first time I'd seen him like that during our entire relationship.'

Rhett remembers the two fighting and Michael leaving the hotel to perform with INXS at the Coliseum. 'I went up to Michael's room and Kylie was in there crying,' Rhett said.

'It was the same time as the Grammies, in February 1991, when Kylie and he broke up,' recalls Martha Troup. 'She came over to the apartment and I had a new-born baby, my daughter Tess, and Kylie just sat there and she rocked the baby, she just kept rocking the baby, she was so upset. Michael talked about Kylie the week before he died. He talked about her a lot. I think Kylie really got to Michael more than she realised,' said Troup.

'I was moving out of our hotel the next day,' Rhett remembered, 'to the Paramount Hotel, and I got Kylie a suite, too. She and I shared a cab. I checked her into her suite and she decided that she was going to stay for a couple of days and we were going to catch up, but she left the next day. That was the end of that. They saw each other again after that and they still got on and they were friends up until he died. He's always had that, he's always been able to keep most of the relationships he's had, most of the girlfriends, always kept on good footing with them afterwards. I don't think that he'd ever been dumped. He'd always done the leaving.' The exception was Michele Bennett, where the split was mutual.

Kell Hutchence never thought Michael was really all that serious about Kylie at the start. 'But obviously it was far more serious than I thought,' he said. 'When they broke up, he phoned me from New York and he told me he felt terrible about Kylie. "I feel terrible, I let her down", Mike told me. So he was clearly sensitive and very upset when Helena came on the scene.'

Kylie remained confused. 'Yeah, I think he eventually wondered why it happened. We had a good thing and I'm sure that he never ever wanted to hurt me either. I don't know, maybe he did indulge himself in too many projects, you know, whether it be seducing women or reading poetry or taking drugs or staying in the most exquisite hotel or, you know... He did normal things as well. I'm sure the greatest sign of that was with Tiger—that doesn't involve being anyone special or having a lot of money, that's the most simplest, most natural thing. He was my first great love and it caused great heartbreak when we split up. And ironically he was the first person I had been extremely close to who's passed away. I'm sure he's laughing, looking down now, knowing that he's still teaching me.'

• • •

Hutchence was an avid reader of erotic and pornographic literature, Marquis de Sade's being among the most thumbed books in his collection. He could have sex of some kind before a show, after a show, and during a show, sometimes side-of-stage during guitar, sax and keyboard solos. Threesomes, group sex, hookers, voyeurism, lesbian sex, sado-masochism, auto-erotica—he was completely relaxed about investigating anything to do with sex.

According to Lian Lunson, 'He was as sexually adventurous as we all heard, and even more so. He had no boundaries about anything.' Martha Troup says that sex was a major priority in his life. 'Michael used to love talking about sex and I'd say to him, Michael when I die it's going to be on my gravestone, "I am the only woman who didn't fuck Michael Hutchence". Women and men would become possessive about him, and I don't blame them, I understand why they would.'

'One-night stands, he did them all the time, he saw them all,' Rhett says. 'He'd be next to them at the bar, you know, and it would happen, just like that. He always had to have somebody in his life, he always had to have somebody there.' As his love of sexual experimentation advanced alongside his increasing experimentation with recreational drugs, Michael just seemed to keep attracting more and more women. The greater his conquests, the more women wanted to be part of the action.

Bill Leibowitz reckons he had it all. 'He projected what I call the triple-S threat,' he told me. 'Sincerity, sensitivity and sensuality. Add to that his incredible voice, charisma, stage moves and the fact that he was a great looking guy. Women just found him completely irresistible. He had many qualities that women would have loved anyway, plus he was a rock'n'roll star, it was an unbeatable combination, you know, he really had it all. When I'm on an aeroplane I can't even get a stewardess to get me a Coca-Cola. Michael blinks and he's in the rest room with her, and I'm still buzzing for a Coke.'

In the beginning, Michael's relationship with Danish model Helena Christensen looked like it was going to be the one where he'd settle down, and he did, for a while. Their romance, on the surface, was a modern-day classic. Rock-god with supermodel. It was heaven on a lens for the paparazzi and the tabloids. She took him into different circles, the social set of the beautiful people, into the world he'd dreamed about, and he in turn took her into his world.

'A photographer friend, Herb Ritts introduced Michael and I over the phone,' Helena told me, 'and we spoke for a month on the phone before we finally met in person in New York City. I fell in love with Michael because of his intensity, the way he could look you in the eyes and you would feel entranced, you would discover a whole new dimension to life.' No doubt Hutchence and Christensen's sex life was also a new dimension for them both. She had no qualms about pornography, as she indicated in 1997 when she commented on the semi-pornographic movie *Inferno*, in which she starred. 'So it's porno, so what? Porno can be great.'

Christensen enjoyed her own life of superstardom and all its trappings. She was one of the world's highest paid and most resilient models. She was independent, was interested enough in sex to keep Hutchence in tow. She once told the media she would marry him and have his children. It was news to Hutchence, but there's no doubt they were in love.

Their base was Hutchence's Valbonne chateau in the south of France. He would cruise the catwalks with Helena, she would be his backstage partner at rock concerts and clubs, and they'd celebrate at the finest eateries in the world. By June 1994, with INXS in an extended recess, Hutchence and Christensen had become the world's glam couple. But while her career kept on going, Michael's was on hold. He slowly merged more into her world than his own, attending fashion shows and designer previews. As Christensen gained further world fame in director Robert Altman's spoof on the fashion industry, *Prêt à Porter*, Hutchence appeared to be simply the man by her side. The couple travelled arm in arm along the world's supermodel circuit.

By October 1994, 26-year-old Christensen was reported to have bought a £1500 wedding dress, but Hutchence started to cool off the relationship. Nevertheless, she still loved him. Like them all, she still does. 'To talk about Michael seems strange to me, still, because it has to be in the past tense. I find that particularly difficult because he was so alive and vibrating as a human being,' Helena said. 'He was one of the most amazing people I've ever met—a combination of having a very sensitive, almost childlike spirit and an old, very intelligent soul. I could watch him converse with people for hours, watch the way he captivated their attention, pouring out his knowledge and feelings. He was very aware of worldly issues and was always reading and observing everything around him. He was so full of information and so interested in it all.'

During his intense affair with Helena Christensen, Hutchence was involved in a serious accident that affected him for the rest of his life. Indeed, in some shape or form it could very well have helped contribute to his death. In Copenhagen in the summer of 1992, Helena, Michael and a group of friends were out one night riding on pushbikes. They were drunk, and they'd just bought some takeaway food. Michael was leaning against his bike, eating his food in the middle of the road, when a taxi driver came down the street. 'He stopped his car and told Mike to get out of the way,' Greg Perano said. Although Perano was not there, Hutchence had told him of the circumstances. 'Mike was drunk and made a joke of it, so the guy gets out of the car and hits him. Mike fell over onto the footpath and hit his head, cracking it on the pavement. It had a very strange effect on Michael. In time, he started being abusive to people and he didn't know what the fuck was going on. He started to have nightmares, sleeping very badly. Helena nursed him for about six weeks, and then he went to a neurosurgeon in Paris, where they told him he had a hairline fracture of the brain and had lost his sense of taste and smell.'

Hutchence supposedly lost around 80 per cent of his sense of taste and smell that night, but nobody seems to be able to confirm this medically. Nobody appears to have any idea who the Paris specialist was that he visited, nor where the X-rays are. Christensen will not talk about the accident in any form, and the entire matter seems to have been brushed off by all but a close few. But that Hutchence did lose a major part of his sense of smell and taste is not in doubt. 'When men lose their sense of smell and taste they can also lose their sexual desire, and he was afraid of that,' Rhett says. 'He was a guy who could afford to taste all the culinary delights of the world, yet couldn't actually taste them anymore. Michael explained to me that he went to see this neurosurgeon, and he drew a picture of his brain and drew ten little strands coming down and he said, "This is the normal human brain." Then he scribbled off eight of the strands and said, "This is what you have left."'

The accident in Copenhagen had a significantly negative effect on Michael's psyche and behaviour patterns for the rest of his life. 'It was obvious after the hairline fracture that Michael could no longer drink very much without his behaviour going really erratic, way beyond drunken behaviour,' says Richard Lowenstein. 'Not long after the accident, when he was still with Helena, she was in a fashion show here in Melbourne. He was here too, and we spent a couple of nights together. Michael became maudlin and he said he'd totally lost his sense of taste and smell and all he had was about 10 per cent, which the doctors would tell him was only his memory of those senses anyway. Of course this was imperative to Michael because he was so sensual, and taste and smell both feature so heavily in lovemaking. Anyway, Michael started crying and sort of collapsed and said to me, "I can't even taste my baby's pussy, I can't even taste my baby's pussy." It was a huge thing which he pretended he was fine about, you know. But he clearly wasn't.'

According to Bono, 'He talked about the accident and it was significant. I think that losing his sense of smell and taste had a marked effect on his state of mind, it was a big thing for him because he was particularly sensual.'

It was at this time that Michael started taking anti-depressants.

'He loved taking anti-depressants because it meant he didn't cum for hours,' Martha Troup says.

'Isn't it fantastic? I couldn't live without it, it's great,' Michael said to Richard Lowenstein of his latest drug find.

Such drugs coax their consumers into a false sense of well-being, a sense that all is well with the world; they give a specious sense of security, but ultimately they create a delusory world. Sometimes the effect is that you sabotage your own life, engineering a kind of self-fulfilling prophecy. In her book *Prozac Nation*, Elizabeth Wurtzel writes, 'I don't know if depressives are drawn to places with that certain funeral ambience or if, in all their contagion, they make them that way. I only know that for my entire junior year of college, I slept under a six-foot-square poster emblazoned with the words LOVE WILL TEAR US APART, and then I wondered why nothing good ever happened in that bed.'

With INXS on hold, the aftermath of the accident, the anti-depressants, the continual usage of cocaine and alcohol and Ecstasy, the dabbling in heroin, together with his occasional affairs and being relegated to the status of Helena Christensen's handbag in the view of some, Michael's self-esteem began to radically diminish. He was now exhibiting regular erratic behaviour, stronger mood swings, spasmodic aggression. The drugs, the transient lifestyle, his increasing need for more exploratory sexual encounters and experiences, the pressure of fame, the frustrations of not being able to kick start a solo career all began to take their toll, just as his relationship with Helena Christensen also began to cool off rapidly. Many of his friends say that Hutchence was bullied by Christensen, but perhaps she was simply trying to push him out of his deepening dark hole and into reality.

'The accident in Copenhagen was a major, major point in all of this,' Lian Lunson rationalises. 'There were changes in his behaviour and moods after the accident, though subtle at first. There was a darkness that had never been there before—not that I ever witnessed. There are some of us who just know this was important. I don't think it's so much a matter of it being covered up or anything, I just don't think people realise how important that accident was to Michael's life. I think it's that simple. I don't think people realise how relevant it was. It was a major, major thing.'

Christensen, however, believes too much has been made of the accident. 'I have no idea what neurosurgeon Michael went to after his accident. He went to see someone in Paris a couple of months afterwards and I was not around at the time. Since he had lost a certain percentage of his sense of smell and taste, of course that will initially make you somewhat depressed. But later he seemed to get more used to it and even mentioned an improvement, which is what usually happens. The remaining nerves improve themselves and try to restore the lost nerves. So I don't think it's entirely in its place to keep trying to blame this fissure, the tiny crack in his skull, for what later happened to Michael. However, there was definitely more important things going on in his head that we will never know of.'

Personally, I think Christensen is totally and absolutely sincere, and is not trying to hide anything, but I also think she misses the point completely. It's not the 'tiny crack in the skull' that is the issue here, but the damage done to the brain. Whilst there certainly were far darker events going on in Michael's mind, some of the effects of the accident had not disappeared when I met with Hutchence a couple of months prior to his death. He briefly spoke to me that night about his failing sense of taste.

Still, the changes in Michael were not just to do with the accident. The relationship with Helena went on too long, some of Michael's friends believe. It should have ended a lot earlier than it did. It was destructive in many ways, and when he came out of that relationship his self-esteem was incredibly low, according to many friends, he had suffered a loss of confidence during his time with Christensen.

Some say Helena denigrated Hutchence, provoked him, placed him on a level below Bono who, along with his wife Ali, was a friend of Helena's. She was also a great fan of Nick Cave, and some of Michael's friends say she told Michael he was not in the same league as Cave or Bono. Yet others say that all she wanted was for him to realise his full potential and that she tried to push him in that direction.

'Sometimes Helena would snipe at him, as she often did with others,' says Greg Perano. 'She would like to keep herself on the pedestal. I went and stayed with them in Paris and she seemed pretty cool, but she demanded to be the centre of attention. Helena idolised Nick Cave and Bono, and sometimes would urge Michael to be more like them.' To be fair to Christensen perhaps she was aware of Hutchence's deep emotional problems and was simply trying to bring him to his senses, to steer him back on track. Christensen still declares her love for his magic. 'It sometimes seemed like he wasn't of this world. I've never met anyone so articulate, caring, humorous, interesting. I'm so proud to have known him. He was and is a beautiful person.'

In an effort to continue preparatory work for his solo projects, Hutchence began spending more and more time in London, a dark city at the brightest of times. London is a sexual explorer's paradise. With outrageous sex clubs of all kinds in abundance, a smorgasbord of legal and illegal drugs on tap, it has an underbelly of addictive proportions. It is the Ecstasy and dance capital of the world. By March 1995 Hutchence had purchased a three-story mews building in Smith Terrace, near the famous Kings Road in Chelsea. Exorbitantly expensive renovations were carried out under the guidance of famed Australian architect, Robert Grace, and Hutchence appeared to be setting up a working base in London, away from his reclusive home in France. He was suffering from massive depression, his anti-depressants by now a part of his life, alongside his unceasing desire to escape, in any shape or form, his mounting emotional problems from which he'd been running for much of his adult life. It was in this atmosphere of change, self-doubt, sliding self-esteem and uncertainty that Hutchence began a dalliance with Paula Yates, wife of one of Britain's modern-day heroes, Sir Bob Geldof.

nine

Paula, Michael, Tiger, Bob

> I found you wanting
> Like everyone
> Always trying
> Happy lying
> To the ways of the world
> I felt like crying
> I felt like dying
> Found in the gutter
> With a knife in her back
> She had a lover
> With danger in his eyes
> I tried to tell her
> But she had the wildest heart
>
> 'Show Me'
> *Elegantly Wasted* 1997
> MICHAEL HUTCHENCE AND
> ANDREW FARRISS

Even before she took up with Michael Hutchence, Paula Yates was tabloid fodder for the British media. Highly intelligent, she also possessed a delightfully wicked, sardonic sense of humour and a keen eye for manipulating publicity. She has always been intoxicated by the famous, with a desire for courting her own fame and mixing with the show-business elite. She is a self-confessed flirt and name-dropper. She is the author of fourteen successful books (some on how to be a successful mother) she has co-presented such legendary British TV music shows as *The Tube* (in its day regarded as overtly controversial, Yates even more so); she has been a columnist, has won awards for her television interviews, and has appeared on the front cover of more than thirty glossy magazines. She has always been outspoken, outrageous, attention-grabbing, and thus has been an easy target for public intruders. She has given birth to four children, and for eighteen years was Bob Geldof's partner. For ten of those years they were married, and she was highly protective and supportive of him.

These achievements are particularly remarkable when one considers Paula's unstable, somewhat transient childhood. Her mother first left the family home when Yates was only eight years old, leaving her, in her own words, 'in the middle of the night to live in London and make some money for us'. Paula was left with her grandmother and her father, who 'just sat in a chair while the rain dropped and picked his nose meditatively. I became an eight-year-old anorexic. I was like a pining dog,' she writes in her autobiography, *Paula Yates*.

According to Oliver James, a clinical psychologist with whom Paula worked in television, Yates was also a borderline personality who took refuge in fantasy during her unhappy childhood. 'Paula has an insecure, shifting void,' he told the *Sunday Times*'s Tim Rayment in June 1998. 'She is liable to feel that she does not exist unless she is at the centre of a crisis, which she likes the tabloids to chronicle because they make her feel significant.' Paula tends to blame external forces for her own problems. In her autobiography she goes to great lengths to explain how her mother chased men, a film career, a career in show business, and how, in the process, became well connected to many of the rich and famous, including the legendary Italian film director Federico Fellini. 'No-one can say she didn't know how to grab a man's attention,' Paula says.

Eventually reunited with her mother for a short while and living in Majorca, the twelve-year-old Paula Yates was walking along one of the island's long winding streets one day when the older brother of a friend pulled up alongside her on his motorbike and said, 'Hey baby, I'm Eric.' According to Yates, 'Eric was intent on corrupting me as quickly as possible. He would give me heroin. We didn't use needles and I didn't smoke or want to inhale smoke, so we snorted it up and lay back comatose.'

Bob Geldof had also garnered headlines of his own. With his attacks on the snobbish, hypocritical London punk-pop set during his early days with The Boomtown Rats, Geldof attracted massive criticism from the trendy alternative London music press. In 1979 he wrote the song 'I Don't Like Mondays', which went to number one in more than thirty countries but was withdrawn by the group's American record company, Columbia, when the Americans realised that it was about an American teenage murderer named Brenda Spencer. Spencer had been leaning outside her bedroom window one afternoon, bored and armed with an automatic rifle, when she began randomly shooting students in her school across the street. When asked by a journalist why she did it, Spencer responded, 'I was bored. I don't like Mondays.' In America for a promotional trip with his band at the time, Geldof wrote the song as the drama unfolded.

Geldof has always been wildly outspoken, blunt, with a brilliant and irreverent sense of humour. His controversial views ensured British, Australian and American newspaper headlines throughout his career. The British liked his cocky attitude, the Americans couldn't figure him out. The British saw him ascend from scruffy, loud-mouthed pop star to scruffy, loud-mouthed, global statesman, a conduit for world knowledge of a terrible famine in Ethiopia. In the process, he became a modern-day British hero.

Yates and Geldof met in 1976 at a restaurant in Fulham Road, London, after she had just completed her A levels at St Claire's in Oxford. A year later they met again at an agent's office in Dublin. 'She was about seventeen, and dressed in an outfit of ragged lace, which made her look like a cross between a hippie and a punk,' recalled Geldof in his 1986 book, *Is That It?* He asked her to that night's Boomtown Rats concert. On the way to the show, according to Geldof, Paula unzipped his trousers in an attempt to give him a blow job. He told her to stop it, and she said she did it because she imagined that's what all rock stars expected. Almost a decade later, in her autobiography, Yates displayed her displeasure at Geldof recalling the event. 'I didn't know Bob had put this in his book until it came out,' she wrote, 'and I rather wish he hadn't. It has become the stuff of legends, like Marianne Faithfull and the Mars Bar.' It has to be said that sections of Geldof's biography, written in 1986, seem particularly derogatory to Yates, especially considering that the pair were supposedly in love at the time, about to get married. Yates evened the score in her autobiography, writing several derogatory comments about Geldof.

After The Boomtown Rats concert in Dublin, Geldof took Paula to a club where she met Bono for the first time. 'My name's Bono and I'm in a band called U2,' said the sixteen-year-old. 'So fucking what?' responded Yates. But the two went on to become solid friends and have remained so. Bono also remains friends with Geldof. As the drama of the Yates–Geldof marriage reached its first crescendo, Bono and his wife Ali tried to help salvage the relationship, inviting Bob and Paula to their house in Dublin so that they could have some time together, away from prying eyes. The following weekend they did the same for Helena and Michael. 'I don't expect human relationships to be logical, I really don't,' Bono would later tell me, 'and I don't expect love to be rational, either. So I just kinda try not to make judgements. I have respect for all parties, and I guess I didn't find it that difficult and neither did Ali. It's not a religious thing, it's just respect. I knew what was going on. I felt for Helena lots, and I now feel for Paula lots. And Bob, actually, and I've known Bob the longest. I met Bob and Paula when I was sixteen. I understand the opera.'

Yates and Geldof became a couple during 1977, and Fifi, the first of their three daughters, was born in 1983. One evening in October 1984, after having bathed their child, Geldof and Yates were watching a television report from correspondent Michael Buerk about the mounting famine in Ethiopia. The television showed heart-wrenching pictures of dying mothers and their babies, seemingly totally beyond help from an oblivious Western world. Next morning Paula set up a donation poster next to the fridge, encouraging visitors to contribute. Geldof told Paula he was going to organise a record to raise money for Ethiopia. The resulting record, 'Do They Know It's Christmas' became the biggest selling pop single of all time, and raised almost £8 million. The American musical elite, relentlessly prodded by Geldof, organised their own record, 'We Are The

World', written by Michael Jackson and Lionel Richie, adding millions more to the Ethiopian crisis fund.

Geldof was now gathering support from politicians and people of the world. In July 1985 the project culminated in a worldwide concert, televised to 132 countries and viewed by an estimated 120 million people. The main concert took place in Wembley Stadium in front of a live audience of 70 000, while similar concerts took place all around the world, broadcast globally via satellite. In Sydney, with frontman Michael Hutchence, INXS took the stage at the Sydney Entertainment Centre. INXS had already begun their world assault but had not yet moved into the big league.

A year later, on the set of *The Tube*, Paula Yates welcomed INXS, who were in London to perform. 'Michael was so heartbreakingly beautiful it made me feel quite feeble,' Yates recalled in her autobiography. Hutchence walked into the studio dressed in black tights and pixie boots, and lisped and stammered his way through the interview as Yates concentrated her attention on his impressive crotch. 'The Taj Mahal of crotches,' was how she actually described it. 'It was impossible to look at anything else, and the whole nation was probably doing the same.' She says he then asked her back to the hotel, to which she replied, 'Crikey, no, I've just had a baby.' Next day, though, she put a photograph of Hutchence up on her fridge door. It stayed there for the next twelve years.

In 1986, following Geldof's knighthood, Paula and Bob were married in Las Vegas. It was kept secret for a while, and on their return the British media had a ball when they discovered Paula was pregnant for a second time. The tabloids were cruel to the extreme with their headlines, one of them reading 'One Geldof Bastard is Enough'. They linked Paula with anyone and everyone, smearing her and Geldof's names at will.

Following Live Aid, Geldof started his own television production company, Planet 24, which produces *The Big Breakfast*. In 1991 Paula was given a segment on the programme where she would interview guests while lying on a bed. Her interviewing technique was flirtatious and seductively abrasive.

In 1988, Yates was dispatched to New York by London's *Time Out* magazine to interview Hutchence, by then the leading contender for the title of World's Sexiest Rock'n'roll Star. The meeting took place in a Fifth Avenue church on Palm Sunday. They did the interview and made arrangements to meet at Michael's hotel later on. When he was late, Yates phoned him in his room. 'Sorry, mate,' Hutchence said to her, 'I'm just feeling up Virginia. I'll be down in a minute.' He strolled in a short time later, and according to Yates said, 'They'll send a load of black girls in hotpants up now.' In her autobiography, Yates says Michael then told her that he'd 'like a baby. But not just one woman. Maybe five women. I guess you'd have to have some kind of arrangement.'

According to Yates, the girl upstairs, the Australian actor Virginia Hey, was sitting in the dark with a pair of scissors, threatening to kill Michael, Paula, and herself. Hutchence and Hey split up that evening; she sold her story years later when Michael and Paula were together. She claimed that Yates and Hutchence had been in bed all day, and that Yates was perfect for Hutchence because 'she was a sex toy'. The two women told different versions of the same meeting. One thing that is consistent with Paula Yates is that she always appears to have a completely different version of events from anybody else.

In 1994 Yates and Hutchence met again in public, this time on her interviewing bed on *The Big Breakfast*. The body language was obvious. It was clear that if a sexual relationship wasn't already happening between the pair, it was imminent. Yates and Geldof had three children at this time: Fifi, aged eleven, Peaches, aged four, and Pixie, just one year old. Unbeknown to Geldof, the marriage was at its end.

'Bob never realised I was unhappy,' Yates wrote in her autobiography. 'He just didn't notice and he just didn't understand. His life was so perfect so it didn't occur to him that I might not be happy. But it was perfect because I'd made it that way,' she wrote, claiming credit for Geldof's happiness. 'We don't behave as though we're in *Who's Afraid of Virginia Woolf?*, she said, rather prematurely, following the pair's split. 'No-one walks away from a relationship after eighteen years without thinking it through for months and without very good reasons. People never destroy a marriage on a whim. It is nothing but pain.' Yates added that she didn't leave Geldof for Hutchence, she was leaving anyway.

According to close friends of Hutchence and Yates, when the affair was in its very early stages he tried hard to persuade her to reconcile with her husband, urging her to save the marriage and protect the children. Indeed, after the affair had been exposed to the public arena, Hutchence stopped calling her so that she would have more time to mend things with Geldof. Paula and Bob went to Jamaica to try and sort things out.

Hutchence had his own problems to deal with, one of which was sitting down with Helena Christensen and explaining that their relationship was all but over, something he had not been able to do with any of his previous women. There was a period before the Yates–Hutchence love affair had been confirmed when the rumours became stronger, the details more distorted. The media, smelling a sensation, were relentless. Geldof and Yates announced a trial separation. Christensen and Geldof must have been smarting at the obvious betrayals and the subsequent furore, neither having been told by their respective partners that they were having an affair. Christensen, obviously the wiser, made her own announcement: 'Michael and I haven't been getting on for quite a while. We most definitely are not seeing each other at the moment. I haven't talked to him. I've heard from mutual friends that he is seeing Paula Yates. All I know is that we are no longer together and I'm not bothered by that.'

Helena Christensen told me that Hutchence did not leave her for Yates. 'Contrary to what the press wrote at the time, we did not break up because he left me for Paula. We had been trying to break it for a while, but it wasn't easy for any of us to take the final step. That eventually happened when they [Yates and Hutchence] publicly were together. The press wanted it to seem like I was in hiding somewhere, heartbroken. That was not the case, although any break-up that is final suddenly makes you sad and thoughtful.'

Michael and Paula continued their clandestine dalliances. The couple were eventually sprung during a 'secret', guarded weekend at the Chilston Park Hotel in Kent in March 1995, a few months after their regular cavorting began. Their first public candlelit dinner together took place in the dining room of the hotel, but they were not alone. More than fifteen reporters and photographers had also booked into the hotel, tipped off by an 'anonymous' source, and when the couple were approached at dinner for photographs, the lovers raced upstairs to their hotel suite. They'd been busted.

As Yates consistently hit the headlines during the next three years, newspapers often as not quoted their source as anonymous. Many believe the anonymous source was Yates. Some believe that it was her way of creating a drama in her life if one did not exist. Some believe she tipped off the press so that Geldof would find out about the affair. She had not been able to tell him herself.

'We didn't want to go public with any of this,' shouted Michael as he was pushed against the wall during the ensuing media frenzy at the Chilston Park. During the night a photographer tried to take photographs when Michael went downstairs to get a bottle of water. Hutchence lunged at the photographer and the police were called. Next morning the hotel was surrounded by the media, most of them heckling the couple. Provoked and angry, Hutchence lurched at the horde, punching and kicking, before getting into a car with Paula and taking off, followed by the paparazzi. Hutchence's tormented images were splashed across the newspapers that afternoon, and the couple's secret was no longer a secret.

The Geldof family nanny, Anita Debney, is one who believes that Yates tipped off the media herself, in an attempt to publicise the affair so that Hutchence would be forced to leave Christensen. Hutchence was later charged with assault over the incident and fined £400 for his trouble. One wonders whether the same justice would have been handed out if it were Hutchence who had made a complaint of assault against a photographer.

On 24 March 1995, INXS publicists Poole Edwards

released a statement saying that Hutchence and Christensen were spending time apart but were sad and still loved each other. 'Despite the current media furore, the parting is perfectly amiable and they still love and are in contact with each other. Both parties expressed sadness at the decision,' the press statement read. On the same day, Yates and Geldof issued a statement announcing their permanent separation. Geldof was devastated, although he did not enter the public debate, preferring to keep his comments for the Family Law Court when divorce and custody of the children became an issue. As the story gained momentum, Geldof made one of his few statements about the affair, telling one reporter, 'I've been made to look like a fool.'

For the following three years, Geldof maintained a dignified silence, concerned for the welfare of his children. The Family Law Court finally granted him full custody of his and Paula's children, a decision which was disclosed on 28 October 1998.

The hoo-ha that followed the public exposure of the love affair between Michael Hutchence and Paula Yates was astonishing, with many private details being made public. The media turned on Hutchence and Yates, stalking them and verbally pulverising them at every opportunity. Yates in particular copped a lashing. She was the whore from hell, according to newspaper headlines, and Hutchence, falling into the trap, retaliated accordingly, defending his new love. He was naive and thoroughly out of his depth; he saw himself as the knight in shining armour coming to the defence of his damsel in distress. This was not a love affair of his making, perhaps, and certainly not one from which he could just move on as he had previously done. When Hutchence began his affair with Yates he was at a low ebb in all aspects of his life. His band was in hiatus, his solo career slow, his self-esteem in decline, his drug-taking on the increase: he seemed to be searching for something but didn't know what. He was easy pickings for someone strong willed enough to take charge and manipulate the weak aspect of his nature—the inclination to avoid confrontation at all costs. And yet strong enough to defend someone he felt was being wronged. He felt Paula Yates was being victimised by her ex-husband because she told him so. He was lured into the custody battle and forced to fight Paula's battle for her. He eventually helped finance it.

Greg Perano has a slightly different twist. 'She couldn't resolve her problems with Geldof, there's no way Michael should have been involved. I'm sorry, but at the end of the day, Geldof was father to those kids. Maybe a couple of hundred years ago Michael and Bob would have had a duel or something. If you open a magazine and there's your children at the beach with another man and your wife, that's going to upset you, that's going to bring out that fatherly instinct. He was the father, after all.

'Two powerful men, one powerful woman and all trying to control the family situation, it's classic. She was as indulgent as Michael was, and that was the worst thing that could have happened to Michael. All his other girlfriends had careers which were on the rise, they all contributed a counterbalance to Michael, all were completely independent, but Paula was indulgent and dependent on Michael financially.

'Everyone attacked Paula, but they have to realise that Michael knew what he was doing, he knew she was as indulgent as he was, it was his choice and that's the way it was. Whether she contributed towards his downfall or not, he was aware of what was happening, deep, deep down inside himself. But it was the last thing he needed in his life at that point.

'No way was he ever going to win. And when Tiger Lily was finally conceived, if he wanted to get away, he couldn't because all of a sudden Paula was the mother of his child. I'm in too deep here, he'd say. It was a public affair. He just could not walk away from her. It was too late, he was trapped.'

Hutchence was portrayed by the media as the young upstart rock star from Down Under who was stealing the wife and children of a British hero. Michael, in a haze of confused fact and fiction, was only hearing one side of the story—Paula's. While some of her claims might have been true—that Geldof was a control freak, for instance—the fact remains that it was during her relationship with Geldof that Yates's career really took off. The minute she stepped outside the stable family perimeters set up by Geldof, Yates's career came to a screeching halt. There were no more television shows, no more newspaper columns, no more books—just stories for sale in tabloid magazines.

While some of Michael's friends say that he was Paula's scapegoat, that she lured him into fighting her battle with Geldof for her, others wonder how she could have drawn him into her custody fight if she truly loved him. Paula's erratic behaviour had begun years before she met Hutchence, and when he finally left her forever she appeared to descend further into her own denial—a dark, deep hole of despair, disillusionment and depression, a place she had been headed for before they began their affair, whenever it was that she had decided her relationship with Geldof was over. At the tail end of 1993, nine months prior to when her relationship with Hutchence officially began, the signs were obvious. She talked about her marriage problems with an old pal of fifteen years, Josephine Fairley. 'We went over all the reasons why she should and shouldn't leave,' Fairley said in London in June 1998. Fairley advised Paula not to leave. 'The anti were that the world would hate her because she'd abandoned Saint Bob, and that she wouldn't find a new partner to take on three kids. And that Bob would make her life miserable. He's always been obsessed with her. I don't think he ever really envisaged a future without her. I honestly believe he would take her back tomorrow.'

Once Paula and Michael's affair was out in the open and under increasing pressure from the media, who were sensing a drama that would provide them with headlines for years, Hutchence, in typical gallant fashion, defiantly said that Paula was his soul mate. 'I've made a choice to go on regardless. I've decided that I want to be with who I want to be with, and that I want to live the rest of my life as I see fit. I know there's a price to pay for that, because I don't play the game.'

People just could not understand why Hutchence would leave horny supermodel Helena Christensen for coquettish supermum Paula Yates. But love is strange, and so were the deep-rooted demons within Michael Hutchence. His own dysfunctional family and its problems would always haunt him, his endless search for the woman who would replace his mother, as well as provide him with everything else he always wanted in a woman, had finally, some thought, come to its end. Others thought quite the contrary—that he did not want to stay with Yates. He had seen his mother leave his father many times before their divorce. He had seen his father suffer. He knew what it felt like to be torn apart from loved ones, for a family to be ripped at the core, yet here he was doing the same thing to another father, another husband, another set of kids, another family. There's no doubt he loved Paula Yates. There's no doubt she was totally in love with him. 'She loved Michael probably too much. If you can love someone too much,' claims Martha Troup.

From the beginning of his relationship with Paula, Michael's friends were alarmed. They could see where he'd been, and to some it was obvious where he was going. Bill Leibowitz perhaps says it best: 'By and large, Michael was the kind of guy who would walk over hot coals to avoid confrontation. He hated confrontation and would swallow a lot to avoid it. The irony is that he ends up getting involved in a personal relationship that ultimately is about confrontation, being caught up between two confrontational and very strong-willed people, ending up being the gladiator for one of them, a role that he was completely unsuited for.'

While it might have been obvious to a few of his long-term friends, Michael appeared not to see the long, dark tunnel he was entering. Then again, maybe he did. Although Hutchence publicly said that Paula was his soul mate, privately many thought he was trying to get out of the relationship as soon as he was into it.

'When Michael started a new relationship he was always excited at the beginning,' Lian Lunson said. 'Whilst the tabloids were filled with reports of his and Paula's affair though, he kept calling me and saying, It's not what you think. I'd never heard him quite like that at the beginning of a relationship before. He seemed to be going down two roads from the beginning. During this period he kept asking me if I could help set him up with a friend of mine. From the very start he worried about his exit. I wish my friend had been available. He was painting himself into a corner and he did not know how to get out of it this time. It's not all Paula's fault, he did it himself. He painted himself into the corner.'

Almost without exception, the friends of Michael with whom I spoke said the same thing: that Michael did not want to stay with Paula, that he never had any real intention of marrying her, that he would leave her sooner than later. But it got to a point where he was in too deep. He simply could not get out of this one, the stakes were already too high, the consequences too dire, sordid details of the relationship having been plastered across every tabloid front page in the UK and Australia.

Michael's legal and illegal drug intake kept increasing dramatically. 'The whole reason why Michael started taking more drugs was purely escapism,' Lian Lunson said. Drugs and booze became the crutch when he could not deal with reality; they took away the pain, hid the problem.

'Michael didn't do heroin in front of me, but he would talk about it,' says Richard Lowenstein. 'I am pretty sure he wasn't shooting it, but snorting or smoking it. Injecting just wasn't sensual enough for Michael, wasn't his style. He was a very oral and sniffing person. That's where the real danger lies, though, because when you are sniffing and smoking heroin, it doesn't seem like you're a junkie or that it's having an addictive effect, but you actually do get addicted, just as if you hit it. I know he would smoke or snort heroin, but I don't know about habitually. I know he would do it if someone put it in front of him. He did most things that were put in front of him. Pre-Paula, though, I never had any experience of him habitually smoking or snorting heroin. I can only surmise it wasn't he who introduced it to her.'

Many more of Michael's friends and acquaintances confirm his occasional heroin and opium indulgences. Michael had conversations with a couple of friends about the ritual of smoking opium, preparing the pipe and smoking it, a particular pastime in Hong Kong. During the emotional torment Michael underwent with Paula and her drama with Geldof, drugs led Hutchence into an area where he thought he was safe. The greater the pain, the more drugs he took. 'I think it snuck up on him,' Lowenstein says. 'It all built on itself, the drugs, the emotional drag with him and Paula.'

His mood swings increased dramatically. He was saying things to his friends that were just not him. He exploded at the drop of a hat; his temper, at times, careered out of control, his bouts of depression became more regular.

'Paula is such a drama queen. It's not funny. If she's not in one, she invents one. Michael would put up with so much. I wouldn't have been able to handle it. I would have walked out,' Rhett Hutchence told me.

'He was sort of fascinated by Paula Yates because she was so full on,' one of Michael's oldest and dearest friends, who didn't want the comment attributed to them, told me. 'But he was a bit frightened of her at the same time.'

Paula began cutting Michael off from his long-term friends. She wouldn't pass on messages to him, she would be curt to them on the phone. 'This woman was manipulative, she got what she wanted. The few conversations I had with him after he had met her, he was saying things that just were not the kind of stuff he would normally say,' the same friend told me.

According to Richard Lowenstein, 'He was the meat in the sandwich of a battle that was so much bigger than he was.' Kell Hutchence laments, 'He travelled down some dark valleys and steep mountains, places he'd never been before.'

By August 1996 Michael Hutchence was locked in with Paula Yates permanently, whether he liked it or not: on 22 July his lover had presented him with a baby girl, Heavenly Hiraani Tiger Lily. Some old friends say that Michael had no intention of having a baby with Paula Yates, that the much publicised fertility treatments were non-existent, the story created by Yates after his death. Regardless, his daughter was born and he loved her dearly; she was an exact replica of Michael. He was completely, unashamedly besotted by his baby girl. And before his paranoia set in, he was blissfully happy.

'Mike rang me and said, "Dad we're thinking up names for the baby", recalled Kell. 'And he said, "What do you think of Tiger Lily?" He told me that Heavenly was Paula's idea. Then they came up with Tiger Lily. In the end, Hiraani became the second name. Paula liked the name Tiger, so when she was born I used to call her just Tiger, and he said, "It's Tiger Lily, Dad." It's really grown on me, Tiger Lily.'

The birth of Tiger Lily quietened down the raging acrimony between Paula and Michael and Geldof, if only for a short time. Yates and Hutchence became reclusive in the first few months. Michael doted on Tiger Lily, telling his friends proudly about what a change she had made to his life, how she had given him a new purpose. The birth of his daughter seemed to spur Hutchence forward, as he suddenly experienced all the wonders and joy that being a parent can bring. Two months before, Bob and Paula had divorced. It appeared all very neighbourly on the surface, Geldof giving his home to Yates and Hutchence and moving into Michael's home just around the corner. Geldof had a second home, in Kent, and a new girlfriend, French actress Jeanne Marine, who was twenty-five years old. 'After three days of complete nightmare in the High Court of Justice, Bob and Paula have with collective sighs arrived amicably at a half-decent solution to their housing arrangements,' the couple said in a press release.

With the arrival of Tiger Lily, Michael played the family man, accompanying Paula and the children on picnics and days out shopping. It was a role he might well have enjoyed, but it was a role he was thrust into nevertheless. By all accounts, Fifi, Peaches, and Pixie adored Michael, but he appeared slightly obsessed with his new father role. He would refer to them as his children in the middle of business meetings, talk about them as if they were indeed his own. 'He absolutely adored them,' said Josephine Fairley in June 1998, claiming that Michael gave them the time Geldof never gave them, that Geldof 'would not get down on the carpet with Barbie and Ken and act out *Brief Encounter*, as Michael did from the beginning. And Michael showered them with gifts. I remember a consignment of dresses from America, real princess dresses that he sent soon after they started the relationship.'

A few days after the couple were caught in the Chilston Park Hotel, the family nanny Anita Debney claims she overheard one of the girls saying to Geldof, 'Daddy, Mummy's been kissing Michael in your bed.' Debney would later figure in the opium bust that would add to the series of events that eventually ended in Michael's death. She was fired by Yates and became a witness for Geldof in the custody battle.

• • •

In September 1996 Hutchence and Yates travelled to Australia with three-month-old Tiger Lily for the christening ceremony of Zoe, Michael's niece by his brother Rhett and his partner Mandy Nolan. 'It was a lovely ceremony, quite hippie in a way,' recalled Rhett. 'We made an altar on the beach and set out a few shells and flowers and offerings of the four elements for Zoe. Everyone wrote down what they wished for Zoe, and we collected them and burned them, rubbed the ashes onto Zoe's forehead and in her feet, and the dolphins came right up to where we were, swimming around in front of us. It was a really beautiful day. It was the first time I'd met Paula.'

Meanwhile, back in London, very early on the Sunday morning of 15 September, the alarm sounded in Michael's green jeep and Anita Debney went to the couple's bedroom to find a manual on how to stop the alarm. Underneath the bed, Debney found a Smarties tube containing opium. She also discovered, inside a box, intimate sexual photographs of Yates and Hutchence. A week later, following an anonymous tip-off, the drug squad raided the house, where Debney and others, including Gerry Agar, a self-appointed publicist for Yates, had been staying while Paula and Michael were in Australia. The media were also anonymously tipped off and the drug bust sensationally hit the headlines. In the week between the drugs being discovered and the raid by the drug squad, Agar went to Geldof and reportedly told him of the discovery.

During the next six months, Hutchence and Yates were

left in limbo as the Crown Prosecution Service procrastinated over the bust, not being able to lay any charges. Firstly, Yates and Hutchence were not in the country at the time of the bust, which put the prosecution's case in jeopardy. Then Agar and Debney withdrew their original statements and the prosecution was left with nothing. But still Paula and Michael were grist to the media's mill: they had a pending drug charge hanging over their heads and the media never let them forget it.

There seems little doubt that the bust was a set-up, but just who was responsible for it is impossible to say.

Michael Hutchence was never quite the same after the drug bust. Yates maintained that it was Geldof who had planted the drugs, that it was his way of getting back at Michael. Although Michael had been preoccupied with Geldof during his illicit affair with Yates, he now became a man obsessed. He began to gulp down massive doses of anti-depressants, increased his Ecstasy intake, and his heroin indulgences became more regular. His moods grew darker, more insular, and he became, for the first time in his life, very bitter.

'I could tell that he was under a lot of pressure,' Bill Leibowitz said. 'There is no doubt that the Geldof thing was the main thing on his mind. He lived with it every day, received calls from Paula about it every day. It was something he couldn't escape from. There just was no respite. They were living in England and the two of them were like prisoners. Every time they walked out of the house there were reporters and photographers everywhere. The only escape was to live in America or somewhere like that, where people don't even know who Geldof is.'

According to Kell, 'Immediately following the drug bust,

Paula jumped on a plane and rushed back to London and left Mike holding Tiger Lily. Michael's sister-in-law Mandy looked after Tiger and went with her and Mike to Mike's house at Surfers on the Isle of Capri.'

Greg Perano claims that Michael was shattered by the drug bust, that it changed him completely. 'It's really easy to fit someone up. Michael was just devastated when the drug bust happened because he came out to Australia to have a good time, to be with his close friends, to show his new baby to everyone. Then bang, he was back in the middle of all the shit. He came to get away from that and be with people he loved, his real friends, and have a good fucking time. And it was just another bad moment for him. He really didn't think that he deserved that.'

A year later, in August 1997, following the final London INXS concert with Michael Hutchence as lead singer, I spoke with Hutchence about the drug bust, Geldof, Tiger Lily and custody of the kids. It was the early hours of the morning and he was tired, depressed and decidedly bitter. He was rambling but he paused to emphasise certain points. 'That whole drug bust last year was a set-up. I hired a detective to investigate the entire affair, and that's how I know.' He claimed that his detective had proof that the drug seizure was set up to discredit the couple. 'We've been battling to keep Paula's children. We think someone illegally entered our home and planted the drugs in a Smarties tube, and ensured that erotic photographs of Paula and I were strategically placed somewhere obvious so the kids and police could see them, then called the drug squad and immediately alerted the London *Sun* and the *Mirror* to inform them of the pending drug bust. The papers were there when the drug squad arrived.'

Hutchence then made the allegation that Geldof had subsequently contacted Social Services. 'He was going to try and get custody of our child, Tiger Lily, following the bust. Can you believe that?' Hutchence went on to explain to me exactly how Geldof was going to take Tiger Lily away from him. The reason why only Paula had come back to London, Hutchence told me, was so that Tiger Lily could stay in Australia just in case the Social Services people were manipulated by Geldof. He told me that he'd found out that Geldof was going to be at the airport with the drug squad and Social Services, and that they were going to do a drug test on him and Paula, and that would justify them taking Tiger Lily away.

Hutchence said that he and Paula were going to take action against her former husband. 'People are going to get a shock when they find out what Bob Geldof is really like. He's the devil in disguise.' He further claimed that Geldof 'was a bullying fascist who lives in the past, where women were treated as being owned by the man. He believed that Paula was part of his goods and chattels. He even offered me £600 000 for Paula, thinking I would take the money and leave her. Can you believe that?'

Hutchence was also particularly distressed about the death-dance which had been done on him by the London tabloids during the previous twelve months. At times they attacked him and Paula in a manner that can only be described as vicious; they ignored his music and tried to crucify his character.

'The stuff about Bob Geldof was completely mad,' Lian Lunson says. 'He got caught up in the custody thing and fighting Paula's battles. He was swept up in all of that before he knew what had hit him. It seemed to me very cleverly orchestrated that he, all of a sudden, was sunk in the level of tabloid journalism that his partner seemed to flourish in. He never belonged there. It devastated him, nothing in his life had prepared him for that. As for Paula, I'm sure she feels this was the love of her life and that they were soul mates, but Michael made every woman feel like that.'

Richard Lowenstein feels like others that Michael was only being told one side of the story, 'That combined with his "knight in shining armour instinct"—most of us have an automatic bullshit detector—I think in this situation Michael's had gone into remission. I got a call, it would have been early 1997, when Michael was in Australia and Paula had been called back to London for some court case. He was in Melbourne with Colin Diamond, and I got a call from him telling me to come to Marchetti's Latin which was his favourite Melbourne restaurant. I went down to see them both and talked about the idea of setting up a little film company. He'd get quite excited about that and talked about getting involved in some low budget and no budget features. He got all vibed up about the idea of being a producer on a feature film. And we're going "Yeah we'll pick the right teams and we'll do it for half a million, a million and it will be cool". Later on we ended up in his hotel room and the nanny brought Tiger down and we played with her on the bed for a while and it was obvious he was a proud father. After a while the nanny took Tiger back to bed and he took a phone call from Paula and he came back bursting with insane frustration saying "Bob is the fucking devil". He'd go on for a while saying this, he's that, and then he said, "You realise he's trying to take my baby". I said, "What? He's trying to take Tiger away from you? They can't do that, Michael."

'"Yes they can, there's a law."

'He explained that there was a fifteenth-century law that hadn't been repealed and I'm going, "Come on Michael, that's not going to happen. There would be an international outrage. It's ridiculous . . ." and he started kicking walls and losing it . . . "fucking Bob! blah blah blah . . ." and he'd go on about how the drug bust was all a set-up and how he was gonna get an ex-CIA man to deal with it. It was obvious that he'd been fed all this crazy information—a mixture of truth, exaggeration and downright lies and it had all mixed together in his head into a chaotic mess, and all he really needed was someone responsible, with knowledge of the facts, to sit there, calm him down and say "that's not going to happen, don't worry about it. He might get custody of his own children, but there's no way he'd get custody of yours." But instead, Michael was there kicking walls and going, "Fucken Bob . . !".

'Then some people arrived in the room that I barely knew. I think they were band related and the nanny gets Tiger up again. It was around 11 pm and they were all chain-smoking as they passed Tiger around, you know, and I'm just sitting back just watching this poor guy, you know, he looked like the loneliest guy in the world. With all these cronies around him in a circle all backing him up like parrots every time he went, "Fucking Bob" and they would repeat, "Yeah, fucking Bob". I just sat and watched them and it was one of the saddest things I had ever seen. You could understand why he said to me "I have no friends, I have no one I can trust, you are my only mate". Even though I know he said that to a lot of people, I just wanted to go over and hug him and say "get rid of these people, and lie there on the bed with your baby—and don't smoke". He was in a real mess. He chilled out after a while because we weren't allowed to go out to a club in case he got photographed and it got back to the court case in London. So we tried to ring a girl he had a crush on here and get her to come over to the room, but she thought it was a joke and kept hanging up on us.'

Bill Leibowitz articulated Hutchence's plight this way: 'Unfortunately, Michael was like a tall skyscraper built on a foundation of sand. His talent was the cement that built and held that skyscraper together. But in time, an overbearing, strong wind relentlessly blew against the skyscraper, dispersing the sand and there was no foundation left to support the building. The skyscraper had to fall.'

ten

Suicide or not— that is the question

> We run
> We hide
> We wait and we want the good life
> Aw sure, you're right
> This ain't the good life
> Ah, Elegantly Wasted
> Ah, Elegantly Wasted
>
> 'Elegantly Wasted'
> *Elegantly Wasted* 1997
> MICHAEL HUTCHENCE AND
> ANDREW FARRISS

On 14 November 1997, eight days before his death, Michael Hutchence sent me a fax from Los Angles—part of an electronic interview he was doing with me—that read 'life is good. Paula and I and the kids love it in Australia. Sydney's the greatest city in the world for the 21st century. London has become very difficult. People in Australia are so real and very friendly. We love it. Also, Paula is doing some TV work there, it's all good.' But, as it turned out, things were not good at all.

Michael seemed far from despondent about the upcoming INXS tour, indeed he was extremely excited about the prospect. 'It was important to us all,' Tim Farriss told me.

'This tour of Australia meant a great deal to us as people and as a band. We all knew how meaningful its success was to our future.' INXS had not toured their home country since the ill-fated Concert For Life in 1993. It was essential, therefore, that their 1997 Australian tour, Lose Your Head, be successful. It was also INXS's twentieth anniversary. The band had a lot to prove in Australia after having been ripped to shreds by some sections of the media for years.

Between July and October 1997, INXS had completed a successful tour of Europe, England and America. While the venues were smaller than those in which they had played in their international boom days, the concerts were sold out, and more importantly the band was beginning to fire again, their style of music influencing many new bands of the nineties. Rock music critics, mainly in Australia and England, claimed that INXS had gone past their use-by date. Yet in London in August 1997 INXS played to 10 000 people at Wembley Stadium, hardly a sign of being past their use-by date. Past their euphoric peak, perhaps, but not a spent force. In America the band had incredible reviews: 'The white-boy funk that propelled INXS out of the Aussie outback and into nearly every major arena on the globe is cranking full charge again', said the *New York Post* in April 1997. INXS seemed to be charging down the track to have a second shot and only the Americans appeared to see it.

After twenty years, INXS were about to enter a new phase and it was important that the band win back lost ground on their home turf. Hutchence was simultaneously on the brink of his long-anticipated film career, following his debut in *Dogs in Space*, then *Frankenstein Unbound* and *Limp*.

During 1997 he was involved in several screen tests and meetings with producers and directors, and he had appointed a Hollywood agent from the giant CAA entertainment agency. He was also excited about his adventurous, on-the-edge solo album, and prior to returning to Australia had squeezed in a further two days' recording with Danny Saber in Los Angeles.

Michael Hutchence's solo album had been a long time coming. Translating his own music to reality had proven difficult, and he needed help from many other musicians. It would be the culmination of at least four years' work, and perhaps he was finding out just how great his own band really was, how hard it is to transform great ideas into great music without the guidance of more experienced production musicians. After the many years it had taken to put together, the album was now dogged by his personal problems, and further delays were inevitable. However, he was moving forward. He had almost finished recording, and from all accounts it is a blistering, explosive piece of work. In short, Michael's career with INXS, his solo music and movie projects all seemed to be going well, giving him no cause for depression.

It was Michael's personal life that had become a monkey on his back. His partnership with Paula Yates had frozen him. His increased drug intake, together with further exploration of bizarre sexual practices, made the situation worse. He became paranoid and had violent mood swings. The indications are that he wanted out of the situation he was in with Paula, but Tiger Lily now made that impossible. It wasn't so much that he wanted to end his relationship with Paula, perhaps, as he wanted to stop being the wedge in an oppressive public battle—a battle about which he really knew nothing, a battle between two people who had been together for eighteen years. In Michael, Paula had her own chivalrous knight to help her escape from Sir Bob. 'Sure she's got his baby,' one of his closest friends told me. 'Basically she was pregnant within a month or so of them actually, officially getting together. Then claiming on the *60 Minutes* television programme that she had gone to fertility treatments for a year was obviously a lie. She knew him intimately for just two years and she then had the audacity to claim that she had this knowledge about him that nobody else has—it is just obscene.'

Michael Hutchence's relationship with Paula Yates was relentlessly exploited by the tabloid media. And there was no solution. From all accounts Michael desperately longed to create his own family. If nothing else, Paula seems to have given him hope, fleeting as it was. She gave a start to his family dream by bearing his baby daughter, and she had an inbuilt trio of stepdaughters for him. Yates had charisma, she had charm; she was highly intelligent, street-smart, and, like his mother, was a strong, independent woman. She also appeared to share his desire to deeply explore sexuality.

Yates says she absolutely worshipped Hutchence. Paula became 'my addiction', the singer once stated. He had changed since meeting Paula Yates, and everybody who knew Michael well could see it. He had become darker, more moody, moving away from many of his old friends, particularly once Geldof and Yates began their highly publicised separation and battle for custody. Paula tried to create a new social life and new friends for Michael. Once she threw a birthday party for Liam Gallagher, who displayed his gratitude by describing Paula as 'double sad'. Not long afterwards, to add insult to injury, the Oasis singer's older brother Noel, in front of millions of television viewers of the 1996 Brit Awards, quipped that INXS and Michael were has-beens. Michael was reportedly deeply hurt by the comment.

Opinion on the Geldof–Yates fiasco was split into two camps—one held that Geldof was a cold, callous, manipulative person; the other that Yates was the manipulative one, an immature drama queen. Michael was hurled between them, believing it his duty to defend Paula, but much of the information he was fed about Geldof appears to have been dubious at best. 'I think she painted herself as the victim, Bob was this big bad man and Michael's job was to save her,' Lian Lunson reckons. 'Geldof was her ex-husband and it was up to her to deal with it, not to bring someone else in to fight her battle for her. She lumped it onto Michael, forcing him to be her saviour. He felt an incredible responsibility to her and he was forced by the press into defending the relationship and fighting for her. He was saying to me, Help me.'

Michael, worn and weary by the lifelong love, devotion and support he had given his proud but sometimes clinging, emotionally dependent family members—precariously glued together by his fame—appears to have become paradoxically dependent yet insecure within the substitute family that was INXS. On the one hand he needed to break free— from what some friends describe as his mother's deep-seated obsession with him, from his father's fame-soaked starry eyes, from his brother's addictions and the guilt Michael felt so deeply from that incident long ago. He seemed to want to split from his lofty position, the fame, fortune, and all its fragile superficial freedom, throw himself with gusto into his fledgling solo careers in film and music, yet not stray too far from the fraternal love and understanding he enjoyed with INXS. It is also evident he wanted to leave London and set up a new home, either in Sydney or Hollywood.

The antipathy between Geldof and Yates, and therefore, by association, Hutchence, showed no sign of abating. For months prior to his departure from London, Hutchence told his friends that Yates was threatening to commit suicide. 'Michael would tell us all that she would threaten to kill herself and the baby,' Richard Lowenstein said. 'We would tell him there is just no way that woman is going to kill herself. She may end up in a psycho home or something, but she'll never successfully kill herself. But she would tell him that and he would believe it, he would feel insecure and torn apart and he'd say, "Oh my god, she's going to kill herself and the baby, I must be a bad person, I must be terrible." Michael, too, had threatened suicide in his final year. Weeks before his departure from London, Paula Yates was telling friends that Michael was on the edge.

When Michael Hutchence left England for the last time, on Thursday 6 November 1997, he was in a confused and traumatised state. He flew to New York on his way to Australia, relieved to be away from London, away from his lover, away from the relentless public scrutiny. But he couldn't get away from himself. He spent five days in New York and spent time with Martha Troup, one of the very few people with whom he could openly relax. He chilled out. With a New York recharge and in high spirits, he left for Los Angeles with Troup, who had organised several meetings and script readings for him. He auditioned for a small part in the sequel to Quentin Tarantino's movie, *From Dusk Till Dawn*. He met with Michael Douglas about a forthcoming movie: 'He seems to think I could sell some popcorn, but it's just talk at the moment,' Hutchence told me. He also spent two days recording more of his solo album with Danny Saber.

'I remember us talking in my hotel room before he left for the airport,' Martha Troup told me, 'and Michael was telling me how he wanted to leave London. He wanted to move to Sydney. He would have moved anywhere, but he also had the situation where he had to continually think of the three children as well. We talked about the fact that the three Geldof children were going to be in Sydney for Christmas. I told him not to worry about it, that we'd figure it out when I got to Sydney the following week. I think he just wanted peace. He wanted serenity. When he left for the airport he turned to me and said, "I love you baby," and that was it, the last time I saw him.'

On Tuesday afternoon, 18 November 1997, Michael Hutchence boarded a flight to Sydney. On arrival he went to the Ritz Carlton Hotel in Double Bay and checked into room 524 under the guise of Murray River, a pseudonym he often used to avoid attention. He had a day off, and drank coffee with his father the following afternoon. Long-time INXS and Hutchence fan Richard Simpkin approached Michael for a photograph, and Kelland Hutchence took the photo of his son, who had his arm around Simpkin. To my knowledge it was the final photograph taken of Michael Hutchence. Kell had also taken the first photograph of his son, thirty-seven years earlier.

'I had been worried about Michael for a while and I wanted to talk to him about his troubles,' Kell told me. 'But it was a matter of getting to him. Since living with Paula, he was becoming harder to contact via phone. After coffee at the Cosmopolitan, he was tired and he wanted to go to bed early, and on the way back to his hotel he said; "You know what, Dad? I shouldn't be here, I should be in Hollywood." I said, "What do you mean?" And he told me he had just got a part in a movie. But he also said that he'd got to do the tour, that he really wanted to do the tour, that he really wanted the INXS tour to be successful. He then told me they wanted him to do more screen tests in Hollywood. He could see a career in Hollywood. He seemed very happy. I'd been looking around at a place for him to buy in Sydney. He rehearsed with the band that night and returned to the hotel and I went up to see him. It was around 11 pm. Rhett and Mandy were going to see him later that night, but he didn't end up seeing them because he fell asleep.'

From 1.30 pm the following day, Friday 21 November, Michael rehearsed with INXS at the ABC studios in Gore Hill, North Sydney. It would be his final ever performance.

'That afternoon he phoned me as he was leaving the rehearsal studio,' Kell told me. "Daddio, I'm leaving the studio, what are you and Susie up to tonight?" He was in a great mood. We decided to go out for dinner at the Flavour of India in Edgecliff. I phoned the manager and asked for a nice table. I picked him up from the Ritz Carlton Hotel at around 7.30 pm and he was all dressed up. He didn't often get dressed up, but this night he was wearing a navy blue velvet jacket and a white shirt. He looked terrific.'

There was a bit of a shuffle when Michael walked into the restaurant, as there often was when he walked into a room. Michael, his father, and his father's wife Susie sat at a table near the window. According to the manager of the restaurant, Ashley Totani, 'Usually with these kind of people, the big stars, they like to sit with their backs to the room. Michael didn't. He sat looking into the restaurant.

He didn't try to hide away at all. He was very, very open and relaxed and natural.'

The waitress was perky. Michael told her, 'I don't have any cigarettes,' and she said, 'We don't sell them.' He asked her if she would be kind enough to get him some, and she soon returned with two on a plate on a silver tray. He got up and kissed the waitress on the cheek then started talking with his father.

'It was vintage Michael,' Kell recalls. 'He was a great mimic and he was mimicking the Hollywood producers and directors. He talked endlessly about Tiger Lily.' But when Susie went to the bathroom Kell grabbed his son's hand across the table and said, 'Hey, Mike, I know that you are very bubbly tonight and feeling great, but deep down I know that you've got big worries.'

'Of course I have,' Michael responded. 'Paula's going into court today to try and get an order that allows her to bring Peaches and Pixie to Sydney on Sunday, with Tiger Lily. I've already made an agreement with Bob Geldof but he changed everything.' Michael told his father that he'd made arrangements with Geldof to bring the girls to Sydney for a few weeks, and then they were to return to London to spend Christmas with their father. Michael was going to get the kids back again in early January so they could all go up to the Barrier Reef with Colin Diamond, a friend and business associate. This may well have been Michael's interpretation of what was going to happen, but it certainly wasn't Bob Geldof's or the Family Law Court's intention, not by a long shot.

Kell said, 'Look, I know that you have all these problems, do you want to talk about them? I can feel that you have a big, big worry, Mike.' He said, 'No, Dad. I'm just naturally concerned, but I think that we are going to win the court case tomorrow, I think that we will get the permission.' Michael clearly did not know the reality of the custody situation.

Kell then said, 'So that means that Paula should be leaving on Sunday?'

'Yeah,' Michael responded.

'But then you are going on tour,' his father said.

'That doesn't matter,' said Michael.

Susie returned to the table and the trio started laughing, changing the subject to other more jovial matters. Michael did not eat much at the Flavour of India that night. They finished dinner and Kell and Susie took Michael back to the Ritz Carlton Hotel. He waved to his father, a beaming smile on his face, seemingly as happy as Larry. That was the last time Kell saw him.

• • •

The hearing for the court case to which Michael Hutchence was referring had been set in London for the afternoon of Friday 21 November. A turn of events two weeks earlier had set the wheels in motion. On 8 November, six days before Michael had told me that everything was dandy, Paula Yates had made an application to the London Family Law Court to remove her three children by Bob Geldof from Britain to Australia for a period of four and a half months. The departure of the children from Britain, the legal request said, was to be in two parts. The children would leave with Yates to join Michael for three and a half weeks before the end of school term, then return to Bob Geldof in the United Kingdom for a seven-day period over Christmas. The three girls would then return to Australia for a further twelve weeks.

Geldof objected to the first part of the application, feeling that the children would naturally suffer if they did not attend school for the final part of the term. This feeling was supported by the girls' headmaster and by their psychiatrist, Dr Hamish Cameron, who had been recommended to Geldof some months earlier by the Family Court presumably to help them cope with the acrimonious custody battle between their parents. Geldof reluctantly accepted the second part of the request, his reluctance stemming from the fact that he believed there was a strong possibility that Yates was going to work and stay permanently in Australia. Geldof expressed his concerns to her legal adviser, Andrew Young, during a meeting between the three held on 12 November.

The response by Yates and Young to Geldof's concerns was to threaten an application to the court in an attempt to take the children from the country despite Geldof's protestations. This was the beginning of the final, much publicised 'custody case' referred to since Michael's death, the results of which he was supposed to be awaiting on the evening preceding his death, and the full details of which he was obviously not aware. Yates and Young followed through with their threat, lodging an application to the court. When Geldof received the application from Yates on 18 November, his fears were confirmed—the application contained a proposal for a documentary series which revolved around Yates settling in Australia.

Geldof was concerned that this might well be an attempt to remove the children permanently from London. Psychiatrist Hamish Cameron felt that the children should not be removed from school at all, whether before or after Christmas. At the time Geldof received Yates's application she had already purchased air tickets for Australia with departure dates set for 22 November, despite having been advised by the court that a decision by that date would be highly unlikely. Did Michael Hutchence know that Paula had been advised that a decision on the Friday was highly unlikely? Indications are to the contrary, as he told his father on Friday evening that he was awaiting the decision. Given the fact that Yates was aware that the court would probably not make a decision on Friday, it is odd that Hutchence was convinced otherwise. Indeed, it was clear to all who saw him that the custody situation had all but taken over his life.

On that fateful Friday 21 November, the London Family Law Court Official Solicitor, through Counsel, made it clear to Geldof and Yates that it was the court's view that the children should not be removed from school. Paula Yates refused to accept the court's view, and immediately applied for an adjournment. So it was in fact Paula Yates and not Bob Geldof whose action in the court that day caused the delay in the children leaving London for Australia. There was no time that day to hear her application so another hearing date was set for 17 December. One has to ask whether or not Yates told Hutchence that it was she and not Geldof who had caused the delay. When the situation had been presented to the President of the Family Division, Yates was asked to give an undertaking not to remove the children from the jurisdiction. Yates refused to give this undertaking to the court, and as a consequence the judge made an order preventing her from removing the children from the jurisdiction without the court's leave. One also has to ask whether or not Yates informed Michael that she had refused to give this undertaking to the court, thus worsening her case. The court decision to stop Yates taking her children by Geldof to Australia was made between 3 pm and 4 pm London time, 2 am to 3 am Sydney time.

Following the court case, Geldof went to pick up Fifi from the school bus.

According to his statement to the Australian Federal Police, the conversation during the first telephone call was precisely this:

'Bob.'

'Who's that?'

'It's Michael, man. Are you happy?' (This was sarcastic, according to Geldof, and he says he chose to ignore it.)

'I'm okay. Listen, can you call back in ten minutes, I'm on the other line.'

'Ah man, can you call me?'

'I can't, I don't have your number.'

'Hold on, I'll give it to you.'

'I'm in the car and I don't have a pen.'

(Sigh of exasperation) 'Okay, I'll call back.'

Bob Geldof was at this time at London's Embankment tube station. The second telephone call from Hutchence to Geldof came, according to Geldof's statement, at 'about 6.40 pm' and ended at 'around 6.50–6.55 pm' London time, which is about 5.40 am and 5.55 am Sydney time. Geldof states that he had only had about eight conversations with Hutchence during the previous two and three quarter years and that this second conversation with Hutchence was the longest he'd ever had with him. Geldof says he told Hutchence that 'the dad part of me, despite my own personal academic record, felt it better they [the three children] finish the school year. He responded, "I'm their father, little man (a term he often used on the phone to me) when are you going to realise that?" I maintained an even voice and responded, "I can understand your feeling that and I know they want to go on holidays, I'd love to go on holidays, but why didn't they [Yates and Young] just wait three weeks, that's all it was? They could go in the school holidays but not during term time." "But it's only three weeks man." "That's exactly my point, Michael, why can't you just wait?"'

Bob Geldof says in his statement that the children's holidays and the need for cooperation dominated the phone call. Then he states that Michael suddenly said, 'You tried to take my own fucking daughter from me.'

"'What are you talking about?'

"'Don't lie to me, man. I've got all the legal documents here."

"'Michael, I can assure you I have absolutely no interest in taking Tiger or anyone else from you. Don't be ridiculous. She's a cute kid but what would I want to take her for?"

"'I have it all here.'

"'Look, I tell you what. I'll sit down anywhere at any time with you and Andrew Young and we will go through it page by page. Just the three of us, okay?"'

In his statement, Geldof also points to the fact that Paula had attempted suicide some weeks earlier, and that Tiger Lily had been 'stumbling around, falling over' following the attempted suicide. The statement also says that Hutchence was 'genuine and normal' when at one point he said to Geldof, 'Please, man. Please, look I'm asking, I'm begging [for the children to come to Australia]—it's only three weeks.' Geldof describes Hutchence's demeanour as 'heartfelt but not heartbroken'. In response to Michael's begging, Bob responded, 'Please, Michael, please don't ask me to do something that I just can't—I can't do it within myself. I don't think it's right. Besides, it's the court who won't let them go now. Even if I said yes, they won't go. You brought the court action, not me.'

Michael Hutchence was not ranting and raving in a loud voice during his conversation with Geldof. His loud shouting was reported by Gail Coward, a hotel guest staying in the room next to Michael's at the Ritz Carlton. She said she heard yelling at around 5 am on Saturday,—around 6 pm the previous evening London time—some forty minutes *before* Michael called Geldof. While Gail Coward might well have heard Hutchence's raised voice, it clearly was not during his telephone conversation with Geldof, the timing of which the police confirmed from the hotel phone records.

According to Geldof's statement, Michael's tone was of a 'hectoring and threatening manner', but he was not shouting. The report by the coroner presumes that Michael's raised voice and expletives took place during his conversation with Geldof. Did Gail Coward get it wrong about the time of Michael's shouting? Was he shouting at someone else in the room? Was he talking to somebody else on the telephone? Was he on his own?

Well-known Sydney actress Kym Wilson and her then boyfriend Andrew Rayment were with Michael in the hotel piano bar following Michael's return to the hotel after dinner. According to Andrew Rayment, a 25-year-old barrister and son of Sydney QC Brian Rayment, he and Wilson drank at the hotel bar with Hutchence as he 'poured out his heart with regard to his devastation over the battle between Yates and Geldof'. The three moved from the bar to Michael's hotel room sometime after 11 pm and stayed until around 5 am, according to Wilson's statement to the police.

It was at the couple's time of departure that the loud shouting was heard by Gail Coward. Yet Wilson made no mention of such a conversation. The coroner's report states that Ms Coward heard the shouting at 5 am Saturday Sydney time and that the Geldof–Hutchence conversation took place at least thirty minutes later. Why then was he 'satisfied that she was hearing the telephone conversation between the deceased and Geldof'? It was impossible.

Hutchence, Wilson and Rayment had consumed copious amounts of alcohol that night, including vodka, beer, champagne and cocktails. Hutchence had also consumed cocaine and other drugs.

According to the coroner's report, Yates claimed that she phoned Hutchence 'before 5.38 am' Sydney time on the morning he died, to tell him she would not be coming to Sydney with the kids. She says he sounded desperate. But exactly how long before 5.38 am did she actually make the call? An hour? Five minutes? Two hours? In her statement Yates said she'd told Michael that the 'custody matter' had not been finalised and had been adjourned until 17 December, and that she would not be bringing the children out to Australia. Was she the person, then, at whom Hutchence was yelling at around 5 am, as stated in the coroner's report?

Hutchence then made a series of telephone calls, none of which were to Paula. His final four phone calls were to Martha Troup and Michele Bennett. On the first phone call to Martha, left on her office message machine, Michael said, 'Martha, Martha, it's Michael. Martha, I fucking had enough.' That was at 9.38 am Sydney time. He then called Michele Bennett and left a message on her answering machine. According to the police who later heard the tape, he sounded 'drunk'. Hutchence once again tried to contact

Martha, this time at her home. She was not there and he left yet another message: 'Marth, Marth, it's Michael, it's Michael.' This was at 9.53 am Sydney time. His voice sounded deep, he was clearly distressed.

As Martha Troup stepped into a cab on a busy Friday afternoon in New York City on her way to Broadway, she phoned her office and heard the first message from Michael. She had earlier received a phone call from Paula in London saying that she wasn't going to Australia, and Martha assumed that to be the reason why Michael sounded upset on her message machine. She immediately phoned tour manager John Martin in Sydney and said, 'John we've got a problem. I've just got the most awful message from Michael and he sounds terrible. I strongly sense that something is wrong.' Martin told Martha that he'd just received a message under his door saying that Michael wasn't going to rehearsals that day.

According to hotel telephone records, at 9.54 am, one minute after he had made his second call to Martha Troup, Michael Hutchence made a second, desperate call to Michele Bennett. He started to sob and cry, and according to Michele was distressed and very upset. She became concerned for his welfare, so much so that she told him she would immediately come to the hotel. She raced to the Ritz Carlton, took the elevator and went straight to room 524. She knocked loudly at his door, but to no avail. She called him from the foyer on the house phone, also to no avail. Not knowing what else to do, Bennett wrote him a note and left it at the reception desk.

About half an hour later, Martha Troup in New York was beginning to panic. She began relentlessly calling the hotel, trying to get through to Michael's room. Her phone rampage began at 10.40 am Sydney time and she called the hotel continually until noon. She told the receptionist that she was Michael's manager and that she had to get through to his room, it was urgent. Finally, the receptionist told her to call John Martin. 'I called the studio where the band was rehearsing and one of the crew members told me that John was on his way to the Rose Bay police station. I said, Why, why? They didn't know why. By this time I was in my bathroom in my New York apartment and I was shaking.'

About ten minutes later came the chilling phone call from John Martin: 'Martha, Michael's dead.'

• • •

At around ten minutes past noon on Saturday 22 November, police and ambulance men arrived at the Ritz Carlton Hotel and declared Michael Hutchence dead. His naked body had been discovered twenty minutes earlier. Although the coroner's report does not give an estimated time of death, I am told the autopsy report puts this between 9.50 am and 10.30 am. Clearly, though, it could not have been the former because at 9.54 am Hutchence was talking with Michele Bennett on the telephone. There was no suicide note.

The hotel maid discovered the body. She had been trying to get a response from Hutchence's room so that she could clean it. When nobody responded she assumed it was empty. At 11.50 am she placed her key in the door and tried to push it, but something seemed to be wedged behind the door, making it difficult to open. She finally managed to enter the room and found Michael Hutchence hanging from the back of the door. He was strung up by his belt, the buckle broken. The belt was looped around the door hinge, a long, self-closing V-shaped brass mechanism seven feet from the ground. Hutchence was facing the door.

Empty beer bottles, cocktail glasses, and a bottle of champagne were strewn across the room. Prescription drugs were scattered across the floor. The names of the drugs were never made public. Police reports originally stated that the bed had been stripped back and there was evidence of sexual activity having taken place, but police could not say when. A day later they changed their mind and said there was no sign of sexual activity. Unofficial reports of sexual activity continued to surface, however.

Kym Wilson, with whom Hutchence had had a brief affair years earlier, gave a formal statement three days later. It was delivered to New South Wales police by her lawyer.

On 27 November, five days after the discovery of the body, London's *Express* newspaper reported that a senior officer from the Rose Bay police had stated, 'We are not entirely satisfied. There are still a number of questions that need answering.' Following the discovery of the body, the police took away a number of objects from the hotel room.

Although we know that Michael had been indulging in legal and illegal drugs in increasing quantities during his final two years, that in his final year he was smoking or snorting larger quantities of heroin, we don't know if heroin was a factor in his death because, strangely, the coroner said there was no 'need to hold a formal inquest, and the police brief of evidence, including the toxicology reports, would not be made public'. And yet some aspects of the toxicology report—but only some—were made public. One has to ask why a formal inquest was not held. And one has to ask why the police brief of evidence wasn't made public.

Michael Hutchence had first been prescribed anti-depressants in 1995. Hutchence picked up his final prescription from a London chemist on 1 November 1997. There were many possible reasons for his recent depression: the overwhelming pressure placed on him by Yates and Geldof, the fact that Paula was not coming to Australia, the hairline fracture to his skull. Says Richard Lowenstein, 'Michael wasn't monitoring the level of anti-depressants he was taking. He would take them like he took Ecstasy—until you feel better. You just pop them in.'

Anti-depressant drugs have been alleged to cause possible side effects including suicidal tendencies, violent rages, insanity, hallucinations, manic behaviour, nervousness, diarrhoea, insomnia, drowsiness, headaches and a lowered sex drive. In America more than three hundred families have so far attempted to sue one anti-depressant manufacturer, claiming that the drug triggered suicide, murder and self-mutilation. In Britain, more than sixty families have taken up civil cases against manufacturers.

Professor John Hilton of the New South Wales Institute of Forensic Medicine believes that a combination of anti-depressants and cocaine and alcohol would have unknown effects on a person's state of mind. 'The effects would be unpredictable—you have stimulants, you have depressants. Put alcohol with any other psychoactive drug and you have a major problem,' Hilton says. Lian Lunson told me, 'I think Michael just could not get out of the situation he was in. I don't think there was any way he could have got out of it. I think, particularly, that he was taking anti-depressants and taking all those drugs was unreal. That's not good for anybody. It has to be a lethal combination.'

Michael's friends are split evenly down the middle when

it comes to whether he committed suicide or died accidentally while engaging in auto-erotic asphyxia. According to the coroner's report, Michael was alone when he died. 'I was quite surprised he died alone,' says Rhett. 'I've never known Michael to be alone.' His mother, according to London's *Q* magazine, said that Michael had been involved with a group of sado-masochists months before his death. It has been suggested by several people that he was involved, during INXS's US tour late in 1997, with two Californian women who were into experimental sex, including auto-erotica, and who also I am told, indulged in heroin.

'I know Michael was into bondage and all that stuff, you know, he was into all of that,' Rhett said. 'After years and years of having sex just the normal way, of course he starts to look for new sensations. He was seeing other girls while he was going out with Paula and he was into bondage and all that. I don't think that's what happened that night, but I have no doubt he had tried auto-erotic asphyxia.' Paula's boasts of trying 'illegal sex' with Michael when she first met him now have an ominous ring about them. Michael's US lawyer Bill Leibowitz just doesn't believe it was suicide. 'I don't think Michael would have given Geldof the satisfaction of suicide. He loved Paula, and the little baby meant more to him than anything in the world. I don't think he would have deliberately left the baby alone. I also think that if he killed himself he would have at least left a note for his baby. I don't think he would have committed suicide. There could have been some psychotic moment where he crashed from any of the drugs he was on, became irrational and there could have been something sexual, but I am sure it wasn't suicide.'

Auto-erotic asphyxia increases sexual excitement by

restricting oxygen to the brain. In Britain the practice claims around a hundred and fifty lives per year. It is not only a common practice, but one that women in particular find orgasmically enhancing. It is particularly common with many high-class, new-wave S&M hookers, and of course, their clients. In 1994 in London, Tory MP Stephen Milligan was found hanging dead from electrical flex with an amyl-soaked orange in his mouth, a device used to keep the air flow going. David Morgan, clinical psychologist at the Tavistock and Portman Clinic in London, is an expert on the phenomenon. 'Auto-asphyxia is self-suffocation,' he says. 'It's a way of sexualising psychological pain, by turning feelings of loneliness and isolation into something pleasurable. It's like a drug, so the need to increase the pain gets greater. There are false fantasies about death—the closer the person is to death, the more exciting it becomes, as they feel they have power over it. Surviving makes them feel powerful, but often this eventually ends in death. Those for whom extravagant sex and brilliant drugs have become a dull commonplace are particularly susceptible to the lure of a dangerous kink. This connection between pain and pleasure is very common in the pop world, especially with performers. I suppose it's a way of making the loneliness exciting.'

'The rumours about this auto-erotic stuff have absolutely no merit,' says Lian Lunson. 'I cannot understand how anybody could come to this conclusion. Even if there were some big secrets in the autopsy report that a select few know about, those secrets obviously did not catch the attention of the coroner. The police at the time said there was absolutely nothing to indicate anything like that.

'Michael was in a desperate state, he'd left messages indicating this. By the time of his last conversation with

Michele, he was in a very deep state of despair. Tell me what person, broken and sobbing, suddenly decides to rig some sort of device and sexually relieve themselves? It's complete madness. Michele knew the state of mind he was in, she did her best to explain this to people, he was as far away from a sexual mood as was humanly possible. I believe she knew him well enough to be certain of that. Michael was heading down a dark road for some time, and the fact that none of us averted this damages us all. Choosing [to believe] that he died via some sexual mistake is of no justice to anybody, least of all the little girl he left behind.

'The great thing about Michael and Michele was that they had their own things to work out, and they had remained such good friends. He really did love her very, very much. When things got dark for him in his last relationship, I think that deep inside himself, somewhere, he was going to head back to her, that he would be safe with her, that it was a safe place to be, that it would be okay.'

When someone commits suicide, close friends often blame themselves, or feel angry with the person for causing so much pain. Sometimes people become angry with themselves for not being there when the person needed them, not being there to help them get through. This is exactly how many of Michael's friends felt, including Martha Troup. 'I blame myself for not being there. I was always there for him. It was like something out of a bad movie,' she told me. His very good friend Bono is still perplexed by the suicide angle. 'I had a conversation with him about suicide and he and I both agreed that it was just a dumb thing to do, and selfish, and in a rock'n'roll context it had a kind of ugly vanity. That it was part of perpetuating the myth of rock'n'roll which we both despised. But maybe he was secretly attracted to it, I don't know. We were talking about Kurt Cobain's death, and we both thought what a loss that was. But we both agreed about how naff it was, that it was so much part of the rock'n'roll handbook, you know, it was rule number 99—when you get to a certain level, to improve record sales, please take your life. We laughed about it. That's why it was a shock to me. Maybe we always talked about it because it was in his head, I don't know. I heard he'd had a few conversations with other people about suicide in his final twelve months, and I was hoping it wasn't true.'

Rhett Hutchence thinks it strange that his brother would have committed suicide. 'A couple of years ago, Michael rented a house in Palm Beach for Paula, Mandy and I to spend Christmas together, and I was telling Michael how a mutual friend of ours and her family had been having Christmas the year before and her uncle had gone into the bedroom in between the main meal and the dessert and hung himself. I was telling Michael how I was feeling for my friend, Rebecca, because of what had happened the year before and how hard it would be on her. When I told Michael, his first words were, "Selfish bastard". So it was odd that he would then go and do it himself.'

His friend Greg Perano says it was too late to turn back. 'At the end of the day, there was not a lot of people he could turn to for emotional support. He just said, fuck it. In that brief period of time, maybe just thirty seconds, he just said I don't care anymore. I've been there and you've probably been there, where you just think, fuck this is an easy way out, and everyone would say it was an easy way out, but he had a lot to die for.

'People say to me, oh no, Michael would have taken a

heroin overdose, but it's not a 100 per cent guarantee that you'll die from a heroin overdose. Neither are a lot of methods of suicide. You take pills and it's a drama. But at some point, no matter what method you choose, there's just no turning back. He was a romantic and he went out that way. In many ways Michael was a tragic figure. To everyone else he had these flash cars, and the house in the south of France, money, but he was a tragic figure, it all meant nothing in the end. He was completely trapped. People think you can buy your freedom, but you just can't. Michael was looking for an answer as we all do. Michael was always quite a spiritual character but he always had a soulful edge to him, too, and that's what made him who he was.'

Perhaps Michael's old Max Q mate Ollie Olsen says it most succinctly: 'In terms of the speculation about whether or not Michael did or didn't kill himself, we all live on a razor's edge. The potential for us to slip up in life is always there—it only takes a split second to slip and make the wrong choice. If you survive, it's an accident; if you don't survive, it's suicide. It's a grey area, I don't know what happened and nobody ever will. As far as I'm concerned, he's not here anymore and that's it. I'll see him again one day, maybe.

'In the end, Michael won't be remembered for the way he died, but for his music,' adds Olsen. 'Drugs, suicides, and all that, are part of the mythology of rock'n'roll, this whole live fast, die young nonsense. In a way it is very much about what the music industry is about too, because in reality a real composer probably doesn't hit their stride until they are sixty or seventy. They put their best work in over a lifetime. So it is an indictment of rock music that they have this sort of obsession with dying young. The life of an artist is a long one. For me, in a lot of ways, that's what made me feel really sad about Michael. He could have been sitting around doing amazing paintings or whatever, he could do anything. Most of us don't have those opportunities, we're so busy just surviving. His number came up, and that's that.'

• • •

Immediately following news of Michael's death, Paula Yates made plans to go to Australia. When she boarded a plane for Sydney on the evening of Saturday 22 November, she was weeping hysterically. On board she reportedly wandered up and down with Tiger Lily in her arms. 'What do I tell this little girl? How do I tell her that her daddy isn't here? That her daddy has committed suicide?' She sobbed so uncontrollably that the cabin crew had to take her to the rear of the plane to stop her disturbing other passengers. As the flight took off from Heathrow Airport, Michael's bunch of red roses, sent from Sydney on Friday afternoon, arrived at his and Paula's home. It read, 'To all my beautiful girls, all my love, Michael.' During the 22-hour flight, Paula was walking up and down the aisle blaming Geldof for Michael's death. 'They call him Saint Bob but that's a joke,' she told reporters who had boarded the flight for Australia. 'Michael obviously flipped out. He was worn down by three years of torture.' Indeed he was worn down by three years of torture, but it's contestable that Bob Geldof should be held solely responsible, if at all. When the plane landed in Bangkok for a brief stopover, Paula, under sedation, said she was feeling unwell. She is reported to have thrown a glass of champagne over a member of the airline staff. Her lawyer, Andrew Young, said of the incident, 'Paula has been on sedatives and was feeling unwell in the VIP lounge.' The plane arrived in Sydney on the morning of Monday 24 November and Paula was immediately taken to the morgue to view Michael's body, before a postmortem was done. The day before, Patricia, Kell and both their respective spouses, along with Rhett and his partner Mandy Nolan, had gone to the morgue.

Richard Lowenstein saw the body with Bono's wife and Lian Lunson. 'Me, Ali [Bono's wife] and Lian [Lunson] went to the funeral home. I got a little sprig of those little white flowers, I think they're baby blossoms, and tied it together with a ribbon. I touched Michael's forehead when I saw him. He seemed so cold and stiff. I wrote him a note and tucked it under his suit coat. I wrote, *"Mikeee..!! Love Rickybaby"*. Whenever he'd call me or when we would meet up, his opening line would always be, *"Rickybaby!!!"* and I'd always respond *"Mikeee..!"*'

Following their son's death, Patricia and Kell, united for the first time in more than two decades, issued a statement: 'We are extremely shocked and deeply saddened by the death. Michael was an inspiring talent who touched many people around the world with his work, and will be greatly missed. To us and everyone close to him, he was a vibrant human being with an immense heart full of love.'

Asked by the media for his thoughts, Bob Geldof said, 'I extend my sincere condolences and sympathy to Paula, daughter Tiger, Michael's mother and father and all his family.' As the media frenzy stepped up a notch during the following week, Geldof was again asked for his personal thoughts on it all. With diplomacy he responded, 'It is better for me if I don't say anything at all. I can live with the whole situation a lot better with myself. As for my thoughts for Paula, those things are private and that is the way to deal with it. Other people are saying things and maybe one day I will. But now is not the right time.'

As soon as word was out on Michael's death, the Ritz Carlton Hotel was besieged by fans. Hundreds of people congregated to share their grief and sadness, leaving a growing shrine of flowers, letters and candles in Michael's memory. Television and radio stations around the globe began tribute programmes, playing INXS concerts, interviews, videos and highlights of Michael's career. Tribute sites sprang up on the Internet. Entertainers worldwide began their homage. Shocked, Kylie Minogue simply stated, 'I can't believe it.' Former INXS manager Chris Murphy sobbed. He issued a statement: 'Michael Hutchence and INXS made an immense impact on me and my family's life. A piece of our hearts was sliced away yesterday on the news of Michael's death.' Australia's Prime Minister, John Howard, threw in his two bob's worth: 'It takes from the Australian and world rock scene one of our most gifted and talented performers, and it's a very tragic event.' Deputy Prime Minister Tim Fischer kept repeating, 'I just don't believe it!'

Bono was first told of his friend's death during a scheduled flight. 'We were flying between shows and someone called and told me. I still haven't figured out quite how I feel about it. I don't know whether I'm angry or guilty. You always think if it's a mate that there was something you could have done. I still find it hard to figure it all out, because I had a conversation with him not that long ago where we talked about something like this, and we both agreed how dumb and selfish it would be, and Hutch was not at all selfish. He was a nice guy to be around. He was very light, whereas I don't think I'm the easiest person to be around, so we balanced each other out. But I hadn't seen him for a while, because we were both off doing our thing. I'm finding the whole thing very hard to understand.

'There's a thing that maybe people don't realise about the process of having yourself enlarged or blown up by success and the concept of being a star,' Bono then told me, 'which is the shrinking of a sense of yourself. It's like your ego is blown up but it implodes, it goes in reverse. I know there is this reversal that happens. Enlarged on one level and diminished on another level. Michael felt sometimes he was ephemeral, and he shouldn't have because he wasn't. He had oxygen—that's one of the reasons why we all loved him so much. But I felt for a while that he might have been scratching away at the surface, looking for an authenticity, which of course is completely bogus. And suicide is really the final act. It's one of the things that really annoys me about rock'n'roll. It's almost like proof that you really were living on the edge, that you really didn't give a fuck, and that you really were the rock star that people really didn't think you were. I don't believe that was in Michael's head when he died, but that notion is in rock'n'roll. There's a constant belief by the media that you've been bought off, you're not the real thing. I heard people say, and Michael say, and it really annoyed me afterwards, this thing about Michael that he didn't give a fuck, you know, that he just went out there and was prepared to jump off the edge because that's the kind of guy he was. Well, fuck that, that's what I say, and I think he was much smarter than that. You have to understand about the mythology of rock'n'roll to really appreciate what I am saying.'

Bono delivered an emotional speech at U2's San

Antonio concert on the Sunday night following Hutchence's death: 'Michael was not only a great singer, but a great friend of ours.' The band then launched into a very stripped down version of 'I Still Haven't Found What I'm Looking For'. Two songs later, during 'Staring At The Sun', a picture of Michael, and nothing else, was shown on a huge video screen. At the conclusion of the set the band played 'Wake Up Dead Man', and before the house lights came on 'Never Tear Us Apart' came over the PA system.

Duran Duran also paid tribute by dedicating their entire show in Cleveland on Saturday 22 November to Michael. At one point, lead singer Simon Le Bon reportedly broke down on stage and started crying, saying that Michael was his 'best friend' in the music industry. He talked about what a beautiful and caring person Michael was, and urged the crowd not to forget Paula and their baby Tiger. The band performed a heartbreaking rendition of 'Save A Prayer' for Michael. Interestingly, one of the tracks on Duran Duran's new album *Medazzaland* is entitled 'Michael, You've Got A Lot To Answer For' and was written specifically for Hutchence as a symbol of their friendship.

Others in the music world also responded. Elton John reportedly spoke of Michael's death at his concert on the Saturday night. When asked for his thoughts Boy George commented, 'If I had to pick one star who was destined for an early death, I would never have chosen Hutchence, despite his obvious love of the high life, the relentless drug rumours and the early morning police raid at Paula's pad. I have been trying to make sense of it ever since I heard the shocking news. I'm honestly very distressed. I had known Michael casually for several years. He was friendly and sociable and I liked him very much. He was one of those people you meet and feel that you've known forever. The last time I saw him was at a Versace fashion dinner. He came and sat at our table and introduced himself to the guests. My young friend Benny, who lives and works in the real world, laughed and said, "I think we all know who you are!" Hutchence played the big pop star on stage and in the media, but one-to-one he was a very sweet, normal man. How sad that someone so young, handsome and talented has died in this way.'

Meanwhile, back in the United States four days later, REM singer Michael Stipe, according to reports on the Internet, hired the Mumbo Jumbo Restaurant in Atlanta, Georgia, invited his U2 pals and threw a thanksgiving Irish wake for the INXS frontman. Ray Manzarek, keyboard player for The Doors, commented on Michael's death the following week during an interview with the *Toronto Sun*. When asked which singers today came close to possessing the same wild, sexy stage presence of late Doors singer Jim Morrison, Manzarek responded, 'You know what? Michael Hutchence. Poor, late Michael Hutchence. I liked him very much. I thought he was very good and I certainly liked the music that band made; INXS was a very good band. What a tragedy. He was going to get married and he was going on a tour and everything. Did you hear anything about anti-depressants? Some people have said that anti-depressants are, for some people, a suicide drug.'

Smashing Pumpkins' lead singer Billy Corgan said on the Internet, 'Listen, I knew Michael and he would be the last person you would think would commit suicide. He seemed to enjoy life as much as anybody. I'm not saying his death is related to drugs, I'm saying you can't keep people from themselves. What people feel inside is their own business. It's not to say it's right or wrong, it's just that there has to be more support for helping people who need help, as opposed to just saying naughty, naughty boy, you know? I hate what happened to Michael, and that suddenly people have an opinion about how he should've lived his life, or what he should've done. Where were those people when he really needed them? I love how certain magazines make his death a completely unimportant event, because "his band's music wasn't important enough". Well, his band's music was important to a lot of people, and I hate the way our society and our value of someone is based on the popularity of their band, or whether or not they're singing about something crucially important at that particular moment. At least Michael and the other guys in INXS had the balls to go out and do something and say something, stand for something. That to me deserves a lot more credit than somebody who sits at home and throws the beer can at the TV.'

It didn't take long before everybody and his dog suddenly had become Michael's best friend. Every day for weeks there were stories about his final hours, his final days, the rumours thicker than a Thames River fog. To set the record straight Kym Wilson sold her story to Australian magazine *Woman's Day* for a reported $150 000, money that was going to be placed in a trust fund for Tiger Lily. In London, Paula Yates sold her exclusive story to the celeb-heavy *Hello* magazine for a reported £500 000. According to reports, she needed the money to cover an expected legal wrangle over Hutchence's estate, believed to be worth more than $20 million. She said she was deeply wounded by reports that her lover had had sex with Kym Wilson the night he died. Wilson herself has emphatically denied this.

Fifteen months after Michael's death the stories still hadn't stopped. There was now more mystery than ever before. His estate was in limbo and its executor leading a clandestine life. Paula Yates was still selling stories. The future of Heavenly Hiraani Tiger Lily was looking uncertain, this tiny little girl whose father had died, whose mother was not well, and who was worth millions.

There are many questions about Michael Hutchence's death and the coroner's report that have remained unanswered. (See Appendix for a full transcript of the coroner's report.) Why wasn't the autopsy report made public? Michael had a CD of some of his new solo productions when he checked into his hotel room. Why weren't they in his room the next morning? How much experience did the Rose Bay police have in dealing with death by suicide? How much experience did they have in dealing with autoerotic asphyxia?

Why does the coroner's report state that Belinda Brewin confirms the substance of the conversation between Hutchence and Geldof, when she did not witness the conversation? In his statement, Geldof says that he told Brewin of his phone conversation with Hutchence when he saw Brewin the next morning. Brewin therefore had only second-hand knowledge and was not in a position to confirm anything. It seems that the investigation into Michael's death left too many questions unanswered. The coroner's report appears contradictory. Whether Michael's death was suicide or misadventure, or yet another method of death, we will never really know.

In that final interview I did with Michael, one week

before his death, he told me, 'I've led a much more decadent life than I've let on for a long while.' When I asked him how he was coping with the media scrutiny of his relationship with Paula, he responded, 'Love conquers all'. Sadly, sometimes, it does not.

> Here we lie
> Looking up to
> Empty sky
> And the promises we find
>
> 'The Gift'
> *Full Moon, Dirty Hearts* 1993
> MICHAEL HUTCHENCE AND JON FARRISS

eleven

The funeral, the eulogy, the wake

> Have we lost direction
> Washed our hands of blood
> I'm in need of sensation
> Is there more to this love
> Saw a mother screaming
> She had lost control
> Of what she once believed in
> And she was not alone
> Oh yeah
> If you could face the pain
> And I could do the same
> It would be clear tomorrow
> But will it start
> But will it start again
> I am searching
> I am not alone
> I am searching
> Please show me some (love)
>
> 'Searching'
> *Elegantly Wasted* 1997
> MICHAEL HUTCHENCE AND
> ANDREW FARRISS

Twenty-four hours after his son's death, Kell Hutchence was in a state of shock and disbelief. 'It seemed to me like some great nightmare that I would awaken from with tremendous relief,' Kelland told me four months later, still shaken but composed. 'The bad dream would go away and life would resume as usual.' On Sunday 23 November, a day after Michael's death, Patricia arrived in Sydney with her fifth husband, Ross Glassop, and booked into the Sir Stamford Hotel in Double Bay, in the street adjacent to where Michael had died.

At 3 pm the Glassops arrived at the home of Kell and his wife Susie. There were emotional outbursts and deep sorrow as the foursome consoled each other, putting aside past differences. All of them were in shock, Kell and Patricia not knowing how to begin to think about explaining the loss of their beloved son. 'I looked at Pat and my heart went out to her at that moment, the light of her life had been extinguished and she was bewildered in her loss,' Kelland told me.

Patricia, Susie, Ross and Kell sat around the lounge room drinking wine and talking through their grief. They discussed the possibility of finding an agent to handle the media, as Michael's death was already invoking a barrage of English and Australian interest. Perhaps naively, Kell suggested they look through the Yellow Pages of the telephone directory and then interview potential agents. A lot of wine was consumed during that afternoon in Kell's Bellevue Hill apartment, and following the departure of Pat and Ross, Kell and Susie fell into a deep sleep.

At about 11 pm, Kell awoke and went for a drink of water, and as he stumbled towards the kitchen he saw a note under the front door. It was from Ross Glassop, who had come back to the house with entrepreneur Harry M. Miller but been unable to rouse anyone. Ross had scribbled on his note that Kell should phone Miller to discuss dealing with the media. About half an hour later, Kell called Miller. It turned out that Patricia had telephoned Miller immediately after leaving Kell and Susie's apartment. Arrangements were made to meet at 9 am the next morning in the Glassops' hotel suite. Michael's half-sister Tina was also to be present, making six people at the meeting. Tina had just arrived from her home in Los Angeles, accompanied by her two sons, Erin and Brent. It was her fifty-first birthday.

Miller was a little late for the meeting, and on arrival immediately placed some paperwork on the desk for Kell to sign. Kell read the documents but felt it was all too quick. Miller then explained what he was going to do for the Hutchence family, mentioning a lawyer friend of his who could help with the inquest. (The report would not be released until two and a half months later, on 6 February 1998.)

'I became uneasy about Miller, and wasn't too sure about his approach,' Kell told me. Pat, Tina and Ross all seemed in agreement with Miller's plans. 'Miller said that unless Pat and I were in agreement he would rather not handle our affairs,' Kell added. Miller then stood up and walked out of the room, saying that if he, Kell, changed his mind he would be happy to return. Pat, Ross and Tina were upset with Kell and said they thought Miller was the man to handle the funeral and the media. Kell says he was too grief-ridden to argue. He relented and telephoned Miller to inform him that he was in agreement with the others. Miller returned to the hotel suite fifteen minutes later.

Kell had already chosen Walter Carter Funerals to handle the funeral, which was to be held at St Andrews Cathedral in the heart of Sydney. With typical shrewdness, Harry M. Miller proposed that he handle the whole funeral for free, that he arrange for one television station to film it and allow other stations to broadcast a feed from it. With firm stipulations from Kell that there was to be no frontal TV coverage and no still cameras inside the cathedral, Pat and he signed an agreement with Miller, giving him the television rights and still-camera rights. The agreement related only to 27 November, the date of the funeral. Another meeting was set for the following morning to arrange the finer details.

Meanwhile, in another suite in the same hotel, Rhett Hutchence, together with members of INXS, Gary Grant, Michael's personal security guard Tony Woodall, and other close friends, were organising the wake and other details, such as which songs were to be played in the cathedral, security and cars. All the people involved were experienced in the finer points of staging events on a grand scale, and were, in many ways, much closer to Michael's character than those at the Miller meeting. When they learnt of the deal Miller had brokered for television coverage of the funeral, they were strongly opposed to it, a view that was later echoed by most who knew Michael well. There were very strong negative feelings about the involvement of Harry M. Miller at all. He had been a successful but controversial Australian entrepreneur for three decades. Amidst controversy, the filming and media deal stayed in place.

The Dean of Sydney, the Very Reverend Boak Jobbins, was to conduct the funeral service in Sydney's beautiful

St Andrew's Cathedral on 27 November. The flowers for the coffin would be Michael's favourites, irises with tiger lilies; the coffin bearers would be the band members plus Rhett. Kell had phoned television personality Richard Wilkins and asked him to give the eulogy and Wilkins had agreed reluctantly. 'I didn't understand the reluctance as I thought he was very much admired by Michael and I always considered him about the best in the business in Australia,' Kell told me.

While his heart had been in the right place, what Kell didn't realise was that Wilkins had not been 'admired' by Michael. 'Michael used to scrub his name off the backstage list, he wasn't a great admirer of Wilkins at all,' insisted one of Michael's closest friends who asked for anonymity. 'We were all gobsmacked,' the friend told me, referring to the reaction from Michael's friends to Wilkins reading the eulogy.

'I was happy with Richard Wilkins reading the funeral eulogy. He is a good guy, and he always batted for us,' says INXS founder Tim Farriss.

Andrew Farriss, Rhett and Tina were to give addresses, and Nick Cave offered to do his song 'Into My Arms', but not without conditions. At 3 am on the night before the funeral, he was wandering around the hotel trying to find the right person to ensure that his performance would not be part of what was perceived as the Miller charade. Cave was adamant that his performance not be recorded, that there be no cameras whatsoever anywhere in sight. He eventually had legal documents drawn up to that effect. His actions brought respect and reverence from Michael's closest friends.

'Paula thought it was a good idea that I sing it,' Cave

would be later quoted as saying. 'I was very good friends with Michael—someone with whom the last thing I'd talk about was music, but I think he liked that song a lot. It was very difficult to play that song at the funeral . . . It's one of the most difficult things I've ever had to do. It was very . . . difficult . . . but I managed to get through it without fucking up, and I'm glad I did it.'

In May 1998 Cave told me, 'Our relationship had nothing to do with music. We got on really well, and hit it off from the start. We had some really good times together and that's about it, really. Our relationship was about having some good times together.'

The horde of media outside the Sir Stamford Hotel, the Quay West Hotel—where Paula and Tiger Lily were staying—and Kell and Susie's Bellevue Hill apartment was relentless. Scores of reporters, photographers and outside-broadcast vans from television stations littered the footpaths, roads, anywhere there was space for them to squeeze into. They stayed firmly entrenched in their chosen vantage points, twenty-four hours a day, until the day of the funeral. They then surrounded St Andrews Cathedral and did the same.

Following Paula's arrival in Australia, Kelland went to visit her and his granddaughter at their hotel. 'I held Tiger Lily and felt so deeply,' he said. 'I felt so sad for her. This tiny little baby didn't know that her daddy was dead. Such irony. She just smiled and gurgled.' Kell then met Paula's closest friend and confidante Belinda Brewin for the first time, along with Andrew Young, who was Brewin's partner as well as legal adviser to Paula. 'I told Paula about the funeral arrangements,' Kell remembers, 'and that I didn't want her to feel out of it all. "I'll leave it all to you," I remember her saying. "Just do what you think is best."'

Colin Diamond, then executor of Michael's estate, had arrived in Sydney, two days after the death, flying in from Indonesia, but he wasn't staying at the hotel he said he would be staying in. He hadn't contacted any of Michael's family since arriving. Kell eventually tracked him down at the Sheraton Hotel through Diamond's brother and business partner, Stephen. He wasn't in the room Kell was told he was in, but he found him in the end. Kell says, 'I thought he was pretty cool for someone who had just lost his best mate, as he often called Michael. But I could have been mistaken.'

Diamond then proceeded to tell Kell that he could not make it to the funeral. This was Tuesday 25 November. 'That really rocked me, and I let him know that I was really surprised he couldn't make it to his best mate's funeral that was taking place in less than forty-eight hours. I could imagine he had a lot of legal and accounting matters that would need to be attended to, but surely Mike's funeral was the top priority as a mark of respect.' Diamond didn't seem to think so, because he told Kell that the following day, the day before the funeral, he was leaving for Surfers Paradise and would be staying on the Isle of Capri in the house that Michael had told his father he half owned with Diamond. Yet in an interview with the Australian magazine *AXS* in July 1998, Colin Diamond, in answer to the question why he hadn't attended Michael's funeral, said that he hadn't been able to go because Tiger Lily 'had a seizure the night before'. He said he spent the whole night before the funeral in 'an emergency ward having Tiger looked at. We had no idea what was wrong,'

Diamond said. 'She had a zillion tests and these results don't come in instantly. The next morning, the day of the funeral, I flew to Queensland to speak to a paediatrician and the doctor who looked after Tiger previously in Australia to see what additional treatment, if any, might be necessary. Paula and I wanted a second opinion. I was more concerned with looking after the living.' Diamond must have got his second opinion without Tiger being present, because Tiger Lily was at the funeral and that was being held in Sydney, not the Isle of Capri.

Two days prior to the funeral, Kell, Susie, Patricia, Ross, Tina, and Kell's sister Croy went to the cathedral to meet the Very Reverend Boak Jobbins. They were given a brief background on the man who would conduct the funeral service, and a schedule of how events would unfold at the ceremony. When mention was made of how Paula and Tiger Lily would arrive at the funeral, I am told Patricia suddenly stood up and stormed out of the room, with Ross and Tina not far behind her. As she left she was heard to yell at somebody, telling them she would not sit and hear that woman's name mentioned. Patricia sat out in the foyer and continued yelling about 'that rotten woman Paula' and that she would not rejoin the meeting if Paula's name was mentioned. Eventually she, Ross and Tina rejoined the meeting and it got under way again, with the Dean no doubt feeling uncomfortable.

On Tuesday 25 November the Glassops and the Hutchences went to the Glebe morgue to see Michael before he was dressed for the funeral. 'It was the worst day of my life,' Kell remembers. He and Susie and Patricia and Ross were picked up by the Rose Bay police, driven to the morgue and led into the waiting area. Susie preferred to stay

The front entrance of the Ritz Carlton Hotel, Sydney
(Peter Carrette, Icon Images)

Paula's friend and confidante Belinda Brewin arriving at the funeral with Paula and Tiger Lily
(PETER CARRETTE, ICON IMAGES)

Actress Kym Wilson at the funeral
(PETER CARRETTE, ICON IMAGES)

A dignified Kylie Minogue arrives at the funeral (PETER CARRETTE, ICON IMAGES)

Left to right: Jon Farriss, Kirk Pengilly, Tim Farriss, Andrew Farriss. Blue irises and a single yellow tiger lily adorn the casket
(PETER CARRETTE, ICON IMAGES)

outside, the other three entered the room where they could view the body. 'Our darling son was on this table in a half-type coffin and we saw his beautiful face with a slight smile, his eyes closed forever. Pat leaned over and kissed him and started sobbing and shaking her head, as I did, and then I leaned over him and said, "Good-bye, my sweet prince, my beloved son. I will miss you more than I can bear," and then I kissed him gently on his lips, oh those so-cold lips, like a signature of death, and I gazed down at him, tears falling over his body. I was still unable to fully grasp that he was there, a lifeless son—never to grace a world stage again, never to compose another song, never to wave to his adoring fans again, never to see his darling daughter Tiger Lily again, nor to hold his beloved Paula, or play with Pixie and Peaches and Fifi again. I was reluctant to leave the room and just stood there looking down at him and thinking so much about this unfolding tragedy and what it meant to lose a son, your own flesh and blood.'

The funeral was set for 2.30 pm. Close friends and relatives were to meet in the first-floor reception area of the Sir Stamford Hotel at 12.30, and the cars were to leave for the funeral at 1.30. Just before departing in a stretch limo, Ross Glassop approached Kelland and told him that the two parents and their spouses were to sit in the front pew to the right; Ross was to enter first, Pat second, then Kell, followed by Susie. The four were to be the last to enter the church.

Along George Street fans were gathered, and members of the media were trying to grab vantage points. The cars turned into the Bathurst Street entrance to the cathedral, pulled up outside, and the foursome entered the cathedral to the strains of Michael singing 'By My Side'.

Michael's friends, and Australian and international music-industry people had already arrived: Michele Bennett, Lian Lunson, Kylie Minogue, Helena Christensen, Tom Jones, Jason Donovan, the five remaining members of INXS, Rhett, Tina, Greg Perano, Martha Troup, Bill Leibowitz, Nick Cave, Dave Edwards, Gary Grant, Chris Murphy, Jimmy and Jane Barnes, Andy Gill—co-writer of many songs on Michael's solo album, among them. Paula was dressed in a black floral-print dress, five-inch stiletto heels and dark batwing glasses. Visibly distressed, sobbing inconsolably, she cradled Tiger Lily, who wore a red-flowered summer dress. One of the last people to arrive was 28-year-old Kym Wilson, by all accounts the last person to have seen Hutchence alive. She'd reportedly been in hiding since giving a statement to police via her lawyer. Following the service she was whisked away by two bodyguards, and later reappeared at the cremation.

The funeral was being broadcast live across Australia. Hundreds of tearful fans, many of them young teenage girls wearing INXS T-shirts, had camped and queued overnight to get a bird's-eye view. Some clutched single white roses. Local radio stations were warning mourners to drink plenty of water in the soaring temperatures, and to wear sun cream and hats.

As the Glassops and Hutchences reached the front row of the cathedral, Ross suddenly stopped. Kell whispered to him to enter the right side, just as Glassop had explained earlier. Glassop was indicating that the four of them would have to sit in the left front pew, not the right. According to a couple of people in the pew behind, Pat was agitated, saying that it wasn't the pew they should be sitting in. As they sat down Paula rose from her seat and walked across to Kelland, lowered Tiger Lily's face so he could kiss her, then said hello and offered her own cheek to be kissed. Paula then moved across and lowered Tiger Lily's cheek to Patricia, who kissed her granddaughter but not Paula.

Taking pride of place in front of one of the altars was a magnificent white floral arrangement in the form of a Claddagh, the Irish symbol of loyalty and friendship. It had been sent by Bono and his wife Ali. The Very Reverend Boak Jobbins urged people to 'take out the memories and share them with each other. Michael, the loyal son and brother who always kept in touch. Michael, the devoted parent who thrilled at being a father. Michael, to those who knew him closely, the gentle and generous one.' A couple of selections from the choir followed, and then Nick Cave sang his moving song 'Into My Arms'.

Just as Cave began to sing, a wild-eyed intruder pushed past the mourners and dashed to a balcony at the back of the cathedral, screeching, 'This is how he did it, Paula, this is how he died.' The man had tied a black cord to a leather dog-collar around his neck. He quickly wound the other end around the balcony before some mourners grabbed him and dragged him to safety. Police ran down the aisle and up to the balcony to bundle away the man, who was kicking and screaming incoherently. 'There were so many weird-looking people in there that he didn't look out of place,' a security guard hired to hold back the ten-deep crowd said later.

The service continued in front of the shocked mourners. Andrew Farriss appealed from the pulpit, 'We don't want the band's fans to react in any way that would hurt themselves. Michael would not have wanted that.' The eulogy was given by Richard Wilkins, then Andrew Farriss paid tribute. 'He loved Australia, he loved his friends, he loved his family. He was a caring father and a passionate family man.' Choking back tears, Rhett Hutchence struggled through his tribute. 'My heart goes out to Paula, to the beautiful Tiger Lily, to his friends and other people who have known Michael and lost a tremendous friend.' Rhett then recalled an early lyric book of Michael's. Inside the book were ten things the rock singer wanted to achieve in life and the first was world domination.

The service was an hour long, attended by 380 friends and family, 500 public mourners, and thousands more lining the streets outside, watching the service on huge video screens. As the ceremony reached its conclusion, the INXS song 'Never Tear Us Apart' echoed around the church, Michael's voice reaching beyond the cathedral, wavering above the outside throng. The coffin was smothered in blue irises, and in the middle was a single yellow tiger lily. Attached to the flower was a note: 'Good-bye, Daddy. I love you. Rest in Peace.' As the coffin was carried outside by the bearers into the sweltering, steamy day, a clap of thunder shook the building, the sky opened up and the rain fell in torrents.

Jason Donovan reckons the funeral was the most moving experience of his life. 'He had six guys, five who he'd been with for twenty years, the sixth he'd been with all his life, and at that funeral service they carried their mate out of the cathedral. I mean, that to me was the most poignant moment of my life. Where you carry your mate on your shoulder and that's the fucking deal with this life, no matter where we go, and that was proof, I couldn't hold it at that point. Michele Bennett was a mess, too. And Chris Murphy, when he was walking out of the funeral, he couldn't walk, he had to be helped. Maybe there was some regret coming out then. It wasn't Murphy's fault, of course. But he may have been thinking that had he been on the scene, maybe it may not have happened, maybe that's how he felt.'

Greg Perano said to me, 'The funeral? I don't know about the funeral, half the people didn't even know him. The funeral was so alien to what he was. I don't think he would have liked it. A few days after he died I took all these irises out on the surf with another friend who knew Michael and we went out and threw them into the water. And the wind came up and the surf came up and there were perfect waves for about an hour. The irises got taken out to sea.'

The coffin was taken to the hearse and from there the funeral procession travelled to the Northern Suburbs Crematorium, where there was to be a private service and cremation. In front of the hearse, leading the procession, was a motorcycle police escort. The cremation was a quiet, quick affair with only twenty-five close friends and relatives present. A short service was followed by a eulogy given by Bill Leibowitz:

'I first met Michael in 1983. I easily recognised the obvious signs of a star beginning his ascendancy. As the years passed and I got to really know Michael as a person, what most impressed me about him and what I most admired about him was not what he had become in life, but what he did not become.

'Michael was man possessed of extraordinary gifts. His voice was beautiful and expressive, and his lyrics poetic. He was one of the singularly great rock'n'roll front men that has ever graced the stage. Michael radiated energy and charisma when he walked into a room. Everyone immediately felt his presence. Michael was a natural star. Unlike many of his peers, he wasn't a media creation. He created media. MTV in the United States in its early years owes much to the magic of Michael Hutchence.

'Michael was a free spirit—sensitive and artistic. He was elegant and stylish—Michael's own unique brand of style. Michael had the rare ability to make an indelible impression on millions of people throughout the world. They heard his voice, saw his face, watched him move on video and the live stage, and they were captivated. Michael moved people on a grand scale—not many people can do that.

'But, as I said, what most impressed me about Michael was *not* what he became but what he *didn't* become. Michael never lost his kindness, his sincerity, his caring and concern for everyone I saw him interact with. He never became arrogant, pompous, hostile, cold or conceited, like so many of his peers who attained international fame. Michael retained his human qualities.

'I was devastated when I heard the horrible news of Michael's untimely passing. I will never be able to truly comprehend why this terrible event took place. It is too difficult to accept and impossible to reconcile.

'Michael's life was short but his accomplishments were great and the impact which he left was stunning. Since last Saturday I have received hundreds of calls from people all over the world, and what is universal in their comments is their personal experience of Michael as a wonderful, charismatic, kind person who was so full of life, charm and sensitivity, and still untapped talents. I don't think Michael truly ever understood how many people all over the world who personally knew him really loved him for being *him*, not because of who he was. This love and high regard was not dependent on whether he had a current hit record—it was because Michael was Michael, the person, not the rock star. Michael was unique; he was extraordinary; his spirit was a blessing to all of us who were privileged to know and love him. He will be sorely missed. He is irreplaceable.'

Boak Jobbins then said the final few words, committed Michael to God's arms, opened the curtains, and the coffin slowly slid towards the furnace and disappeared.

It had been arranged that Kelland and Susie would travel separately from Patricia, Tina and Ross, but a mix-up in the car arrangements meant that the five of them ended up in the same stretch limousine. Patricia sat between Kelland and Ross, Susie and Croy were opposite Kell, and Tina sat opposite Ross and Pat. No sooner had the car set off than Pat started berating Paula and her behaviour at the crematorium. During the service, Paula had stood up from her seat and without saying anything to anyone proceeded to walk out, stepped into her waiting limousine, and returned to her hotel. The rest of the occupants of the limousine remained silent. Once the car turned into the highway, Pat started criticising Rhett.

'She told me that he'd invited hundreds of his friends to the wake that was about to be held at the Pacific Blue Room in Oxford Street, Darlinghurst,' Kell said. 'Rhett was on the organising committee for the wake. I told Pat that she was exaggerating and that Rhett wouldn't have invited so many people.' Pat then told Kell he should have a talk with Rhett because he was 'out of control around the hotel'. Tina butted in and said the only person who could talk to Rhett was her son Brent. Kelland looked at Tina and told her that he resented what she had said because none of them had helped raise Rhett, and that if anyone could talk to him it was Kell, not Brent. Pat continued to berate Rhett, so Kelland said to her, 'Why don't you talk to Rhett if you're such a know-all?' Apparently things in the limo degenerated even further—but all the family members I talked to about this remained pretty tight-lipped.

• • •

Michael's mother first met Paula Yates in London in late 1995. 'I thought she was perfectly lovely,' Paula recalled in her autobiography, remembering the meeting. 'Patricia and I decided to peruse Chanel.' Inside the store, near a perfume counter, Peaches turned around to Patricia, 'fixed her with a piercingly interested gaze and said in a loud voice, "Do you think Michael has seen Mummy's knickers?" Luckily, Patricia is a mother of three too, so she knew about this sort of thing,' Paula wrote.

According to Martha Troup, 'Paula was very nice to Patricia during the first year, and Michael told me that his mother was better to Paula than she was to any women he ever went out with. I personally think that the mother would just get jealous after a while. The jealousy was weird to me.'

'Ross and I were on our way to Michael's home in the south of France,' Patricia said in May 1998, recalling her meeting with Paula. 'He invited us to stop over in his apartment in Belgravia—Paula was living in Chelsea with her daughters by Bob at this time. I was, to say the least, curious to meet Paula and I was pleasantly surprised.'

Greg Perano claims, 'The mother's not interested in anyone who's not wealthy or famous. I've met her twenty times and she wouldn't know who the fuck I was. She was never interested in any of his girlfriends, only Kylie because she was a big name in Australia and London. She was always quite distant with Helena—almost to the degree that she was jealous of her.'

'Pleasant' and 'lovely' are not the best words to describe the behaviour of Glassop and Yates during the verbal battle that took place between them following the death of Michael. It took only a couple of days before the two women publicly declared war. A war in the tabloids, a war on the telephone; a vicious, vitriolic, bitter war that tore the memory of Michael to shreds. Both women were completely obsessed by Michael Hutchence, and after his death Patricia scorned Paula, who in turn was utterly contemptuous of Patricia. It was a battle of the matriarchs.

At first the words they used to lash each other came from their own mouths. Then they took to talking by proxy, at times through lawyers, at times through their appointed spokeswomen—daughter Tina in the case of Patricia, friend Belinda Brewin in the case of Paula.

The slanging match between mother and lover revolved around everything from the reasons why Michael died and the method of his death to the distribution of his ashes, the seating placements at the funeral, matters concerning the Michael Hutchence estate, the welfare and custody of Tiger Lily, and the moral status of both women. Kelland Hutchence bought into the mess when Tiger Lily's custody came into the equation, but bowed out when his personal health became an issue. He entered hospital to undergo a triple bypass operation, and was also suffering from nervous exhaustion and bronchitis.

The first signs of conflict between Patricia and Paula had appeared during Michael's final year. That was the year when some of Michael's closest friends and family began to wonder about his state of mind, his welfare, and exactly what he'd got himself into with Paula Yates, even though he said he adored her. There were threats of suicide from both Michael and Paula, consistent rumours and tantrums. Whether or not these rumours reached Pat, the tension between the two matriarchs began to seep out.

Later their disputes were more open. Patricia, for instance, publicly aired her distinctly different memory of the incident that took place in the cathedral before Michael's funeral service. 'Someone said I pushed Paula,' she said in a London magazine interview, 'but there were cameras there, and if that really happened it would have been recorded. Paula came over to me with Tiger Lily. I kissed Tiger Lily and suggested that Paula take her seat. I think she must have been upset when the minister insisted Michael's immediate family walk ahead of her when entering and exiting the chapel. He was only following procedure.'

In a letter to Australian rock magazine *Juice*, Tina wrote of the incident: 'The only time my mother saw or spoke to Paula was in the cathedral. She came over to the family and made a big display in front of the cameras. Paula never once contacted my mother during that terrible week in Sydney.' Tina then went on to discuss the funeral arrangements. 'Paula was not present for she was neither Michael's wife, nor his fiancée, she was "medicated" in her hotel room. It would appear that those closest to Michael, the people left with the decisions on his passing, would be our parents, Patricia Glassop and Kell Hutchence, since Michael was not married and did not have a child old enough to make the decisions.'

In an interview with London's *Hello* magazine in May

1998, Patricia defended her daughter's letter by saying there was nothing in it that hadn't been said before. 'I think Tina was setting the record straight. Everyone, including Paula, knew Michael did not want to get married. There are plenty of men who feel that way. He even had his manager put out a press release to that effect last October, 1997.'

Then came the christening of Tiger Lily, in Sydney in April 1998. The two women continued to trade insults via the telephone in the lead-up to the christening, and eventually the police in two states were dragged into their squabble. The Surfers Paradise police were asked to investigate harassment calls allegedly made to Patricia.

Paula Yates launched a blistering attack on Michael Hutchence's mother which included the comment, 'For Patricia to suggest I would neglect my child is disgraceful, especially when one of her sons hung himself.' Paula went on, 'Michael used to call her the bitch, or the witch. I am leaving out worse stories in the interest of Michael's memory. However, people who dislike me on other levels have never accused me of being a bad mother.'

Later in the year, Paula was reported as saying that Patricia had claimed that Michael had never loved her, Paula; that he was in fact in love with two other women in America, both of whom he was going to marry. 'She said other things, too, that I won't even repeat. I just felt sorry for her.' Paula then said that Pat's non-attendance at Tiger's christening was a rejection of her granddaughter. 'Look at the mother's two sons,' Yates said, 'one is dead, the other is in detox. She should question her own mothering skills, not mine. Her behaviour is shameful.'

In an interview with London's *Hello* magazine in May of 1998, Patricia said, 'I don't know why we have fallen out so badly.' She went on to say that during the previous twelve months Paula had had many mood swings and that she, Patricia, just happened to have been in Paula's line of fire. 'Paula has said some hurtful things, but my focus is on picking up the pieces and getting on with my life. But as far as my feelings for Paula—she cannot hurt me any more than I am hurting now. Hopefully, some day she will remember the nice times we had.' Pat was also reported to have said that she had been devastated by press comments about Michael being distanced from her. 'Michael and I had a really lovely relationship and I know the things being said would have upset him terribly. It has been written that Michael said I was senile and a witch. It was not in his nature to say those things. It's easy to make comments when he cannot defend himself.'

Patricia claimed that the first she knew of Michael's depressed state was in June 1997. He had called her from Europe when INXS were touring and she said she could 'feel' his unhappiness. She then went on to say that she felt that the pressures of Paula's ongoing custody battle were 'really getting Michael down at the time of his death. He was the sort of person who did not like conflict. His suicide was, and still is, beyond comprehension to his family and friends.' Patricia claimed that she had never witnessed 'Michael indulging in anything illegal. Our time together was fun, we went out, had dinner and drinks. But I'm past being a party girl, so he went his way. I never witnessed his wild life. He would have wanted his daughter Tiger to grow up out of the spotlight and be her own person. Right now she is only a baby and the attention is overwhelming. He would have wanted her to have fun and enjoy being a girl.'

Around July 1998 it was reported that Patricia Glassop was in London to have a meeting with Bob Geldof. The meeting has never been confirmed or denied by either party, but it has been suggested that the reason behind it was an attempt by Patricia to try for custody of her granddaughter. In the same month, according to London newspaper reports, Paula Yates tried to hang herself in a copycat suicide bid. Since Michael's death she had been treated for acute depression. Late one evening, she took an overdose of pills and then tried to emulate the death of her lover by hanging a noose from the back of a door and putting it around her neck. A London Ambulance Service spokesperson said that Yates did not need hospital treatment; instead, the mother of four was taken to Roehampton's Priory Clinic, where she received psychiatric help. This was also the time when the London Family Law Court granted Bob Geldof residence rights to their three children. The court's decision was accompanied by a media blackout order, and was not made public until October. Belinda Brewin has since said that Paula did not attempt suicide but Paula has said many times in interviews that she has contemplated suicide on a daily basis since Hutchence died.

The Priory Clinic was the place where Paula was admitted earlier in 1998 for what was described as a nervous breakdown. At the time, Yates said the only reason she did not take her own life was because of her children. There seems little doubt that Paula has suffered greatly, no matter which way you look at it. Her mother left her stranded, her beloved family life is in ruins, her lover is dead, her identity seemingly shattered. But for her to suicide would condemn her children to the same abandonment that helped form her own character.

A month later, Paula was admitted to Clouds, a prestigious rehabilitation centre for gambling, drug and alcohol addictions. It is not, as some have suggested, a rehab centre for depression. When she was admitted she was informed by doctors that she would have to do it on her own, without distraction. She missed Tiger Lily's second birthday because she was in the clinic. Tiger Lily was sent to Australia with Belinda Brewin and her two daughters, Montana and Indiana, in order that Paula have time on her own to rehabilitate. Tiger Lily was in the care of Brewin during her Australian visit. Belinda Brewin, granddaughter of socialist baron and landowner, Henry 'Harry' Walston, on the surface of it has appeared quite the hero in this saga. She is no stranger to controversy, marriage splits, custody wrangles; she has famous friends and a taste for the high life.

Paula and Belinda first met when they enrolled their children in a play group/day-care centre in Battersea, southwest London, in the early nineties. Soon after their initial meeting, Brewin's own marriage collapsed and a bitter custody battle began between her and her husband, a bankrupt hotelier named Tony Murphy. Murphy was facing an uphill battle. Even in the liberated nineties, it seems that the English courts mostly favour the mother in child residence battles. While child residence is not always awarded to the mother, it seems to be a rule of thumb that, if in doubt, they favour the mother. This quirk of the system notwithstanding, Brewin, when faced with the possible loss of her two children, asked Yates to tell the court she was a worthy mother. Paula jumped at the opportunity to help her pal, and Brewin repaid the favour during the 1996 Drug Squad raid on Paula and Michael's home.

Paula and Belinda quickly became firm friends. Brewin is Paula's agent, confidante, best friend, and procurer of lucrative media deals, as well as Tiger Lily's main carer when Paula has problems.

During a group-therapy session inside Clouds rehabilitation centre, Paula met 29-year-old Kingsley O'Keke, a tall, dark-haired, handsome former heroin addict and jail inmate. They were immediately attracted to each other and gave each other support. They fell in lust, and the London *Sun* headlined the news that the couple were 'at it like rabbits in the woods'. Paula's friends say that Kingsley showed her that life can go on. However, rehabilitation for the couple did not go on, as the two were asked to leave the centre. For clinical rather than ethical reasons, administrators of the centre frown upon personal relationships between people undergoing rehab.

'It's very easy in early recovery to swap one addiction for the other,' Deidre Boyd, editor of medical publication, *Addiction Today*, said at the time. 'Call it sex addiction or co-dependency, it's a classic situation. You spend time on the other person, where you should be spending the time on your own recovery. You can block the feelings you need to experience with a high from love or lust.' A Clouds spokesperson said that the pair were released 'with great sadness'.

In Australia, Brewin took Tiger Lily to see Kell, but not Patricia. She also took her to see her cousin Zoe, daughter of Rhett and Mandy. 'Tiger Lily was calling Belinda, mummy,' Rhett told journalist Di Stanley during Tiger's visit to Australia. He said that Belinda was becoming increasingly concerned about Paula, something that has been repeated by several people who saw Belinda during her visit. 'Belinda told me she's reached the end of her tether. From what I can gather the thing with Paula and Kingsley was the last straw,' said Rhett. Brewin was reportedly very angry when she heard that Paula had fallen for Kingsley.

So too was Kelland Hutchence. He was outraged when he read of Paula's affair with Kingsley O'Keke, which caused her to be asked to leave the clinic. He accused Paula of betraying the memory of his son and he feared for the future of Tiger Lily. Kell subsequently launched legal proceedings for temporary custody of his granddaughter, believing that she would receive a better upbringing in Australia than with Paula and a recovering heroin addict. Perhaps because she was tipped off about the attempt to gain custody, Belinda tried to leave Australia secretly. After telling Kell she was going to visit her sister in the country, she went instead to the airport, where she was quizzed by Australian Federal Police. The plane's departure was halted while police phoned Kell at his home and asked him what he wanted to do. They told him he had one minute to decide as the plane was about to leave.

'I pulled out at the last minute,' he told me, 'because I thought it was unfair on Belinda and her two children to be messed around like that, but I now wonder if I did the right thing by letting them go. I only ever sought partial custody, and hoped that Paula would come out to Australia and tell me she was cured. Tiger seemed to have a continual cold on her trip to Australia and appeared underweight to me. I wanted to ensure she had regular eating and sleeping patterns.'

Kell says he simply wanted to protect Tiger Lily and give Paula another chance at rehabilitation. Perhaps he went about it the wrong way, but he had little other alternative. When Paula found out about his custody attempt, she called Kell and screamed at him down the telephone line, calling him a fucking cunt. This was the same expression she had used a few months earlier to Richard Lowenstein after he had taken part in an interview with a London newspaper. Lowenstein said in the article that he believed Michael was in love with Michele Bennett. Paula repeatedly called his home, abusing him or leaving horrendous messages on his answering machine, and at one stage she told him that he would have 'her blood on his hands'.

After being stopped at Sydney airport by the police, Belinda Brewin decided not to return to London as planned, but instead stopped off in Bangkok for two weeks. When she eventually flew back to London in early September, she quickly instigated the departure of Kingsley O'Keke from Paula's home. Paula realised that she had to pull out all stops if she intended keeping custody of Tiger Lily. She determined to stay away from drugs and drink.

A little more than a year after Michael Hutchence had bowed out and kissed the sky, the emotional wounds caused by his death were still raw. Clear thinking and good judgement are not necessarily characteristics of those in shock after the death of a loved one, especially when that death is the result of suicide or misadventure or, indeed, unknown causes. What some people said following Hutchence's death might very well have been tainted with the venting of hidden grievances, the avenging of past confrontations, thinly veiled personal turmoil, or guilt. But the fact remains that both Patricia Glassop and Paula Yates are tough, ambitious and seductive women. Both can be manipulative, explosive and, at times, irrational. Both effectively blamed each other for Michael's final act. They have traded insult for insult. They are still at each other's throats, still scratching and clawing, still fighting over his money, his morals, his ethics and his child. Both have enough ammunition to keep firing until one of them keels over and dies. And the one who will suffer the most will be Tiger Lily. What will Tiger Lily go through when she grows up and reads of the cascade of insults between her mother and her grandmother?

Michael Hutchence was pivotal to the lives of both Patricia Glassop and Paula Yates; some would say he was a crutch to them. His mother doted on him, prompting some of his friends to call her INXSessory; his lover entangled him in a web from which it was impossible for him to escape. In some ways, all the other people in Michael's life have since his death become bit players in the drama between these two women. They have dragged Michael into the murky depths of sensation in the tabloid newspapers, a place he had successfully avoided for most of his career. Tabloid sensationalism had never been the domain of Michael Hutchence before he met Paula Yates. He featured in the tabloids, yes, but only on the arms of his girlfriends, not in the quagmire of hatred, bitterness, venom and sleaze that Patricia and Paula pulled him down into.

One person who could have helped repair the situation was Colin Diamond, overseer of the Michael Hutchence estate. What happens in a normal estate settlement is that family members and beneficiaries are called together by the executor and informed of how and when the estate will be divided. But instead of doing this, Colin Diamond steadfastly maintained his silence. No matter how honorable his intentions might have been, one has to question his methods, especially since, as he has himself acknowledged, the family and Yates are in dispute. He could have quelled much of the emotional heat had he been more out in the open with the Hutchence family about the estate.

twelve

Money, that's what I want

> Money can buy almost anything
> But anything's nothing
> When you're dead
>
> 'Just Keep Walking'
> *INXS* 1980
> INXS

Michael Hutchence and Colin Diamond first met in 1986 in a restaurant in Hong Kong. The tax lawyer and the gypsy rock singer had an instant rapport and soon became firm friends, going fishing, paragliding, socialising and doing business together. Colin Diamond was an associate of a barrister named Gordon Fisher, the man who had built a set of complex worldwide investments, shelf companies, and trusts for Hutchence, diversifying his finances in order to minimise taxation.

Originally from Glasgow's working-class suburbs, Fisher joined the Royal Navy to escape unemployment, and soon proved to be a robust and devoted sailor. In 1975 he threw aside his merchant life and enrolled at the University of New South Wales, where he showed a natural aptitude for the laws of taxation. By 1979 his expertise had landed him in the established Sydney law firm of Allen, Allen and Hemsley, and he was soon made a partner in the company. One of Fisher's clients was a man named Brian Ray, whom he'd met in the same year. Ray had been introduced to a tax-saving scam by one Ian Beames, who had been convicted for fraud and given a stiff jail sentence. Ray was to take over Beame's business interests while Beames was in jail, becoming the director of several international companies in the process. Gordon Fisher became intricately involved in the worldwide money movements of his new client, who had also been charged over questionable money practices as a result of a Royal Commission but was eventually acquitted.

By 1982 Fisher had left the legal firm of Allen, Allen and Hemsley to set up business with a growing number of his own clientele. During this time he was investigated by the Australian Federal Police and the Australian Taxation Office for alleged involvement in a A$19-million global fraud. Fisher was found to control at least eight hundred companies, which in turn controlled hundreds of millions of dollars which were shuffled all over the world. Police urged that Fisher be charged for his part in the scam, but public prosecutors felt the charge was too difficult to prove. They dropped the case. The New South Wales police also had reason to question Fisher concerning one of his clients who had been charged with trafficking heroin and suddenly disappeared while released on bail. A few years later, Fisher mysteriously left Australia, basing himself in Hong Kong, where Michael Hutchence was one of his top-shelf clients.

Not long after his meeting with Colin Diamond Michael had a bitter falling-out with Fisher over money. Hutchence swore he'd never again have any future financial dealings with Fisher. In 1988 Fisher, facing legal action over other of his dealings, suddenly and unannounced, hightailed it to the tax haven of Monaco, where he stayed for almost four years. In 1991 he once again cleared everything out of his office and home overnight and returned to Hong Kong. Since his departure in 1986, Gordon Fisher has never returned to Australia, not for his daughter's wedding, not for his divorce.

At the time of Gordon Fisher's departure from Hong Kong, Colin Diamond and another associate of Fisher's, Andrew Paul, made guarantees to Hutchence that they would have nothing further to do with Fisher, but in reality they continued their liaison, either directly or indirectly, with the man at the centre of Hutchence's international financial jigsaw puzzle. Hutchence handed Colin Diamond control of his personal business affairs, and when he died his vast fortune was hidden in a web of trusts and companies spreading from West Africa, through Europe, to South-East Asia, the British Virgin Islands, then back to the Pacific Islands. In most cases, either Andrew Paul or Colin Diamond or both were listed as directors or executors of the companies, with Diamond listed as trustee. Paul and Diamond were also listed as executors of Michael's will. The two men had every corner covered, absolutely controlling the Michael Hutchence estate.

Organised-crime investigative journalist for the *Sydney Morning Herald*, Kate McClymont, along with finance journalist Ian Verrender, discovered that during Gordon Fisher's time in Monaco he shared office space with an Englishman, Norman Leighton. According to McClymont, Leighton was a director of a company called Rodman Plastics, which also listed Andrew Paul as a director. The company operated out of Hong Kong and owned some of Michael Hutchence's assets, including his French villa in Roquefort Le Pins where Tina was married in 1996. In July 1995 Leighton sent a fax to Michael Hutchence requesting that he send further funds for work on the villa's 'swimming pool, Aston Martin and costs associated with a tax audit'. Leighton also asked Andrew Paul to 'remit a further 100 000 French francs to meet the unusual expenses'. It seems strange, then, that six weeks after the death of Hutchence, Colin Diamond's brother Stephen, himself a beneficiary of some Michael Hutchence trusts, wrote a letter to Michael's mother, an excerpt of which states: 'The executors advise to the best of their knowledge and belief that Michael Hutchence did not purchase and more particularly at the time of his death, did not own a villa in the south of France.'

The house is not listed in his estate. Nor is the house he supposedly 'doesn't own' at 48 Smith Terrace in London, where Hutchence personally authorised, in writing, massive extensions to be made on the home. The owner of this home is a company based in the British Virgin Islands. Technically speaking, Hutchence did not own the houses. But it was his money, held in a trust account or business company accounts, that paid for the purchases. It was also his money that set up the trusts and the businesses. It was also his money that was directed into whatever cover company was used to pay for ongoing expenses on the homes. This was the pattern. This is what caused the outrage over his estate—not the terms of the will, not the percentage breakdown, but the clandestine ownership of assets not listed in the will.

To get a full picture of the much-publicised dispute over the Hutchence estate, it is important to understand that money he accumulated during the last twelve years of his life, perhaps £8 million, did not simply go into a bank account but was directed into an extremely complex net of discretionary trusts. When money is placed in a discretionary trust it ceases to be owned by the person who places it there, and so do any assets purchased by the discretionary trust. It is called discretionary because what is done with the money is at the complete discretion of the trustee, who controls the trust. The trustee decides who gets what and when they get it. It may be, for example, that one year one beneficiary receives income, while in another year a different beneficiary receives the income. Beneficiaries have no rights whatsoever to view the trust's accounts, nor do they have any rights to see how income or assets are distributed. Clearly, the person who is placing their money and assets in a discretionary trust needs to have complete faith in the trustee.

There are two main reasons why high-income earners choose to put their finances in a discretionary trust: to minimise tax payments, or to block creditors from making a claim against assets or cash. This blocking effect is far-reaching and includes beneficiaries to a deceased estate. In other words, beneficiaries of a will have absolutely no rights at all to anything held in a discretionary trust. In most cases, and certainly in the case of the Hutchence estate, it is almost impossible for anyone who is a beneficiary in a will to make a claim against the discretionary trust. Even the executor of a will has no rights to see the accounts of the discretionary trust in most cases—this is the law. Unless, that is, they also happen to be the trustees of those trusts.

Andrew Paul and Colin Diamond, along with Andrew Young, Belinda Brewin's partner, had complete control over Michael's estate. Paul and Diamond have been variously named as trustees, executors, legal representatives, or financial representatives of Hutchence's estate, the trust companies he set up and the businesses he directed others to run. They are named as co-executors of the will and Diamond is appointed guardian of Tiger Lily during her minority.

In his will, Michael Hutchence left A$250 000 to Amnesty International, A$250 000 to Greenpeace, with Tiger receiving 50 per cent, Paula, Kelland, Patricia, Rhett and Tina receiving 10 per cent each of the remainder.

Since Michael's death, each member of the Hutchence family has individually and repeatedly tried to pin down Colin Diamond in order to assess exactly what Michael's assets were—not such an unusual request from the beneficiaries of a will. However, they either have not been able to locate him, he would never return their phone calls, or he would not turn up to meetings. He has never personally explained to any of the family the exact situation with regards to the Michael Hutchence estate, something which is standard practice between executor and beneficiaries in the matter of wills and estates. Diamond's high-handed attitude is seen by many as the main reason for the ongoing acrimony over the Hutchence estate.

But a few of Hutchence's friends say that Diamond has acted the way he has because he feels the entire family is money hungry, and that all they care about is how much each one of them is going to receive from the estate. Some friends say that Michael financially helped each one while he was alive; he helped settle some of his father's debts when he left Hong Kong for Sydney in the early nineties; his mother was supposedly always trying to coax him into buying her flats and apartments—this was prior to her fifth marriage to millionaire Ross Glassop.

'He bought me a car when I was in Los Angeles,' Rhett told me. 'He helped me out lots. He got me a job on tour. I'd hate to think how much money he spent on me—probably $200 000 over the years. But Michael's estate means nothing to me without Michael in it.' One very close business associate of Hutchence told me in confidence that 'his family leached off him from the minute he became successful, leaned on him to buy apartments and stuff like that. They were like an albatross around his neck. If only he'd told them to get lost years ago. But when he died it was like, We haven't got Michael to hit on anymore, so we better make a beeline for the estate because the gravy train's over. If he cut them off years ago, they would have got used to it by now.'

Andrew Young echoes these sentiments. He claims he advised Michael on 'any matter he required'. He said in July of 1998 that he was a barrister 'with a roving brief'. So roving was his brief for Hutchence that he used the offices of a Sydney magazine, *AXS*, with which he has an association, as Tiger Lily's playground in August 1998. At the time, Brewin and Young were lovers. In an interview with *AXS* in July 1998, Young said that he thought the best way for Michael's mother and sister to reflect any love they had for Michael would be to abide by his wishes, referring to the conditions of the late singer's will. 'I know, as did most people who were genuinely close to Michael, what his views on his family were. I think it fair to say that Michael's will reflected those views accurately. One way or the other they had their pound of flesh while he was alive. But it's time to accept that he's unfortunately not with us and that he made these financial arrangements specifically with Tiger's well-being in mind. As I understand it, none of his family have been forgotten but, not unnaturally, Tiger was his prime concern and that is clearly reflected in his affairs.'

Eventually, after months of bitter public acrimony between Diamond and the Hutchence family, Patricia instigated proceedings against Colin Diamond and Andrew Paul. 'It's for my son's sake,' the teary-eyed mother told the *Australian* on 6 August 1998. A few months earlier she had said that she felt like she'd lost Michael twice. She said his houses had been closed down and personal effects locked away. 'I do not even have one of his shirts to remind me of him,' she said. It has been stated by some of Michael's friends that Patricia Glassop tried to retrieve many of Michael's smaller belongings, such as chairs, clothing, and in one instance a motorbike. Andrew Young, in a reference to Michael's mother, said in July 1998, 'Some of the beneficiaries approached the staff of his villa in France and arranged for some things to be sent to them before the executor could seal the assets. One beneficiary in particular has been phoning people claiming personal items Michael left with them were now hers and should be sent to her immediately. I believe the executors are expecting some items presently with friends and family members to be delivered to them.'

In January 1994, Hutchence's London home, his French home, the assets of a company called Nextcircle, a Mercedes-Benz, an Aston Martin, investments to the tune of almost US$300 000, and a bank balance of US$2.25 million were listed as his assets. Four years later, following his death, the beneficiaries of his will were informed that Hutchence owned very little. Missing from the estate listed in the will were his London home, his French home, his Surfers Paradise properties, the Aston Martin, the Mercedes-Benz— in fact, almost no assets were listed in a statement of account accompanying the will. Listed amongst the various liabilities, however, were ongoing debts to a company called Pokfield, based in Liberia on the west coast of Africa. Astoundingly, the amount of debt to Pokfield was listed as 'yet to be quantified'. Pokfield could, at any given time, legally list any amount of money as a debt. Andrew Paul is listed as a director of the Pokfield company. I am led to believe that another of the listed ongoing liabilities of the estate is a personal guarantee from Hutchence to cover all costs associated with Paula Yates's continued legal battle with Bob Geldof, rumoured to be almost half a million pounds.

But it was the Hutchence properties on Queensland's Gold Coast that finally aroused the ire of Patricia Glassop, causing her to instigate a legal investigation into the affairs of her late son. One of the properties, a sprawling waterfront home on the Isle of Capri valued at A$1 million, was not in fact technically owned by Hutchence, contrary to what he'd told his family and friends. The property is actually owned by a trustee company called Sin Can Can Pty Ltd on behalf of the Isle of Capri Development Trust. Colin Diamond is director, his mother Gloria Diamond is named as the major shareholder, and his father Clifford Diamond is listed as principal of the trust. Colin's two children, Liam and James, are primary beneficiaries. Kelland Hutchence is also named as a beneficiary.

Another Sin Can Can director, Gold Coast accountant Anthony Alford, wrote in a letter to Pat and Tina's lawyers, 'the late Michael Hutchence was not involved directly or indirectly with the purchase of the property and no part of the purchase was made by him'. However, a statutory declaration signed by Colin Diamond in November 1997, three days after Michael's death, gave Hutchence's address as 13–17 La Spezia Court, Isle of Capri. It is also interesting that, despite claims that Michael did not have anything to do with the purchase of the house, his father is listed as a primary beneficiary.

Ownership questions have also been raised about another Gold Coast property, a bowling alley bought for A$2.25 million in January 1994. Michael Hutchence had lunch at the complex the day the contracts were signed. Anthony Alford wrote another letter denying the rock star was involved in the purchase, or that his money was invested in the business. The bowling alley is owned by a trustee company called Nexcess Pty Ltd. It holds the title on behalf of the Broadwater Trust. Once more, Colin Diamond is director, his mother is the main shareholder, his father is listed as principal of the trust, and his two children are primary beneficiaries. Nexcess also owns a Bentley, which was part of the Isle of Capri purchase. The third Surfers Paradise property under question is a huge commercial development site worth A$1.3 million, owned by Nextcircle. The shareholders are Citipak and Red Light Ltd, both registered in the British Virgin Islands.

Hutchence's French villa, Ferme de Guerches, was owned by a network of companies stretching around the world and into Monaco. The same pattern of ownership applied to his London home at 48 Smith Terrace. Royalty payments and record sales are believed to be operating through a series of shelf companies and discretionary trusts emanating from Hong Kong and the British Virgin Islands.

Until his death, Michael Hutchence's address, according to the Australian Securities Commission, was listed as Redburn Street, London and Tai Tam Road, Hong Kong—contrary to popular belief, Hutchence did not own property in Hong Kong. Three days after his death, Colin Diamond changed Michael's address to the property in the Isle of Capri. Hutchence was also listed as having dealings in at least four other companies, mostly with INXS members; Fibuso Pty Ltd, an investment company; Tizine, a trustee company; Truism, a production company; and Jet Trash.

Soon after Patricia lodged her and Tina's legal challenge to the Hutchence estate, Andrew Paul made a successful application to the Queensland Supreme Court for administration powers so that he could defend the challenge. He also successfully sought for all his legal costs to be paid for by the Michael Hutchence estate. Patricia and Tina are attempting to determine the exact ownership of many properties around the world. They have requested details of assets from ten defendants and have demanded that Andrew Paul furnish accounts held with regard to the estate. Patricia's lawyers have argued that the assets owned by several trust companies should be included in her son's estate and divided according to his will. She is not challenging her son's will, she says, but rather the contents of the disbursement of the will.

When he heard in May 1998 of the pending court action, Colin Diamond resigned his long-held post as executor of the Michael Hutchence estate. Diamond, who describes his profession as a practising international lawyer, said he resigned because 'the lawyers in Australia felt that there was a possible conflict of interest, or at least there was the potential for such perception if I remained an executor of the will or a director of a trustee company'. In an interview with *AXS* magazine, with which he also has ties, the elusive barrister said, 'I was one of the directors of the trustee companies because that is what Michael wanted. With what's going on at the moment,' he said, referring to pending court action at the time of the interview, 'the last thing that's needed is anything that detracts from the welfare of Tiger Lily. Obviously Michael didn't think it unreasonable for someone he trusted to retain an element of responsibility over financial decisions that impact on the future of his two-year-old girl, and, indirectly, her mother. Whether these trusts could have benefited members of his family, or anyone else for that matter, is not for me to say. I am trying to ensure that Michael's instructions are carried out. In spite of this, I have renounced my role as executor. I have also resigned as a director of any relevant trustee company.'

Andrew Paul, in legal terms, is now the sole executor of the Hutchence estate, but it is clear that Colin Diamond is still actively involved in its affairs, if only because he also happens to be one of the legal guardians of Tiger Lily.

In May 1998, prior to instigating legal proceedings, Pat Glassop said, 'We have never ever disputed Michael's wishes, they are very clear and the division fair. We just want his wishes adhered to. We are ensuring all beneficiaries are treated as Michael intended. This action is being brought especially for his daughter and her mother. We have never fought with Paula over this—in fact we have not even spoken to her about it. In Michael's will, Tiger is to get half his estate, kept in trust until she is twenty-five. The other half is divided between Rhett, Tina, Kell, Paula, and myself. There is no dispute. We just want to make sure that the wealth he accumulated in his lifetime is distributed the way he wanted it and not the way other people want it.'

Patricia's comments are a very pointed reference to Colin Diamond and Andrew Paul. Perhaps this is why Diamond and Young have kept saying they are looking after Tiger Lily's interests. When you think Diamond, Paul, Young and Tiger Lily, you must also think Yates. Obviously the more money that is distributed, the more taxation will need to be paid and the less money will be received by Tiger Lily. 'He [Michael] was very clear who was to receive what,' Diamond insisted. 'The will was written in accordance with his specific instructions. He knew what was in his estate and what was in trust. He knew what the will meant. He was very clear in his instructions as to what should ensue should anything ever happen to him, and that those instructions should be followed to the letter. As far as I am concerned I owe it to Michael to retain a long-term interest in his affairs, and that means most importantly, to the best of my ability, ensuring that Tiger is properly looked after.' Given this pledge, it is understandable that Diamond and Paula Yates have forged a firm friendship. Belinda Brewin, as Yates's right-hand woman and Young's partner, is also intricately involved. It would be fair to say that Brewin is now more involved in the inner workings of the Hutchence estate than the family members who are beneficiaries, and her agenda, if she has one, would surely be to aid Tiger Lily and Paula, not the Hutchence family.

In his interview with *AXS*, Diamond was flippant about suggestions that some of the Hutchence money had vanished. 'Nothing's vanished. If it's not in his estate, it's in trust.' Andrew Young has stated that he was under the impression that Michael's family 'simply assumed that anything that associated Michael with what was his would be included in the estate. They don't seem to be aware that Michael's affairs were structured in a fashion that is quite common around the world and that only those things that were personally owned by Michael could be included in his estate. They have their grief to come to terms with. I can understand that. I understand that grief can manifest itself in many different ways. I just wish they would respect Michael's wishes without suggesting Mr Diamond is acting contrary to them. Explaining a situation is one thing, getting people to accept something they don't like is another,' Young concluded.

While nobody from the Hutchence family is questioning the terms of Michael's will, they are questioning the way in which his trusts have been created. But according to Andrew Young, if the trusts were to be declared part of the estate, 'it would definitely not be to Tiger's benefit, not fair to her, it would be to her considerable detriment. It seems to me that they must know that and that in spite of this they are in fact seeking to have the court rescind Michael's legally expressed wishes. Wishes that are particularly evident by the legal structures he established to ensure they would be carried out.'

Colin Diamond claims he is not being paid for his work on the will and that he is doing it as 'a service to Michael'. He further claims he is out of pocket. Hutchence had utmost faith in Diamond, to whom he gave specific responsibility to look after his daughter's wealth and welfare until she is twenty-five years old. Under those terms and conditions, any amount of spending could be attributed to Tiger Lily's welfare. What obviously wasn't one of her welfare costs, however, was the funeral of Tiger's father.

Walter Carter Funerals claim that the Hutchence estate still owes them A$49 587.94. According to Stephen Diamond, Colin paid over A$60 000 from 'his own personal funds to the funeral and associated expenses', but a spokesperson for the funeral company claims that Diamond has not paid them a cent. Far from paying the bill, in fact, Diamond instructed lawyers in Hong Kong to tell the funeral company that it could 'stand in line with the other unsettled creditors'. The cost of the funeral is now listed as a liability against the Hutchence estate.

It is unclear exactly when the matters of Michael's estate, his will, and his various discretionary trusts will be settled, but it is clear that they will not be settled amicably or quickly. The entire affair could end up being settled in the courts of Hong Kong, where Michael spent a great deal of his life and where he was once listed as a resident. Hong Kong is also the location of the law firm overseeing his estate, and the source of many of his trusts and shelf companies. The Hong Kong company appointed as solicitors for the executor of the Hutchence estate is Boarse, Cohen and Collins. A grant of probate has to be issued by the Hong Kong solicitors before executors can even think about beginning to distribute the estate. Once the probate is granted, the executor's solicitors independently value the estate. That process won't begin until the legal dispute is settled and litigation for that could take literally years. Until the grant of probate is made, personal assets can't be valued or touched.

One of Michael's lesser known assets—which is potentially a legal minefield, financially valuable and a source of embarrassment to some—is his photo album collection. At the end of 1998 nobody seemed to be aware of its whereabouts, but many people were on the lookout. Hutchence was known to have a large collection of very personal and intimate photographs of both himself and some of his friends. He was always discreet about the photos, but that does not mean someone else would be as discreet, particularly if a large amount of cash were offered.

Colin Diamond still looks after the affairs of INXS drummer Jon Farriss, who swears by the man's integrity. Tim Farriss told me that as far as he is concerned, 'Colin Diamond is definitely one of the good guys.'

Martha Troup believes Diamond and Hutchence were as close as any friends could be. 'There was nobody that Michael admired more than Colin Diamond, I don't care what anybody says. Michael trusted him and Michael was thirty-seven years old, and if he trusted him, everyone should shut up. No matter what you hear, no matter what you read, Michael knew what he was doing,' Troup told me in April 1998. 'I don't care if Colin had no money left in the world, that last dollar would go to Tiger Lily. If one thing angers me more than anything it is people who are attacking him. The only time Colin was concerned was when Michael was spending a little too much. That guy did many things for Michael, and Michael knew it. He respected, admired and loved him.'

Bill Leibowitz added weight to Martha's judgement. 'Michael was an astute businessman, a very smart guy, a very intelligent guy. He understood business. I spent a lot of time over the years explaining deals to him, answering his questions, and they were perceptive questions. He knew what it was all about. He wanted to know what the deals were all about. He also understood investing and the importance of investing. But you must remember I represented INXS, never Michael or his personal financial matters. I never represented him in tax matters. I am not involved with this thing between his family with regard to the estate.'

It is Colin Diamond, along with his associates, who without question holds the key and the power to the Hutchence estate. He's the main man at the centre of the emotional, financial, legal and controversial furore surrounding the legacy of Michael Hutchence, but the estate is so confusing, his assets so well hidden and so widely disbursed, that the full list of corporations, trust companies and businesses controlling his assets may never be known. It is almost impossible to come to grips with the structure of the hidden millions, and the legal battles to find out may indeed go on for years and run into millions of pounds in costs. Tiger Lily could end up being a millionaire and Colin Diamond a hero. But it's also sadly conceivable that Michael Hutchence's daughter becomes a debt-ridden pauper.

thirteen

The christening, the photos, the money, the mag

> I'm standing here on the ground
> The sky above, won't fall down
> See no evil in all directions
> Resolution of happiness
> Things have been dark for too long
> Don't change for you
> Don't change a thing for me
>
> 'Don't Change'
> *Shabooh Shoobah* 1982
> INXS

'I just felt utterly, utterly alone, because that's something every mum and dad does together, isn't it, you christen your child.' The words were from Paula Yates, two weeks after the christening of Heavenly Hiraani Tiger Lily. They were strange words, coming from her, because not once during the traditional ceremony did she mention Tiger Lily's dad—not at the christening, nor at the reception afterwards in one of Sydney's most expensive restaurants. Neither did the Reverend David Luke mention Michael's name during his gentle, succinct service. Maybe Paula just couldn't bear to mention Michael, either by name or by inference, the pain of his death being still too strong. Nevertheless, one wonders how Michael Hutchence would have felt had he known that he was not mentioned at his daughter's christening.

Tiger Lily was christened at 11 am on 31 March, the same day that Paula's eldest daughter Fifi turned fifteen. The christening was held in a tiny little church in the picturesque Sydney Harbour suburb of Watson's Bay, a beautiful setting. It was a strange affair, this christening of Tiger Lily. An interview that Paula did a few weeks later for the London magazine *OK!* was even more bizarre, with Paula using the opportunity to vent her vitriol against Bob Geldof, Patricia, Rhett, Tina, and the media from which she had made a literal fortune during the past months.

The idea for the christening was first hatched by Paula in February 1998, with early details being sent to various people in Australia and America via Belinda Brewin. I was in Australia when I first heard about the christening from a friend in London, and I asked Kelland if he knew where it was to be held. At first he thought it may take place at the Uniting Church in Frenchs Forest, where Michael was christened in 1962, but eventually he told me he was unsure about the location, or even if there was to be a christening. He said that Paula was coming to visit Australia so that Tiger Lily could see him.

I knew from my source in London that there was indeed to be a christening in Australia, and that Belinda and Paula had arranged to bring out the photographer from *OK!* magazine because he had done such brilliant photos of Tiger Lily and Paula in London. Belinda had told everyone who was invited that there was to be no publicity, which was unusual for any venture undertaken by her and Paula, and that three or four photographs of the christening were to be published in 'a UK magazine'. Paula was emphatic that no personal cameras were to be allowed into the ceremony, and this applied to family members too—an unusual demand for a family christening. Instead, to compensate for the loss of family participation, all family members would receive a copy of each photograph taken.

When the *OK!* article was finally published a total of nineteen photos were featured, and as of February 1999, eleven months after the christening, no member of the Hutchence family had received a single photograph of the event, or even a copy of the magazine article.

Belinda, Paula, Tiger Lily and a group of photographers arrived in Sydney a week before the christening and booked into the expensive Quay West Hotel, despite the fact that Paula had been consistently stating that she was broke. According to Paula, the trip to Australia was to allow Tiger Lily to see her grandfather, but up until the day before the christening he was able to see her only twice, briefly. Paula was either not well, or the doctor was coming, or she was asleep, he was told.

A few days prior to the christening, rumours about the event were out, but when questioned about it by the media Brewin's response was 'Bollocks!' As clandestine arrangements began to take shape, Martha Troup arrived in Sydney; Rhett, Mandy and Zoe Angel flew in from their home in Byron Bay; and Colin Diamond also arrived, anonymously, later disappearing as quickly and quietly as he'd come.

According to Patricia, Paula did not personally invite her to the ceremony, opting instead to pass the task to Belinda Brewin. 'Paula never phoned to ask me, her friend did,'

Patricia told Australian magazine *Woman's Day* on the day of the christening. She claimed it was difficult to 'make arrangements to fly to Sydney as there were no details of where or when it was to take place. It's all too silly. It's crazy, that cloak-and-dagger stuff.' She said she felt bad about refusing to attend but she thought it would be a circus. (She was right, it did become a three-ring circus.) 'I felt very sad knowing Tiger was being christened and I wasn't there. This is my son and nobody seems to care.'

Paula Yates, of course, has different recollections. She claims that she personally called Patricia to invite her. 'I rang Michael's mother three times and begged her to come,' Yates claimed in *OK!* magazine. 'I just felt sorry for her. I've turned my back now, because this was a monumental moment for Tiger, and to reject Tiger—that's nothing to do with a family feud. It's all right to throw a million horrible things at me when I'm trying to raise four children without the father they worshipped. And not to turn up at the christening? That's just shameful.'

The weekend of March 28–30 was an interesting three days, a sensational series of events providing a melodramatic prelude to the christening. During the weekend, Kelland was phoned by Belinda and told he could see Tiger Lily at the Quay West Hotel. He went to the hotel and played with his granddaughter for a couple of hours; this was only his second contact with her in almost seven days. The Hutchence family was annoyed by Paula's apparent obstructions. When Mandy and Zoe were summoned to visit, they got all dressed up and, full of anticipation, went around to the hotel, only to find on their arrival that Paula and Tiger Lily were 'unavailable'. Again. The tension increased. Frustrated, Rhett went around on his own and unannounced to see Paula. Paula was depressed and suffering emotionally, had been drinking champagne like water and was constantly inebriated, so much so that Belinda Brewin and Andrew Young had all the alcoholic drinks removed from the mini bar.

Patricia, following a particularly vicious phone call with Paula shortly after Rhett had left the hotel, decided that Paula was not competent to look after Tiger Lily, so she called the Rose Bay police, who in turn telephoned The Rocks police, who went to the room to investigate. Tiger was playing happily on the floor, being cared for by Belinda, and Paula was asleep in the bedroom. The police found nothing out of order. Somebody leaked the story to the media.

'When I made that call I was assured the report would be private and confidential,' Patricia said in a London interview almost two months after the christening. 'The report was leaked, which was embarrassing to me and Paula. It should never have happened, and how it did is being investigated. Paula was upset at the time. She made many phone calls to my home which were very unsettling. I'm not going to discuss what was said. As Tiger Lily's grandmother, I obviously care about her very much.'

The reason Paula did not want other photographs taken at her daughter's christening was because she had struck a reported £150 000 deal with *OK!* magazine, with the proviso that the photographs be exclusive. Rhett had learned from his father of the rule banning all personal cameras at the christening and understandably did not like the idea. This was his beloved brother's daughter; this was supposed to be a family get-together. 'I was angry and very upset at the no-photo rule,' Rhett told me. 'I was being told that I couldn't take photos at my own niece's christening.'

On Tuesday 31 March, the morning of the christening, Patricia called Rhett from her home in Surfers Paradise and asked him to take photographs of the ceremony, knowing that this contravened Paula's no-camera rule. Pat had hatched a deal with *Woman's Day* magazine worth $20 000, and following her call an assistant from the magazine came to see Rhett at his hotel and gave him a loaded camera, a mobile phone, and a contract for $20 000.

Rhett says of the incident, 'I had planned to take shots even before Pat set up the deal. It really bugged me that this entire christening was a sham, set up for a London magazine. There was nothing real about it—simply one of Paula's many publicity stunts using Tiger as her trump card.'

The British, German and Australian photographers following the story were having a picture frenzy, shadowing Paula's every move. The christening had created such media attention that it became anything but a private affair. So obviously was it an orchestrated public relations exercise for the British magazine, that some of Michael's friends grew doubtful about the sincerity of the event. There were more than a few who went purely out of respect for Michael and Tiger Lily that sunny March day.

On the morning of the christening guests were picked up at 10.30 by chauffeur-driven cars, whose drivers refused to tell their passengers where they were going, and all the time communicated with security guards via mobile telephones. It was essential for Paula to keep the location a secret; the event had to be kept totally exclusive or the deal would fall through. Even the reception afterwards was a secret until the last minute. About thirty people attended the fifteen-minute ceremony at St Peter's Church. There were no hymns. There were no speeches from family members. There were no family members and none of Michael's long-term, close friends were in the official christening party who stood before the altar, with the exception of Martha Troup. She was accompanied by Colin Diamond, Andrew Young, Belinda Brewin and, of course, Paula. On the certificate of baptism Belinda Brewin, Martha Troup, Colin Diamond, Andrew Young, Nick Cave, Jo Fairley and Catherine Mayer—a friend of Paula's—were listed as sponsors.

No-one spoke other than the Reverend Luke. 'The baby cried but she was very well behaved, she is adorable,' he said. 'It was a very usual baptism.'

The beautiful twenty-month-old Tiger Lily wore a frilly pink dress for her big day. Following official group photographs at the church, the official christening photograph did not feature any Hutchence family members, any members of INXS, or any of his closest friends except Troup. Photographer Brendan Esposito from Sydney's *Daily Telegraph* newspaper claims that during the ceremony he was pushed off the church wall by a private security guard. He was taken to St Vincent's hospital after an ambulance crew spent thirty minutes stabilising him. 'I was standing away from the other media, standing on the church wall, when a fellow came up to me and asked me to leave,' Esposito was quoted as saying later. 'I told the security guy that it was a public place and that I was within my rights to stand there. I then felt an almighty shove and found myself falling off the wall and then lying on my back smashing my head on the ground.' But an onlooker maintained that the photographer faked the fall, while Paula Yates said of the incident, 'The only problem was we had so many German paparazzi outside. And they were all terribly chubby and kept falling off their ladders and accusing everyone else of pushing them.'

Rhett Hutchence had managed to use an entire roll of film photographing the christening. On the way to the reception he met up with the *Woman's Day* assistant, gave her the film, and then loaded his own personal camera. As the official photographic session at the reception proceeded, Rhett began taking photographs with his camera. When he went to the bar to get a drink, Colin Diamond took the camera and removed the film, but of course the photos of the christening were already on their way to *Woman's Day*.

As a consequence, Paula's deal with *OK!* magazine was cancelled. So she sold the photographs to *Woman's Day*'s opposition magazine *New Idea* for a reported A$30 000. *OK!* then came back and offered £75 000, half their original fee, which Paula accepted. Paula was claiming that the proceeds from the English magazine were to form the basis of a school fund for Tiger Lily. According to her, she was broke, she was not being supported by the Hutchence estate, and she had to do story deals to cover living costs. Rhett was now accused of having messed up Tiger Lily's education fund by taking the photographs. He was devastated and, I was told by a source at *Woman's Day*, begged them not to print the photos. But of course they did.

'If I could turn back time I would,' Rhett told me. 'Morally it was a bad decision I made that day. Due to my addiction I was not thinking clearly and therefore did not think of the consequences of my actions. I have since felt deep shame and guilt about my part, and that is something I have to live with.'

The official photo session by *OK!*'s photographers took

just over an hour to complete, and once done Paula immediately left the premises, without saying thank you or goodbye to anybody. I spoke with five people who were at the reception and without exception they told me it was not a happy occasion. A feeling of disappointment, sadness and emptiness filled the room. Paula later told *OK!* magazine, 'I must admit that I didn't expect the reception to be quite so miserable. Not for everyone else—everyone else was having a complete riot playing with Tiger, but I felt sad that Michael was not there.'

fourteen

The ashes: torn apart

> We could live for a thousand years
> But if I hurt you
> I'd make wine from your tears
> I told you
> That we could fly
> Cos we all have wings
> But some of us
> Don't know why
> I, I was standing
> You were there
> Two worlds collided
> And they could never tear us apart
>
> 'Never Tear Us Apart'
> *Kick* 1987
> MICHAEL HUTCHENCE AND ANDREW FARRISS

On 22 January 1998, exactly two months after Michael Hutchence's death and on what would have been his thirty-eighth birthday, one third of his ashes were scattered near Vaucluse in Sydney Harbour. The ashes had been split three ways: one third going to his father, one third to his mother, and one third to Paula Yates.

It was the decision of the erstwhile trustee of Michael's estate, Colin Diamond, to split the ashes three ways. Patricia and Paula had been arguing over who should receive the entire ashes, so Diamond telephoned Kell, who had not entered the fray at this stage, and asked him whether or not he thought splitting the ashes was the best solution under the circumstances. Kell agreed that it was, and so three urns were prepared and the ashes placed in three countries: Australia, the United Kingdom and the United States. Michael Hutchence, as was the case during his life, was torn apart even in death.

'Colin Diamond put an independent seal on the ashes as a result of a move by Paula to take them back to the UK,' Patricia told London magazine *Hello* in May 1998. 'Notification was sent to me from the office of Stephen Diamond, acting on behalf of his brother. A question was put to me about division and it made me ill to have to even answer a question like that. I felt it beneath my dignity to fight over my son's ashes, so I made the decision to allow Paula to share in the ashes. America is where Michael wanted to be, and that's where my share of the ashes are. He was always a nomad.'

A month earlier, in an interview with *OK!* magazine, Paula Yates, in typical style, said that she slept with her one third of the ashes. 'They're actually in my bed, and they're wearing a pair of Gucci pyjamas. I've taken them out of the urn because the urn's a bit tricky to sleep with.' She didn't reveal what she was keeping the ashes in. 'It's secret. I'll tell you one day when I've decided what I'm going to do with him when he's taken his pyjamas off. But he's happy at the moment.'

Kelland and Rhett chose to conduct a Sydney Harbour ceremony and share their one third of Michael's ashes with the people of Sydney, Michael's place of birth. They planned an intimate twilight evening on board a luxurious chartered boat, *The Ambience*, inviting thirty close friends to take part in the ceremony. Following his son's death, Kell had gone to Bali to try and garner his spiritual strength, and on his return he waded through thousands of letters from INXS fans and the public. One of the letters was from Pastor Dennis Patterson.

Patterson had been a rock musician during the seventies and eighties and understood only too well the pressures, the temptations, the troughs, the loneliness and the emptiness that can be part of being in a rock group. In 1979, at the Central Coast Leagues Club north of Sydney, Patterson, full of sorrow and self-pity over the break-up of his six-year marriage, looked out into the sea of faces through the noise of poker machines and the smell of smoke and spilt alcohol, and the turmoil inside him was more than he could bear. On the spur of the moment he decided he would leave the band. He telephoned an old Christian friend and asked him to meet him at their local church. 'As I drove away from the club, I remember feeling a strong beckoning in my heart and I knew that nothing could convince me to turn back. I was going to church and I felt as if God was pulling me towards him.'

In 1987 Patterson began studying to be a pastor. At the same time he was a supervisor of trainee music teachers at Davidson High School, the very same school where Michael Hutchence and Andrew Farriss had first met all those years before. Just two weeks before Michael's death, a friend of Patterson's, also a minister, had booked into a hotel and committed suicide by taking an overdose of sleeping pills. He had planned it all, leaving a detailed suicide note. Patterson's friend had been prescribed anti-depressants for deep depression, and when Michael Hutchence died the coincidence was just too much for Patterson. He wrote to Kelland expressing his heartfelt sorrow at Michael's death. Kell felt that destiny had called, and contacted the pastor to set up a meeting. They met a few days later and discussed Michael's boyhood days, when he and Rhett would have Kell drive them to a paddock to ride their dirt-bikes. 'We talked incessantly during the following weeks as we planned what to do with the ashes. Kell was able to bring strength to everyone at this time, he showed such courage in the patriarchal role,' Patterson told me. Eventually it was decided to scatter the ashes in the waters of Sydney Harbour.

As the evening of the ashes ceremony drew closer, Kell became concerned about the inclement Sydney weather. 'I had an undesirable experience when I scattered the ashes of my dear father into the sea all those years ago,' he remembered, 'so I was a bit worried that the same thing would happen scattering my son's ashes.' Pastor Patterson came to the rescue via the Internet, and contacted a Christian university in Ohio, USA, asking 2000 students, staff and friends to pray for clear weather. On the afternoon of the ceremony, thousands of fans were globally linked via the Internet, and thousands more gathered at Hard Rock Cafes in cities around the world.

As the guests arrived to board *The Ambience* the weather was perfect. It was a warm, calm Sydney summer evening, pink clouds set against a pastel-blue sky, the Opera House and the city skyline silhouetted against Michael's sunset. In attendance were Andrew and Shelley Farriss, Tim and Buffy Farriss, Kirk Pengilly and partner Louise, Garry and Jodi Beers, Rhett Hutchence and Mandy Nolan, Kell's sister Croy, his cousin from England Sonya Hutchence, Michele

Bennett, Jenny Morris, Jimmy Barnes and his wife Jane, Richard Lowenstein, Paul Ellis, long-time friend Greg Perano, INXS tour director David Edwards, Tony Woodall—Michael's personal security man—former co-manager Gary Grant, Andrew Young, Hiraani and John Clapin, old friend Paul Horton, Kelland and Susie, Pastor Dennis Patterson and his wife Joy, and Maori singer Erana Clarke. Erana had been a back-up singer for INXS during the eighties.

The Ambience anchored opposite Milk Beach, a small beach on the Vaucluse peninsula, and Dennis Patterson called the group to the bow of the boat. As the mourners left the cabin, an eerie silence hung over the proceedings. Rhett held the beautifully crafted wooden urn containing his brother's ashes. The pastor began the ceremony by recalling stories from Jenny Morris, Tim Farriss and Kirk Pengilly, linking their tales to passages from the Bible. Following the reading, Andrew Farriss thanked the pastor, saying, 'Michael would have liked that. I don't care what anyone thinks now, but Michael and I loved the years we spent together as teenagers in a church youth group.'

'Let us not waste this moment, but let his death motivate us all to dig deeper spiritually,' the pastor said.

The gathering then recited The Lord's Prayer, followed by a brief pastoral prayer for the committing of Michael's ashes. Rhett and Kell scattered the ashes from the urn into the still waters of the harbour. Susie and others threw brightly coloured flowers after them, followed by a minute's silence in honour of Michael. As the weeping of the guests became audible, Erana Clarke braced herself and began a haunting Maori lament, her powerful voice reverberating around the harbour. She then rolled into the ageless hymn 'Amazing Grace', slowly building to the final verse:

When we've been there ten thousand years,
Bright shining as the sun,
We've no less days to sing God's praise,
Than when we first begun.

Just as Erana's final note drifted across the harbour, the sun sank behind the glowing horizon. The end of the day, the end of an era.

On that very day, thirty-eight years before, Michael Hutchence had entered the world. When Erana had finished singing, Kell asked the group on *The Ambience* to raise their glasses. 'Happy birthday, Michael,' he said.

As people were leaving the boat, the beautiful dark-haired woman who Michael's closest friends said was always his true love, approached Pastor Patterson. She hesitated for a second as if to hold back her tears. 'I just wanted to thank you for tonight,' she said. She turned away, walked down the gangplank, along the jetty, got into a friend's car, and drove off.

appendix

The coroner's report

The following report was made public on 6 February 1998, almost three months after the death of Michael Hutchence:

I have received a completed police brief into the death of Michael Kelland Hutchence on 22nd November, 1997, at Ritz Carlton Hotel, Double Bay. I am satisfied that the cause of death was 'hanging'. I am also satisfied that there was no other person involved in causing the death.

The question of whether the death was a suicide or not has to be considered.

The deceased was found at 11.50 am naked behind the door to his room. He had apparently hanged himself with his own belt and the buckle broke away and his body was found kneeling on the floor and facing the door.

It has been suggested that the death resulted from an act of auto-eroticism. However, there is no forensic or other evidence to substantiate this suggestion. I therefore discount that manner of death.

With regard to the question of suicide I have to be satisfied on a strong balance of probabilities before I am able to come to such a conclusion. There is a presumption against suicide. Having considered the extensive brief I am satisfied that the standard required to conclude that this death was a suicide has been reached for the following reasons:

(1) Michele Bennett, a former de-facto of the deceased, received two telephone calls from him on the morning of the 22nd November. The first was on an answering machine and Mr Hutchence sounded 'drunk'. During the second call at 9.54 am, the deceased commenced to cry and according to Ms Bennett sounded 'very upset'. She was concerned about his demeanour and for his welfare and told him she would come immediately. However, when she arrived at the hotel she was not able to rouse him by knocking loudly on his door, nor by ringing him. She wrote a note and left it at reception. Ms Bennett stated that Mr Hutchence never expressed previous inclinations regarding suicide.

(2) The deceased's father, Kelland Hutchence, dined with him the previous night. The deceased was in good spirits, however appeared very worried in regard to the outcome of a custody suit in London. Mr Hutchence could offer no explanation as to why his son would take his own life.

(3) Ms Kym Wilson and Mr Andrew Rayment were with the deceased in his hotel room from sometime after 11 pm and left about 5 am. According to Ms Wilson the deceased appeared to want both of them to remain with him to offer support if the result of his custody hearing was unfavourable. His mood was described as 'elevated, however pensive when discussing court proceedings'. All three persons consumed alcohol, including vodka, beer and champagne, together with cocktails at this time.

(4) Whilst Ms Wilson and Mr Rayment were in the room Ms Martha Troup, the deceased's personal manager, rang from New York. Then later at 9.38 am she received, via voice-mail, a call from Michael Hutchence in which he said, 'Marth, Michael here. I fucking had enough.' She rang the hotel immediately and the telephone rang out. A further call was received at 9.50 am on Ms Troup's telephone answering machine. The deceased sounded as if he was affected by something and was slow and deep. This call worried Ms Troup and [she] spoke to John Martin, the tour manager for INXS, about her concerns. Mr Martin refers to a note received from the deceased saying he was 'not going to rehearsals today'. The rehearsal was to be the last one prior to the start of the tour and was quite important.

(5) Ms Paula Yates provided a statement. She provided background to the custody dispute between her and Sir Robert Geldof. She stated that she rang the deceased at some time prior to 5.38 am on the 22nd November and he told her he was going to beg Geldof to let the children come out to Australia. She had told the deceased that the custody matter had not been finalised and was adjourned until the 17th December and she would not be bringing the children out. Ms Yates stated that the deceased sounded 'desperate' during the conversation.

(6) Sir Robert Geldof received two phone calls from the deceased, the first at about 6.30 pm London time on [the] evening of 21st November. It was of a short duration and Geldof asked the deceased to call back. The second call was received by Geldof about 5.30 am on 22nd November, Sydney time. This call was of some length. Geldof refers to the deceased's demeanour as being 'hectoring and abusive and threatening' in nature. He refers to the deceased as 'beg-

ging' to allow him to let the children come to Australia. He did not sound depressed during the conversation. A friend of both Geldof and Paula Yates, Ms Belinda Brewin, confirms the substance of the conversation between the two. A statement obtained from Gail Coward, the occupant of the room directly next to the deceased's room, alludes to hearing a loud male voice and expletives emitting from the deceased's room about 5 am that morning. I am satisfied that she was hearing the telephone conversation between the deceased and Geldof.

(7) A statement obtained from the mother of the deceased, Mrs Patricia Glassop, confirms her opinion that the deceased was in a depressed state.

(8) In December 1995, Michael Hutchence was first prescribed anti-depressants by Dr J. Borham, a London medical practitioner, to treat a pre-existing depressive problem. He was last so prescribed on 1st November 1997. A London psychiatrist, Mr Mark Collins, was consulted by the deceased on 17th October 1997 in regard to a minor depression being experienced by him. According to the doctor there was no hint of suicidal thinking by the deceased.

(9) An analysis report of the deceased's blood indicates the presence of alcohol, cocaine, anti-depressants and other prescription drugs.

On consideration of the entirety of the evidence gathered I am satisfied that the deceased was in a severe depressed state on the morning of the 22nd November 1997, due to a number of factors, including the relationship with Paula Yates and the pressure of the ongoing dispute with Sir Robert Geldof, combined with the effects of the substances that he had ingested at that time. As indicated

I am satisfied that the deceased intended and did take his own life.

I am also satisfied that this death is one in which nothing will be gained by holding a formal Inquest. The identity of the deceased, the date and place of death and the manner and cause of death are clearly set out and the time and expense of holding an Inquest is not warranted and therefore such will be dispensed with.

May I offer to the family of Michael Hutchence my sincere condolences on their sad loss.

Inquest dispensed with.

(D.W. Hand)
NSW State Coroner
Glebe, 6th February 1998

Acknowledgements and sources

RESEARCH
Ms Jacqui Daniels—beyond the call of duty.
Ms Tiffany Bakker
Ms Trudi Dadswell
Ms Phoebe Ashton
Ms Caroline Hirons
Mr Rod Willis
Mr Scott Howlett
Mr Anthony O'Grady
Ms Holly Lovegrove

INTERVIEWEES AND CONTRIBUTORS
Bono
Richard Lowenstein
Ollie Olsen
Lian Lunson
Bill Leibowitz
Gary Grant
INXS
Greg Perano
Martha Troup—friends
Rhett Hutchence

Mandy Nolan
Kelland Hutchence—without whom the book would have been an even more difficult task.
Hiraani Clapin
Karen Ansell
Kylie Minogue
Helena Christensen
Jason Donovan
Susie Hutchence
Mabs Terry (Hutchence)
Pastor Dennis Patterson
Kate McClymont
Mary Woodsmary
Scott Howlett
Ian Verrender
Andy Gill
Rod Willis
All those who preferred to remain anonymous—thank you.
My apologies to anyone I have omitted.

PUBLISHED QUOTES FROM:
Boy George, Billy Corgan from the Smashing Pumpkins, Simon Le Bon from Duran Duran, Bob Geldof, Danny Saber, INXS, Liam Gallagher from Oasis, Elton John, Ray Manzarek from the Doors, Paula Yates, Michael Hutchence, Belinda Brewin, Patricia Glassop, Tina Hutchence, Andy Gill.

SONG LYRICS
The author and publishers gratefully acknowledge the following for their kind permission to reproduce song lyrics: 'Just Keep Walking' (from *INXS*, 1980), 'Original Sin' (from *The Swing*,

1983), 'Golden Playpen' and 'Don't Change' (from *Shabooh Shoobah*, 1982) reproduced by kind permission of MCA Music Australia Pty Ltd; 'Searching', 'Show Me', 'I'm Just a Man' and 'Elegantly Wasted' (from *Elegantly Wasted*, 1997), lyrics reprinted by kind permission of PolyGram Int. Music Publ. BV.; 'Rooms for the Memory' written by Ollie Olsen, published by PolyGram Music Publishing Australia and reproduced by their kind permission; 'The Gift' (from *Full Moon, Dirty Hearts*, 1993), 'Never Tear Us Apart', 'Need You Tonight' and 'New Sensation' (from *Kick*, 1987), 'What You Need' (from *Listen Like Thieves*, 1985), 'Men and Women' (from *Welcome to Wherever You Are*, 1992) all reproduced by kind permission of Warner Chappell Music.

SOURCES
Spin
Rolling Stone
Ram
Penthouse
Sounds
Juice
Who Weekly
New Weekly
Vox
New Musical Express
Melody Maker
Q
Sydney *Telegraph*
The Australian
The Sun Herald
The Age
The West Australian
The Advertiser
Hello

OK!
Woman's Day
New Idea
TNT magazine
The London *Daily Mirror*
The London *Sun*
The London *Sunday Times*
The Observer
The Guardian
Perth *Sunday Times*
The Internet
New York *Times*
New York *Post*
AN EXCESS OF INXS Internet site
Prozac Nation Elizabeth Wurtzel, London, Quartet Books, 1994
Is That It? Bob Geldof with Paul Vallely, London, Sidgwick & Jackson and Penguin Books, 1986
Paula Yates: The Autobiography, Paula Yates, London, Harper-Collins, 1995

THANKS

Mr Jim Young, without whom this task may not have been completed. Thanks a trillion. Jonathon Wright; Richard Sampson; Sarah Fitzpatrick; *TNT* magazine; Tina, Paula, Patricia, Belinda, for special inspiration; Peter Lynch; Peter Carrette; Icon Images; Lisa Carrette; Alison Urquhart; Jane Burridge; Alex Tippetts; Ian Wakeling; Ian Jackson; Genevieve Stewart; Tin Tin; Thomo; Kelland Hutchence; Angie; Nigel; Sharon Salmon and Sharon Thompson and Martin Reid; Ghadir Razuki; Nadia; Rocky; Kathleen Eridani; Baz and Trish; Anthony and Linda O'Grady without whom I wouldn't have been able to wade through my own shit; Rob Hirst—Rob, I owe you a lot; Nina Stephenson; Jeremey and Kate Fabinyi; Phil Tripp, Lisa and the dogs; Troy

Lovegrove Foundation; Sam Corrie and the Corrie family; Jacqui Daniels; the Head family; Simon, Sue and family; Rick, Marcia and family; Jo; Jason; Julie and Bill; Phillip and Cydney Frazer, Lori Eastside; Meredith Rose, Karen Ward, beyond the call of duty. Thankyou so much; Sophie Cunningham who showed patience beyond the beyond, and faith—despite my impatience and my temper and my verbosity and my emails; everyone at Allen & Unwin; everyone at Faber & Faber; all the girls at Immedia Pty Ltd; the girls at Jigsaw Day Care Centre, Hammersmith, London; Sharon Johnston for being a life saver for me and a second sister, shining light and shining example for Lilli Rae.

THANKS ALSO TO
Troy and Suzi for shining over me from above. Lilli Rae for keeping me on the straight and narrow. I love you. Holly for faith, for belief, for love and for knowing that the best is yet to come. Helen's forgiveness, strength and greatness. Aubrey Corkill; Arlo—onya mate; Rick, Joan, Paul, Stephen and the Fry families; Pauline, Ken, Geoff, Nicki, Bradley, Julia, Jason, Sonny, Alex, Ted, Ella, Pat, Jean, the late Tommy Lovegrove; Betty, Dudley, Christine and Susan—for still loving wandering, prodigal black sheep.

Index

Index compiled by Russell Brooks
AC/DC 58, 64, 71, 72, 84, 113
Addlestein, Joan Von 4
Agar, Gerry 188, 189
Alford, Anthony 264, 265
'All Around' 135
Amphlett, Christina 77
Angels, The 58, 68, 69, 70, 71, 81, 84
Atco 79

'Baby Don't Cry' 135
Barnes, Jimmy 121, 238, 286
Beames, Ian 257
Bee Gees, The 64
Beers, Garry Gary 50, 51, 120, 127, 128, 131, 135, 285
Bennett, Michele 73–6, 93, 146, 148, 156, 159, 210, 211, 217, 238, 240, 253, 285–6, 289
Birthday Party, The 71, 97
Birtles, Beeb 65
Black, Cilla 46
Bono 124–6, 135, 146, 164, 167, 172–3, 217, 222–4, 239
Boomtown Rats, The 171
Brewin, Belinda 227, 234, 245, 249, 250–2, 253, 260, 268, 274, 276, 279
Browning, Michael 64, 72, 73
'Buckethead' 105
Burgess, Tina 4, 5–6, 7, 10, 14, 22, 26, 60, 231, 233, 243, 245, 246–7, 266, 274
'Burn For You' 93, 96
'By My Side' 237

Campbell, Hiraani 147–8, 286
Cave, Nick 71–2, 97, 167, 233–4, 238, 239, 279
Charles, Ray 137
Christensen, Helena 77, 134, 136, 138, 155, 157, 158, 161–3, 164, 165, 166–7, 173, 176, 178–9, 182, 238
Chrysalis Records 71, 78
Cold Chisel 58, 68, 69, 70, 71, 84
Conroy, Nick 74, 75
Corgan, Billy 225
Coward, Gail 209, 210
Crocodile Dundee 122

'Dancing On The Jetty' 96
Davies, Iva 69
Davies, Roger 64–5
Davies, Troy 92, 93
Debney, Anita 178, 187, 188, 189
Deluxe Records 72
'Devil Inside' 123
Diamond, Colin 192, 235–6, 254–5, 256, 257, 258, 259, 260–1, 263, 264, 265, 266–7, 268, 269, 270, 271, 272, 275, 279, 280, 282–3
Dirty Pool 69–70
Divinyls 70, 71, 77–8, 81, 84, 86, 121
Doctor Dolphin 48–50
Dogs in Space 39, 90–1, 94–7, 98–104, 196
Donovan, Jason 138, 150–1, 238, 240
Duran Duran 224

Easybeats, The 64
Edwards, Poole 178
Elliot, Jenny 69

Fairley, Josephine 182, 187
Farriss, Andrew 32, 44, 45, 46, 47, 48, 50, 60, 70, 74, 84, 86, 112, 116, 123, 127, 129, 135, 136, 139, 233, 239, 285
Farriss, Dennis 46, 60
Farriss, Jill 46, 60
Farriss, Jon 45, 46, 47, 48, 50, 54, 60, 74, 75, 120, 127, 128, 271
Farriss, Tim 45, 46–8, 50, 51, 52, 54, 59, 60, 61, 73, 82, 123, 127, 130, 135, 195, 233, 271, 285
Farriss, Wendy 46
Farriss Brothers, The 50–5, 56–7, 58, 59–60, 61–2
Farriss family 32, 42, 45–6
Fine Young Cannibals 106, 107
Fisher, Gordon 128, 256–8
Flowers 69
Frankenstein Unbound 128, 196
Full Moon, Dirty Hearts 137
funk 70, 81, 85–6, 89

Geldof, Bob 139, 140, 168, 170, 171–82, 185, 186, 188–94, 198–200, 203, 204–9, 220, 221–2, 227, 249, 264, 274, 290
'Gift, The' 137

Gill, Andy 140, 238
Glassop, Ross 6, 230, 236, 237, 238
Glassop, Patricia 2–11, 14, 17–18, 19, 21–3, 26, 33–8, 39, 40, 43–4, 55–6, 57, 58, 60, 221, 230, 231, 236, 237, 243–5, 246–8, 249, 253–4, 262, 263, 264, 266, 267–8, 274, 275–6, 277, 278, 282, 283
Goble, Graham 65
Grant, Gary 82–3, 85, 86, 92, 93, 122, 136, 232, 238, 286
Gregory, Diana 7
Guthrie & Co. 1, 7

Hanna, Arnie 109
Harris, Rolf 46
Harrison, George 46
Hearn, Ray 69
Heavenly Hiraani Tiger Lily 147, 181, 186, 187, 188, 190, 191, 192–3, 197, 203, 208, 220, 226, 227, 234, 238, 239, 245, 247, 250, 251, 252–3, 254, 261, 263, 267, 268, 269, 272, 273–81
Hey, Virginia 175
Hines, Deni 135
Hong, Colin Lee 61
Hutchence, Kelland 1, 2–4, 5–20, 24–7, 33, 34–8, 40, 42, 43–4, 55–6, 57, 221, 231–2, 233, 234–5, 236, 243, 245, 252–3, 264, 275, 276, 282–3; relationship with Michael 37–8, 40, 42, 55, 60, 159, 186, 201, 203–4, 230, 237, 261, 283–5, 289
Hutchence, Mabel 5, 10
Hutchence, Michael: accident in Copenhagen 162–4, 165–6;
in America 35, 39–40, 42, 43, 48, 85, 124–5;
death 187, 212–13, 227, 288–92;
and drugs 43, 46, 51, 85, 117, 132, 134, 156, 160, 164–5, 167, 180, 184–5, 187, 188–90, 197, 213, 214–15, 291;
education 14, 20, 22, 30, 31–2, 40, 44, 55;
estate 226–7, 235, 254–5, 258–72;
first recording 23;
friendships 117–18, 132, 144;
funeral 232–3, 236, 237–43;
in Hong Kong 11, 12, 13–14, 15, 18, 19–21, 22, 23–5, 40, 128, 147;
in Perth 51–5;
relationships with women 38, 43, 75–7, 143–59, 160, 175, 176–7, 179, 180–1, 183–4, 192;
scattering of ashes 282–7;
and sex 43, 50, 94, 120, 132, 144–5, 154, 159–60, 164, 167, 175, 197, 215–16, 226–7
teenage years 28, 30–2, 33, 35, 37, 39–40, 49, 73
Hutchence, Patricia see Glassop, Patricia
Hutchence, Rhett 8–9, 10, 11, 12, 13–14, 15, 18, 19–21, 22, 23–6, 27, 29–30, 35–8, 40–3, 43, 44, 48, 49, 54–8, 60–1, 137, 147, 188, 232, 243–4, 274, 276–8, 280
relationship with Michael 8–9, 22, 26, 27, 36, 38, 48–9, 54, 56, 60–1, 137–8, 157, 185, 218, 240, 262
Hutchence, Tina see Burgess, Tina
Hutchence family 3, 7, 8, 11, 13, 18, 26, 28, 34–9, 56, 60–1, 221, 255, 261
Hunters and Collectors 76, 77, 92

Icehouse 69, 71, 78, 81
INXS 23, 31, 32, 40, 46, 48, 51, 53, 59, 61–2, 63, 68, 70–1, 72–4, 78, 79, 81–9, 90, 92, 96–7, 99–102, 106, 110–12, 113–14, 115, 119–24, 128, 129–31, 132–3, 135–7, 139, 140–1, 165, 174, 190, 195–6, 202, 222, 225
INXS 73

Jackson, Michael 80, 174
James, Oliver 170
Jonny 148–50, 152
'Just Keep Walking' 73

Kennedy, Patricia see Glassop, Patricia
Kerridge, Vicky 58
Kick 84, 107, 110, 119, 120, 121, 122, 123, 124
Kinski, Klaus 23
Kinski, Nastassja 23
Knuckles, Frankie 108

Lees, Vivian 76
Leibowitz, Bill 86, 123, 132, 133, 160, 183, 189, 194, 215, 238, 241, 271
Leighton, Norman 258, 259
Lewis, Brent 26, 243
Lewis, Jim 6, 26
Limp 139, 196
Listen Like Thieves 87, 88, 99, 101–2, 120
Little River Band 65, 71
Loiterton, Barry 33
Loiterton, David 33
Lowenstein, Richard 39, 75, 90, 91–3, 94–103, 113, 146, 164, 184, 186, 192, 200, 221, 253
Lunson, Lian 74, 75, 144–5, 150, 160, 165, 183, 191, 199, 216, 221, 238

McDonald, Bill 109
McDonald, Richard 69
McEntee, Mark 77
McGuire, Duncan 73
Magee, Croy 10
Manzarek, Ray 225
Marine, Jeanne 187
Marshall, Sonny 9, 34, 35
Martin, John 211, 212
Max Q 104, 106, 108–14, 115, 116, 117, 128, 132
Men at Work 71, 79, 80

Mental as Anything 70, 71, 81, 121
Midnight Oil 58, 61, 68, 70, 71, 84
Milburn, Lyn-Maree 92, 93
Miller, Harry M. 231, 232, 233
Minogue, Kylie 60, 77, 129, 134, 150–9, 222, 238
Morris, Gary 61, 71
Morris, Jenny 127, 129, 286
MTV 80–1, 100
MTV Music Awards 124, 130
Murphy, Chris 33, 61–2, 63, 65, 71, 72, 79, 82–4, 86, 89, 90, 100, 101, 109, 110, 111, 113, 114, 122, 128, 132–3, 136, 222, 238, 240–1
Murphy, John 109
Mushroom Records 68
music industry 58–9, 63–73, 78–89, 97, 105–6, 107, 109–10, 112, 219

'Need You Tonight' 123
'Never Tear Us Apart' 124, 240
'New Sensation' 124
Nolan, Mandy 36, 188, 285

O'Keke, Kingsley 251, 252, 253
Olsen, Ollie 91, 103–9, 112, 113, 115, 116–17, 149, 219
'One Thing' 70, 85
Opitz, Mark 84–5, 135
'Original Sin' 86, 87

Patterson, Dennis 284–5, 286
Paul, Andrew 258, 259, 260–1, 263, 264, 266, 267, 268
Pengilly, Kirk 46–8, 50, 51, 52–3, 59, 70, 82, 115, 127, 135, 285
Perano, Greg 75, 76–7, 111–12, 113, 146, 163, 167, 180, 190, 218, 238, 241, 244, 286
Perth 51–5
'Please (You Got That?)' 137
punk 67–8

Ray, Brian 257
Rayment, Andrew 209–10, 289, 290
Richie, Lionel 174
rock'n'roll 3–4, 58, 70, 83, 85, 89, 120, 122, 135, 141–2, 217–18, 219, 223
Rogers, Nile 85
Rolling Stone 132–3
RooArt 33, 128
'Rooms For The Memory' 91
Rowe, Glenys 98
Russell, John 22

Saber, Danny 140
Scott, Bon 72, 113
Shabooh Shoobah 70, 73, 85, 120, 123
Sherbert 64
Sheridan, Michael 109

Shorrock, Glen 65
Simenon, Tim 140
Simpkin, Richard 201
'Simple Simon' 72
Skyhooks 66
Smith, Roger 5
'Stay Young' 81, 83
Stigwood, Robert 64
Stipe, Michael 225
'Suicide Blonde' 129, 130
Swift and Company 10, 14
Swing, The 86, 87, 123

Terry, Todd 108
Thomas, Chris 87–8, 99, 120, 129, 135
Till, Gus 109
Townsend, Pete 97, 98–9
Troup, Martha 86–7, 134, 139, 140, 145, 150, 157, 158, 160, 183, 200, 201, 210–11, 217, 238, 244, 271, 275, 279, 290

U2 124, 126, 172, 223
'Underneath The Colours' 70
Underneath The Colours 81

Vanbro Pty Ltd 33
Vanda, Harry 64
Vaughan, Mike 64
Vegetables, The 50
video making 79–81, 91, 92–4, 96, 99–100, 102, 112

Walker, Johnny 1–2
Walter Carter Funerals 270
'Way Of The World' 105
'We Are The Vegetables' 72
Welcome to Wherever You Are 135
'What You Need' 88, 99, 100, 101, 121
Wheatley, Glenn 65
White City 98, 99
Wilkins, Richard 233, 239
Willis, Rod 68–9, 71
Wilson, Kym 209–10, 213, 226–7, 238, 289, 290
Woodall, Tony 232, 286
Woodruff, John 69, 71

X 129, 131

Yates, Paula 77, 138, 139, 140, 155, 168, 169–92, 195, 197–20, 201, 203, 204–6, 208, 210, 211, 215, 220–1, 226, 227, 234, 238–9, 243, 244, 245–8, 249–50, 251–2, 253–4, 268, 273–81, 282, 283, 290
Young, Andrew 205, 208, 220, 234, 260, 262, 268, 269, 277, 279, 286
Young, George 64